An Autobiography of a Pioneer Business Woman

Nothing by Chance

An Autobiography
of
A Pioneer Business Woman:

Nothing by Chance

by

Eleanor Macdonald

ISBN 1-85259-090-4

Typeset by:
Betagraphics, The King's House, Bow Street, Langport, Somerset TA10 9PS

Printer: Ptarmigan Printing

NIMROD PRESS LTD
15 The Maltings
Turk Street, Alton, Hants

Contents

Chapter One   1

Early Memories and Events   1
Love and Security   2
My Brother, Ian   3
Repairing Early Damage   3
About my Parents   4
Robert Glover, the Martyr   5
Getting Rid of Victoriana   6
My Aunts   7
The Pre-1914–18 World   7
Household Drudgery   8
Building My Confidence   9
The Air Raids   10
Going to School   11
Attitudes to My Father   11
The Fun of School   12
Being Ignored   13

Family Reading   13
Recognising Style   14
Patterns of Behaviour   15
Friends   16
Music Comes into Its Own   17
Theatre Going and the Films   18
Becoming Aware   20
Animals   20
Religion   21
Ian Goes to Work   22
The Stage   23
The Start of Fencing   24
Special Lessons in French   24

Chapter Two   33

Perceptions of the Outside World   33
My Father's Unemployment   33
The Mood of the Country   34
Vulnerability   35
Family Possessions are Sold   35
The Fencing School   36
Fleet Street — Learning to Think   36
Using Imagination   38
A Plethora of Jobs   39
Modelling   40
An Audition   41
Outside Events   42
Finding my Feet   43
Men and Romance   43
Shyness and Ignorance   44
My Love of London   45
Eve's Wedding   45
Holidays   45
The Fascination of Light   47

Chapter Three   52

The Fencing Era and the French Influence   52
Building up the Fencing School   53
Teaching in Different Locations   54
Going to Paris — Fencing in Exclusive Clubs   56
La Famille Bourdon   58
Other French Friends   59

Back to England   60
Fencing — a Training for Management   61
Coaching duels for Stage and Screen   63
The Lord Mayor's Show   64
Domestic and World Events   65
My Father's Changing Fortunes   65
War is Declared   66

Chapter Four   **76**

The War Years   76
The Paraphernalia of War   77
Joining the Censorship Department   77
I do "Time"   78
Personnel Increase   79
A New Pattern of Life   81
The Fall of France   81
Dunkirk   82
The Battle of Britain   83
My Responsibilities are Enlarged   85
Managing Staff   86
Meeting Senior Officials   88
Gaining Recognition   89
I Take Over Another Department   90
Inter-Departmental Difficulties   91
Work Most Secret   92
Lectures at Provincial Branches   93
Doodlebugs and VIIs   94
Allied Liaison Officers   95

Chapter Five   **98**

Taking my Degree — Early Post-War Jobs   98
Preliminaries   99
Degree Choice   100
The University   101
The Practical Approach   103
D-Day   104
Personnel Work   105
My First Post-War Job   106
Escaping to a New Opportunity   108
Buckingham Palace   110
Making the Job My Own   111
Negotiating and Making Things Work   111

Continued Study   114
Store Personalities   115
I Become Uneasy   115

Chapter Six   **121**

Unilever — a New World   121
Getting to Know the Company   124
I Take My Exam   124
A Paris Visit   126
The Experimental Salon   127
Social Activities   129
Working on the cosmetic range   130
Changes in the Company   133
Exploring Perfume in Italy   134
We Visit Grasse   137
The Launch of White Lady Cosmetics   138
Looking for New Ideas   139
I become a Director   141
The launch of Skinfare   144
Staff Management   144
The Bond Street Pageant   145
Links with Hartnell and the World of Art   147
Hospital Beauty Scheme   147
Domestic Problems   150
Personal Feelings and Philosophies   151

Chapter Seven   **166**

The African Era   166
My First African Tour   168
I Meet African Women   171
Schools Lectures   172
I Travel to Sierra Leone   174
Lagos   175
Developing Ideas for the Store   178
"Live by Beauty"   179
Creative Energy   181
Furthering Management Training   181
External Activities   183
A New Assignment   184
Practical Aids   187
Results of the Nigerian War   187

Chapter Eight

200

Launching my Own Business 200
First Women Managers' Course 202
A Personal Loss 204
Developing Further Courses 206
The Training Years 207
Delegation 208
Considering People 209
Power Play 211
Finding the Balance 212
Important Personalities 213
WIM Activites 215
"Fact Sheets on Career Building" 217
Weekend Events 218
WIM Newsletter 218
Home Affairs 220
The Office 221
Personal Back-Up 223
Preparation for the States 224

Chapter Nine

230

Overseas Work with Travel and Ongoing UK Assignments 230
I go to America 230
Travelling in the States 232
American Friends 236
Ireland 239
United Nations Assignments 241
Team Building and Personal Effectiveness 243
Important Colleagues 245
Putting Ideas on Paper and Other Workshops 250
Damaging Management Styles 251
Learning from Others 252

Chapter Ten

263

Building a Life Philosophy   263
Risk Taking   266
Exercising Choice   267
A Self-Discovery Course   268
The Role of Leisure and Pleasure   269
Faith and Belief   272
I Re-Visit Nigeria   273
Feminism   275
The 300-Group and Working Woman   277
Two Outstanding Women   277
Girl's Education   279
Results   280

List of Illustrations

Chapter One

(1)   Ian and I, aged 7 and 1
(2)   Aged 3
(3)   My rocking horse
(4)   With Ian and my teddy bear
(5)   My mother
(6)   Jack
(7)   Ian
(8)   Ian in *Madame Guillotine*
(9)   Ian and I fencing

Chapter Two

(1)   Fencing salute
(2)   Modelling
(3)   More modelling

Chapter 3

(1)   Shadow of the Sword
(2)   Fencing ballet
(3)   City Fencing Club
(4)   Fencing — en garde
(5)   Fencing — the lunge
(6)   Elizabethan duel
(7)   A fencing film
(8)   Fencing — the Lord Mayor's Show

Chapter Four

(1)   On holiday

Chapter Five

(1)   Selfridges — at my desk
(2)   Buckingham Palace

Chapter Six

(1)   Atkinson's salon
(2)   Testing a perfume
(3)   Lavender fields
(4)   The Bond Street Pageant
(5)   Norman Hartnell and White Lady cosmetics
(6)   The White Lady fashion show
(7)   Beauty salon
(8)   My portrait by Francis Marshall
(9)   Judging a beauty competition

Chapter Seven

(1)   Arriving in Africa
(2)   Meeting the Ashanti Hene
(3)   Talking to market mammies
(4)   An African party
(5)   In Yoruba costume
(6)   A literacy class in Africa
(7)   Visiting a market in Africa
(8)   Lady Kwali, a famous potter
(9)   A group of Northern Nigerian women

Chapter Eight

(1)   Running a management course
(2)   Peter Mulcahy-Morgan attending a New Office Technology cou
(3)   WIM Executive Committee members at an AGM
(4)   My staff

Chapter Nine

(1)   At a course in USA
(2)   Betty Jay in USA
(3)   Ann Wohl and her sons
(4)   Ann and I towards the Grand Canyon
(5)   The Grand Canyon
(6)   Arizona Desert
(7)   Bill and Libo
(8)   A course at Henley
(9)   Pauline Graham

Chapter Ten

(1)   Organising an event
(2)   Building Personal Effectiveness Course
(3)   *Thrushes* by Mary Elliot Lacey
(4)   Osprey nesting in USA
(5)   Pets
(a)   Snooky
(b)   Sammy
(c)   Nicky
(d)   Alex
(6)   My garden
(7)   S.L. Moore — my gardening mentor
(8)   On Dartmoor
(9)   In India with Philippa, my godchild
(10) Nigerian Women Managers Course

By the same author:

"The Successful Secretary"
– jointly with Julia Little

Price: £3.50

"Building Confidence"
– Audio Tape, complete with Notes

Price: £12.50, inc pp.

Both of these are obtainable from:

Eleanor Macdonald EM Courses
4, Mapledale Avenue, Croydon CR0 5TA

Telephone: 01-654 4659

Introduction

This book is an enlargement of the thinking which both consciously and unconsciously has occupied my mind for at least the last 20 years.

It is based on the deep conviction which I hold that everyone is a unique and valuable person with abilities and potential often far beyond their own perception. Although, unfortunately, this potential often lies dormant, I believe it can be released, and with enlarged perspectives and some help from others, people can reach for their stars.

All too often negative, or even no development occurs as a result of unfavourable and hurtful circumstances or destructive personal relationships, which produce a lack of self-belief and motivation.

I have chosen to describe some patterns of my growth and achievement, which as I have said are possible for everyone, in an autobiographical form, because I can now see much more clearly the trigger points which during my life enabled me to move forward, and my failure at times to perceive opportunities which certainly altered and probably minimised my achievement.

The conclusions that I arrive at are obviously personal ones; other people may not draw the same inferences as I have done, but the important thing I would like to show is that by sharpening our perceptions we see that there are options, although initially we thought there were none.

Our lives are not the haphazard jumble we sometimes feel they are. If we think deeply enough and have confidence, we can make things happen and prove to ourselves the maxim, 'Nothing by chance'.

Writing the book has in itself been a voyage of self-discovery. I have found many new perspectives as I have dredged my memory for fact and impressions. In many instances, I have for the first time compared events with most illuminating results.

I hope everyone who reads these pages will be able to do the same.

My grateful thanks go to all those who have helped with the creation of this book. First Pauline Graham, whose promptings set me to work on it – all those who have read drafts and made helpful suggestions – but especially to Hilary Cook who, with great perception and no impatience, has taken illegible writing and upside down drafts and converted them into a readable script. I am also very grateful to the other members of my team who, by correcting, criticising and commenting, have made a major contribution.

Croydon, January 1988   *Eleanor Macdonald*

Chapter One

Early Memories and Events

I was born in Wanstead, Essex, in 1910. What a convenient year, because it makes calculations as to when events happen very easy. I remember nothing of Wanstead, because my parents moved to Croydon when I was two in order that my only brother, Ian, six years older than I, could go to The Whitgift School.

We were not well off and pennies always had to be watched carefully. Later these difficulties increased, but in spite of this I believe that I was really a very fortunate person. It could be said that this early good fortune belies the sub-title of the Book, "Nothing by Chance", my interpretation of that is that it is what we do with what we've got which is the significant thing.

Few of us are granted the innate abilities that made Mozart, eg: into a genius, but we all have our own endowments which can be developed if we so wish. There is no such thing as equality; so some of us have more than others of talent — parental care — riches, but how we deploy those things — leads to good or poor development.

One of the aspects of good fortune with which I believe I was endowed was described to me by my mother. When I was only a few days old, her nurse, an austere lady, who did not usually fuss over her charges, would walk me round and round the room, humming happily to me and saying to my mother, "You know this child has been here before — she is an old soul, she will have a very interesting life".

There are those who utterly reject the idea of life after death being a progression, that we move from one existence to the next on an improvement path. While I may not be wholly convinced of this, I have to confess that I have frequently had the sensation of having "been here before" and even with simple pedestrian tasks, which I am seemingly tackling for the first time, I get the feeling that I already know how. This is both good and bad — bad because people can get very irritated thinking that I have the intention to prove them stupid, because I sometimes get there before them. Indeed, later in life I learned not to speak or act too quickly, even though I had the answer, so that others did not feel inadequate.

Love and Security

More important than this, however, my early years were completely surrounded by love — love of different kinds, which without my being fully aware of it, enable me to "feel safe", "understood", "appreciated". Our close-knit family unit was made up of my mother and father and my brother. My mother's love was unstinting — nothing was too much for her to sacrifice for our advancement — yet she had a very just critical faculty and very high standards; so that my brother and I knew the limits, felt the bite of discipline, yet never lacked support. My father's love for me was inevitably different — not so perceptive, yet very deep and genuine; but I sometimes felt that it embraced an uncritical admiration which, had it not been for my mother's firmness might have led to my becoming conceited.

I was also aware that my father did not give Ian this same warmth, that there was always an edge of criticism and a lack of tolerance between father and son, administered perhaps in order to make my brother tough and manly. I also asked myself in later years whether there was not also a touch of jealousy of my brother, because my mother was deeply caring of Ian, because he had been such a delicate baby; indeed there had been times when he could have died.

My father was deeply concerned with Ian, but I doubt whether he ever really understood his character. The lightheartedness which made Ian such fun to be with, my father perceived quite wrongly as triviality — I have come to observe such latent feelings often exist between fathers and sons, making communication almost impossible.

My Brother, Ian

My relationship with Ian was deeply affectionate, and as we grew up increased in sensitivity and understanding, although my quick temper must at times have been hurtful.

There was, however, always a vigorous rough and tumble of opposing points of view between us, yet linked with respect. So, although at a superficial level we maddened each other at times, arguing ferociously, when the situation had cooled, there was always a return to the warmth and mutual admiration which resulted in sharing ideas, aspirations and material things too.

In later life, pre-occupied with training and developing people, I have become more and more aware that many children when small do not have the advantages I have described — they are not loved, they are not made to feel wanted — and they are not disciplined. Many parents it seems are too stiff and self- conscious ever to fling their arms round their children and say, "Darling, you're lovely", or they are neither interested nor imaginative enough to say "Now children, what are we going to do today?", as if it was going to be the most exciting event ever. Equally, they are not strong and consistent enough to say firmly and without rancour, "No" to the silly things children get up to.

So I see people who lack a feeling of serenity which love and thoughtful attention provides; they have not learned to develop relationships by participating and sharing. They are also not able to accept discipline and standards with a good grace, so they are often quite devastatingly badly behaved and selfish.

Repairing Early Damage

Such early deprivations can sometimes be overcome at least in a measure, but it takes time which, whether the need to change is discovered at 18 or 28, ought by then to be devoted to other things. It is not that it can't happen, but it all takes so much longer and is so much more difficult.

It is well known that one of the tenets of the Roman Catholic Church, held also oddly perhaps by modern psychologists, is that if children have not been given a solid basis of sympathy with control, by the time they are 5 or 7, it is doubtful whether they will every acquire the discipline which life demands.

It has to be said that the scars from fear of punishment, fear of not succeeding — not pleasing, being constantly belittled or compared unfavourably with others or being left alone without support, are often very deep and have to be worked at if they are to be eradicated. I had few, if any, such hang-ups. I do not believe that this was so true of my brother.

It would be utterly stupid to leave the impression that everything in my family background was serene and peaceful. There were strong divisions and disagreements. Whether more or less than other families, who can tell — I suspect that conflicts happen, even if behind closed doors, in most households.

About my Parents

My parents came from very different backgrounds. My father was the second son in a family of three brothers and a sister. His father, who was Scottish, died before the youngest child was born and when Daddy was only six. My grandfather was a young man, who, having come to London from Scotland, was only getting established when he died, so his widow and children were left in very poor circumstances. I never met my grandmother, who remained a shadowy, and I was led to believe, a not very pleasant person.

For reasons which were never clear to me, when my father got engaged to my mother, a feud started. Daddy's family resented my mother — were rude to her and intrigued against her in a very disagreeable way. My mother, who was proud and had a quick temper, could not accept this kind of treatment.

I think the reason for this disharmony may have been the totally different manners and lifestyle of the two families. My father's family was blunt and down to earth, although Daddy was not like his brothers, being gentle and courteous. His elder brother who took on the role of head of the family, was shrewd and able and, I believe, very self-opinionated. I think he despised my mother's stylish elegance and my father for marrying such a person

My uncle was beginning to be commercially successful, and money meant a great deal to him. My mother and my aunts were all teachers and, therefore, not well off. Another cause for disdain was the pride that my mother's people had in their old long- established family.

The comments which were circulated round the Macdonald clan were along the lines of, "Fred's wife has lots of airs and graces, but not much substance"

Moppett, as we often called my mother, on the other hand, and my aunts too, found the brusque, crude manners of Daddy's family completely unacceptable. There was no common ground of respect and affection.

Disagreement and dissension blossoms all too quickly where there is prejudice and unkindness, and rifts grow wider. Eventually, even my father who had a strong sense of loyalty to his family, became disgusted with this behaviour and cut himself away from them.

My father did keep in touch with an uncle who had been very kind to him, when as a youngster he had endured a very poor and lonely childhood. Because money was so limited, my father's education was very brief. He attended St. Clement Dane's Church School, just off the Strand, leaving at the age of eleven.

This was another source of hurtful comment. Daddy's elder brother had already been put down for the Merchant Tailor's School, before my grandfather died. A scholarship to allow him to continue was granted; he felt, therefore, that this education was far superior to Daddy's and very unfairly never missed an opportunity to comment on it.

As soon as he left school, Daddy went to work at once as an office boy in different firms in the city. In the brutal city which London was in the 1890's, it must have been a shattering experience — but a kind of impish mischievousness sustained him, and he set to work to make his way. He tried very hard to overcome the meagre level of his education and to a large extent succeeded. I greatly admired the way he must have worked, determined to learn all he could and, largely self-taught, he read and read and became very knowledgeable.

He devoured books of every kind on trade — business — the classics — Roman history. He also acquired skill in commercial arithmetic and learned to keep books and accounts in a remarkably skillful way.

My mother's family, whose name was Glover, were completely English, coming from the Staffordshire-Derbyshire borders. It was a very old family of yeoman stock, who for generations had owned farms or followed professional careers.

Robert Glover, the Martyr

Robert Glover, a staunch supporter of the Protestant or Anglo- Catholic faith, became a martyr. He was burned at the stake in Coventry in 1555. As children, we were told the story how at the time of Mary, who reinstated Catholicism in England during her brief reign 1553-1558, Robert Glover resisted any attempt to interfere with his religion.

This stalwart was warned that if he did not forsake his prayer book, he would be punished. He refused to be diverted from his faith and in an old book which is still on the shelves in my house, the lurid description of his imprisonment in a miserable little cell and his final death on the stake, obstinately clutching his prayer book, made a lasting impression on me.

I thought I saw the same kind of integrity and determination in my mother, which gave her great strength of character with considerable dignity. I believe that some at least of my independence of character sprang from this tradition.

My grandparents on my mother's side were real people to me, although I did not see a great deal of them. My grandfather, even as an old man of over 80, which is how I remember him, had great charm and a sharp sense of humour.

He had not lived a very profitable life. He was, in fact regarded by his brothers as the ne'er do well of the family, having early in life been spoiled by an uncle, who promised him an inheritance, which never materialised and left him with expensive tastes and little except great skill with horses.

My grandmother was a gentle, courteous lady who during the course of her life had had to compensate for my grandfather's impracticalities and recklessness. Grandpa was a handsome and dashing horseman — not averse to a glass or two — but he earned little money. She kept the family going by earning money from her skill as a beautiful needlewoman. I only met her a few times, but I found her delightful and was very pleased when people said I bore a strong resemblance to her.

She died when I was four and I remember my mother being very quiet and sad and wearing a black feather boa, (which later one of our cats discovered in a box under a bed and tore it to pieces!).

It is small things like this as well as major happenings which form the basis of one's growing up, and I have very clear recollections of all sorts of trivia that filled my early years. For example — not being allowed to grizzle when new shoes hurt me, loathing having my cheeks pinched by elderly male acquaintances, but being too polite to comment, or Ian being given a Meccano set. I never played with this. I recognised that this was Ian's territory and with no sense of deprivation I respected it and did not meddle.

Getting Rid of Victoriana

There was also the time when my mother, with great zest, got rid of some draped mantel boards. Most people today have never even heard of these hideous things, a hangover from the Victorian era, which decorated, or rather cluttered, dining and drawing room mantelpieces. They were intended to make the mantelpiece look broader and more important looking and were covered with swags of fabric ending in tassels to give a final decorative touch! In fact, all they did was to create a fire hazard and gather dust. Understandably, my mother intensely disliked these monstrosities, but having been given them as wedding presents when she and my father married, she endured them for many years, then one day in a fit of exasperation she took them down and gleefully we shared in their annihilation.

It was a typical gesture of quick decision which my mother would engage in. I am sure that these actions were a model for me. If you really don't like a thing, then *do* something about it and do it quickly, even if you risk some displeasure from someone.

Then there were visits from my aunts — Auntie Emmie and my favourite Auntie Norah, frequently accompanied by her great friend with whom she lived. We called this lady Great Aunt Emma, although she was no relation. I sensed the tension which these visits caused my mother, for while my aunts were well intentioned, they were strong minded ladies who didn't fail to criticise things they did not approve of. They had straight backs, wore large hats and frequently dressed in black.

My Aunts

If I am honest, I did not like Great Aunt Emma and, because I thought she was ugly, she showed up one of my weaknesses — I do not like ugly things! It was not however, so much her unattractive featureS and screwed-back hair, but it was the way I felt that with a seemingly very mild manner, she tried to dominate people. She had something of a reputation as an artist, based, I perceived later, on very insubstantial grounds. On one occasion, I had been given a box of beautiful crayons for my birthday. I was thrilled at the gorgeous graded colours in their little box and cherished this gift. "Now you must take care of those and use them properly," Great Aunt Emma said in her humourless voice, "I will show you how. " Picking the prettiest picture in the colour-in book which accompanied the crayons, she broke three of them. I was terribly upset. While I had been taught never to comment or show annoyance in such situations I was angry and a little bit of me closed up inside and I said to myself, "I'll never forgive you for that." Such are the vengeful thoughts that children can harbour about grown-ups.

By contrast, Ian and I communicated in a very different way. On one occasion we were playing together, and by accident he knocked over one of my dollies and broke it. He was terribly upset and I cried a little, but then I said, "Well, never mind, she can be mended, and in any case I have always preferred playing "robbers" with you", which was true. Robbers was a private game we had devised, which brought down my father's wrath, particularly on Ian's head, who being the older was supposed to know better. It was a rough game which entailed a fearful amount of rushing about; I have to confess to no great purpose.

The Pre-1914–18 World

I recall other incidents from this period, the setting of which belongs to a social era which is very different from today's. Because one's mind was uncluttered and the pace of things more gracious, often quite small happenings absorbed my attention and conditioned my attitude. One such experience happened when my brother and I were staying for a holiday with Auntie Emmie and grandfather in the country at Theydon Bois in Essex.

The road from Epping to my aunt's house was down two hills. The hill on the horizon was higher than the one closer to us and there was a dip between them. The road was only intermittently visible, because of high hedges and trees, but sound carried clearly in the unpolluted air. One afternoon we were expecting guests to tea − a major event in a world where there were no children to play with and, of course, no radio or TV − so great excitement. We knew they would come in a pony and trap.

We waited expectantly at the gate and at last, although we could not see the trap, the clip-clop of the pony's hooves sounded clearly coming down the distant hill. The sound grew louder until it suddenly ceased as the trap went down into the dip between the two hills. Then suddenly the sound was renewed, the clip-clop, that most endearing of country sounds, came back.

We knew by this that the guests had almost arrived. Then the pony rounded the corner and came into sight. The build up of excitement from these moments of expectancy was tremendous. In today's terms a very simple happening, but one which left a lifelong joyous impression.

Household Drudgery

Although there were many pleasurable things at this time, running a house entailed a great deal of sheer drudgery which took up a great many hours. My mother did have people to help her, two notable characters were Mrs Blythin, who had strong political interests and stood at street corners and shouted. She and we always referred to her husband, who brought us lovely vegetables and flowers from his allotment as, "Old Blythin"; I think because he looked so old and walked with such a lumbering gait, although I don't think he was more than 50.

Later, Susan came several days a week to clean and polish. She was a very sweet person who must have been very pretty once, but when we knew her, she had a sadly faded appearance and long years of scrubbing and washing had coarsened and reddened her hands. In some odd way, her short blouses never quite met her long trailing skirt. But I loved to hear her tell how when she was in her teens she walked on in crowd scenes at the old Croydon Grand Theatre.

My recollection of the chores which made the household routine, were horrendous. Blacking a hideous old kitchen range, whitening the front door step with hearthstone, the annual washing of venetian blinds which were made of thin sheets of wood to which dust clung like glue, carrying pails of boiling water upstairs for baths when the boiler failed to work, which was quite often, washing blankets and using an old-fashioned carpet sweeper or a hard brush on carpets!

My mother was an excellent cook, so all jams, jellies, pickles and chutneys were made at home. No tinned foods ever came into the house. She taught me how to do things in the kitchen. Her formula was an excellent one. "Cook things so that they taste as they are at their best. " She showed me how to capture the true flavour of fish, meat and fruit dishes. Sauces augmented, never masked the true taste.

At Christmas time there was the ritual preparation of Christmas puddings which we all had to stir. The results were marvellous, wholesome, but it took forever and with old-fashioned stoves and no refrigerator, it amounted to real hard labour.

Sometimes my mother would get very tired and then, if Ian and I scampered about in an irritating way, she would scold us. But she never generated any long lasting anger, even when she was cross with us. She somehow contrived, whatever the initial indignation, to make us see the justice of what she was saying, and I came to love her generosity and fearlessness.

Her determination to pass this last vital quality on to me has stayed with me always. Once Ian, who was by now at Whitgift School, had a friend to tea. The first World War was on and I would be about six. Ian went out of the room to get something, leaving me with the friend, whose name was Bayley. In a threatening voice he said, "Do you know what you've got upstairs?" I did not answer. "Under your bed is a German!" There had, of course, been rumours of escaped German prisoners or spies hiding in all sorts of places, so this was a terrifying thought. I was struck dumb — I did not know what to do.

Ian came back and eventually Bayley left, and the awful thought of having soon to go upstairs to bed filled me with horror. My mother soon noticed that I was unusually quiet and asked what was the matter. I tried to pretend it was nothing, but she soon got me to tell the story.

Building My Confidence

There was no derision, no brushing off as of no account what was obviously to me very upsetting. Taking my hand she said that it was not true, but we would investigate. In a solemn little procession we went upstairs, Ian bringing up the rear. We looked under every bed, in every cupboard and in the loft for good measure. "So you see, darling, you don't ever have to be frightened at the silly things people say. " This meant that there were no "fright hang-ups" which she could clear, so I had the great good fortune to have the foundations of my confidence laid at a very early age.

Of course, later there were all the usual fears and doubts which beset people, before exams, in one's teens etc, but there was always a concept of fearlessness to hang on to.

But to return to the war — its true devastation did not touch me as deeply as it did many people. My father was not called up. He was the Manager of a cigarette factory, and I suppose as the men at the front wanted cigarettes so badly he was exempt.

The Air Raids

The air raids remain very clear in my mind. Croydon is only ten miles from London, and as it was the main target of the enemy attack, we were within the danger zone. We would be woken up when the sirens went at three or four in the morning, and would come downstairs in our dressing gowns to drink cocoa and play cards and watch the play of the searchlights over the city. It was a great adventure!

One night, the air was filled with an all pervading hum, which grew louder and louder, and then in the beam of the searchlights as it seemed, very close we saw a Zeppelin floating by. The emotion was excitement rather than fear, for although one or two houses within a few miles were wrecked by bombs, compared with the 39/45 conflict, the civilian involvement in the Great War was slight.

Not so the trench warfare. Dimly I knew that something awful was going on, and sadness hit me deeply when on some days a cavalcade of Red Cross ambulances went up and down our road to a school, which had been converted into a clearing hospital. The wounded were being brought over from France, via Dieppe to Newhaven and transferred from trains to ambulances at East Croydon station.

When an ambulance went very, very slowly down the road we guessed that a terribly badly wounded soldier was passing. It was deeply upsetting, even to a little girl. On the return journeys the ambulances tore up the road, making haste to collect the next batch of wounded.

My mother entertained soldiers and sailors from time to time, to give them a break and a few good meals. I loved helping to prepare these. One of our favourite visitors who came on several of his leaves, was a delightful New Zealander, Captain Nicholson, Uncle Nick to us. The last time he came he had been wounded in the knee, and I can still see him limping down the stairs, his black curly hair and smart uniform turning him into a complete hero for me. He was to go back to the front the next day.

My mother was standing in the hall and he said, "Guess my share of luck has run out. " I asked afterwards what he meant, and my mother said very quietly, "He fears he may not come back — war is a terrible thing, darling. " I think it was good that my mother was so frank with me — I was able to respond by being treated so responsibly. He did not return.

Going to School

I had by this time gone to Woodford, a small private school. I remember my mother taking me to be interviewed by the Headmistress before I joined. She was a very precisely spoken, but a very frail looking lady, who told us about the various facilities at the school. She then said, "I can assume, can I not, Mrs Macdonald, that your husband is not in trade?" My mother chose to interpret this as meaning, "Is he a shopkeeper?" To which she answered, "No", and I was accepted.

This kind of snobbery irritated my mother greatly. She said to me, "You will ignore it — you are going to the school for the excellent education that is offered. Learning is the important thing".

Attitudes to My Father

My father was equally liberal in his outlook, and treated his work people in the cigarette factory very fairly, often protecting them from the rather mean vindictiveness of the owner of the business, which took quite a lot of courage.

He was very ill once, with a double quinsy, and to present him with a get-well gift, which the staff had collected together to purchase, one Saturday afternoon a little Russian Jew, one of his work people appeared at the door. I was enormously intrigued by this little man, who had a large beard and a lot of grey fuzzy hair. He spoke with a strong accent and told us that he had come from Odessa in 1912. These cigarette makers worked tremendously hard, rolling cigarettes with incredible skill and speed with their agile fingers, and then cutting off the shaggy ends of the tobacco. The result was a most beautifully shaped fragrant product, often tipped with gold.

Each London store, Harrods, The Army and Navy etc, had their own special blends, which my father created. His palate was so refined that he could combine the finest Virginia tobaccos with say a rare Latakia from Syria, to produce a unique blend — stronger or milder — to a particular requirement.

This was the kind of expertise which existed in Britain in that era. Infinite care and precision were exercised and experience carefully built up to produce — beautiful tailoring — exquisite hand-made shoes — delicious coffee and tea varieties, which could meet the most exacting tastes. The same precision existed in engineering and furniture workshops up and down the country. To achieve this perfection people worked long hours and there was slavery in such a system, but to set against this there was pride of achievement which people found highly satisfying. They enjoyed working and knew that each of them was making a unique and personal contribution to the final product.

The little Russian cigarette maker left me with the feeling that he was an artist, and the courtesy and appreciation which he showed to my father for the way he was treated was very touching. All this is quite clear in my mind, as was his comment that British people take their freedom too much for granted. "You are so lucky and you do not realise it. I never walked down a street in Odessa without looking over my shoulder with fear. That does not happen here!"

1912 was a long time before the Bolshevik Revolution.

The Fun of School

I enjoyed school enormously. I found the lessons interesting and I think I learned quickly. I liked making things — cardboard models, little stuffed animals, and the mess I made cutting up paper or gumming together matchboxes infuriated Ian, who tried to boss me into clearing up the bits, only to be told by my mother, "You do your thing and she will do hers!"

One of my favourite subjects was Natural History including Botany — Auntie Norah was a great flower person and on holiday we would gather flowers and I would press them. I was early introduced to Hooker and Bentham, the famous early Botanists, whose British flora gave the classification of plants which appealed to me very strongly. It made it easy to identify flowers, grouping them according to particular features, so I not only loved their beauty, but enjoyed being able to categorise them even if in a very elementary way. This approach both responded to and developed the logical streak which I had and which subsequently has proved very useful.

The children at school stay in my memory for particular attributes — there was Marjorie, who was so rough I avoided playing with her; there was Sheila, who have very little chin and sounded as if she always had a cold; there was Leonard, a thin little creature with almost invisible sandy/white eyelashes. His mother was an enormous intimidating lady who came to fetch him. I felt he was not very happy. He also had a way of walking straight into trouble. I could often see it coming before it happened.

For example, on one occasion we'd all been given new exercise books. A quite ridiculous fuss was made about this. "Beautiful new books — you must take care of them — aren't you lucky to have them", etc. I was aged about eight at the time and I thought all this was a lot of nonsense, but was wise enough not to say anything, but sit quietly.

Poor old Leonard, equally disgusted, couldn't restrain himself, he seized a pencil and I knew what he was going to do, he scribbled all over the first page, venting his annoyance on the clean white sheet, with great swirls of the pencil which became blacker and blacker.

I watched with combined feelings of horror and an almost irrepressible desire to laugh. Then the teacher spotted this sacrilegious act, outraged, she hauled Leonard out of the class. We heard her angry voice through the partition. I don't think the sharp tones were accompanied by a slap, but in a minute or so Leonard returned, his pale face, pink, tears dripping off his sandy/white eyelashes. I admired, though deplored, Leonard's bravado which revealed his awareness of the teacher's pomposity. But I have to say that nothing would have induced me to do that.

I think children have a unique gift for spotting the humbug which some grown-ups dole out to them, and I have always been sorry when this clear perception and truthfulness gets clouded over to meet absurd conventions, often making children deceitful and dishonest. This has nothing to do with honest discipline which then, as now, I greatly respected. I determined that when such things happened to me I would watch very carefully, not get trapped, but equally not engage in sham if I could avoid it.

Being Ignored

Another lesson I learned at this time was in the gym class, which was an "extra". Initially I wanted to do it. At eleven years of age I doubt whether I had a very well co-ordinated body, but I never received one word of encouragement or praise from the thick-legged gym teacher. She didn't correct me either, but if there was rather a lot of girls to use one piece of equipment and there was not time for everyone to have a turn, I was always one of the ones to be left out. After two terms, I said to my mother that I would rather do Art.

The message which this left with me and which I made into a personal rule of conduct, particularly when much later I was training people, was — to be praised is good — to be corrected is tolerable — to be ignored is devastating and totally kills motivation.

Family Reading

Another very important experience in these early years was our family reading sessions — mostly my father read, or sometimes my mother. There was, of course, no TV or wireless, but we were never bored. After lunch on

Sunday, the current book was produced. Sunday lunch was always memorable, not only because of the food, but also the conversation, in which we all joined. There would be roast lamb or beef, sometimes hot, sometimes cold, which would be followed by gorgeous old-fashioned puddings — spotted dick (suet pudding with raisins or sultanas), homemade lemon-curd tart and real egg-custard.

The lovely repast over, we would settle down as a family to read. It was delightful. A roaring fire in the fireplace in winter, or French-doors open in summer — and the delights of Dickens, Blackmore, Thackeray were unfolded. I would sketch, Ian would draw geometric figures, or design complicated electrical circuits, my mother would knit, while my father's voice, often with dramatic inflection, rolled on. We all found it thrilling and, although I was unaware of it at the time, these treasured sessions laid the foundation for my lifelong love of words.

There was no coercion about this, the close-knit family feeling and my parents unselfish interest in our development just led to this shared experience, which we all enjoyed.

Later on with some disdain from my father, Ian and I wallowed in Sherlock Holmes and Sexton Blake, waiting every month for the four paper booklets of mysteries and crime stories, which were really thrilling.

My father, as well as being a great reader, had considerable skill with woodworking tools and made, among other things, a beautiful chess-board in different coloured woods. He was, however, no gardener. When seized with vigour (or guilt?), because the hedge or the ivy on the house was badly overgrown, he would attack them with momentary zest, but with little skill and often forgot to change his clothes! My mother was then annoyed that better suits were soiled and spoiled.

Recognising Style

My mother, Moppet, was a fastidious person. She protected her very limited wardrobe by wearing aprons or pinafores, but when dressed for visitors or going out, I early recognised that she had that elusive quality "style". Something about the tilt of her head, the way she always tied a scarf, or had a touch of lace at her wrists which gave her small hands much grace, all added up to a picture which delighted me. One of my earliest recollections of her, was on her return home after a visit to my aunts — she was dressed in a black and white voile dress with a large black picture hat and little button boots with patent toe caps.

I have to confess that when I was young I often felt clumsy and untidy beside her, and I have had to work pretty hard at getting tidier. Even today I have to check a streak of carelessness in my nature which, while I love and aspire to the "bandbox" look, I cannot always be bothered to spend the extra time it requires, when other things at that moment seem to have acquired greater importance. The same thing applies to practical matters as well as appearance, where from enthusiasm and a capacity for seeing the objective very clearly and *finished* before the task has began, I respond too quickly.

I have had to learn that mistakes can come from rushing at things, because the patient preparation which leads to real success has been sometimes skipped over. Contradictorily, however, I have always been able to stick at things for ever until they go just as they should. I learned to control my hurry tactics very slowly and here my brother was a very important example as he was orderly and exact.

I was, outside home, a rather serious child, and at school I was conscious of being a little "different" from some of the other girls. I was basically optimistic and happy, but I think I reserved my laughter for home consumption; so in the junior school I daresay some of the children found me rather dull.

Patterns of Behaviour

As I moved up the school, however, I worked hard, because I liked it — not because I was what we used to call a "mark grubber". I saw things quickly and I didn't mind making quite creative, very much to the point, observations in class, which teachers sometimes found infuriating. Snubbed — I would then sit silent for a while — but not for long I suspect, and so I climbed into the top two or three in the class. This meant that gradually I found a place for myself, although I never thought of myself as in the top league and certainly never as popular.

On one occasion, therefore, when there was need for the form to be represented by one person, to my astonishment the girls spoke out and chose me. "It's obvious Eleanor is the one", they said. I was, of course, very pleased, but utterly amazed and slightly embarrassed.

In the next year I was made a prefect, but I made a hopeless hash of the task. I didn't really understand what I was about, no-one explained how I should proceed and I felt out of place telling other girls what do do. My confidence was at an all time low. By mutual consent my prefects badge was removed!

Another aspect of this may have been my consciousness that most of the girls at Woodford came from families who were very well off. They brought huge bunches of gorgeous flowers to school from large gardens and seemed to have things which I did not possess. This did not worry me or make me feel jealous, I just thought of myself as "different" and felt I had to try very hard to keep up.

Woodford, which had a very high reputation, provided a good basic education, but typical of many girls' schools of the period, there was far too little maths and science. Later in life I was to find this a disadvantage. Considerable emphasis was, however, laid on courtesy and good manners, which eventually made moving in different social circles easy. English, History and languages were well taught and there was a wide range of art subjects from which to choose.

Friends

One of the happy school experiences was the friends I made. One particular girl, Eve Forgan, was my very special buddy. Her father, who was a wonderfully skilful and sympathetic GP, had not long come down from Scotland, so Eve spoke with a delightful accent. She was small, erect, vigorous and goal-orientated from the age of nine. She wanted to be a doctor, like her father, and of course, succeeded.

I went to parties in her house; she came to mine and we played endless card games with her, her parents and younger sister. There was a speed and sharpness about this which was very different from the pace of my home surroundings. To begin with I was left behind by the quick calculations and the rumbustious grabbing of the counters or the cards, but I quickly latched on and gained so much from this rough and tumble. At other times, Eve and I talked for ages about our ideas and beliefs and the future. She adored her father, but could not get on with her mother at all. This astounded me, because my relationship with Moppet was so rewarding. I thought all children were the same.

Eve found my mother a warm friendly person and from those early days they struck up a great friendship and she sent Moppet postcards wherever she went. When I was thirteen and she was twelve, it was decided that Eve should go away to boarding school. She wanted this to escape the home conflict. I was very sad, because I felt rather alone. But holidays came around and there were more meetings and comparing of notes and parties, in a lovely old Victorian house where the Forgans lived.

After boarding school, Eve went to Switzerland for a year and then to the Royal Free Hospital, where she qualified. This progression meant, of course, that over the years we did not meet all that frequently, but we were together whenever possible and 'phones and letters kept us very close. In our teens we shared books, particularly Galsworthy, and went to theatres together or out on picnics. Vicariously we shared each other's lives and I came to meet a lot of medical people, which gave me an insight into another world.

There were other girls at school whom I liked very much and am still in touch with, because constancy is something I value very highly. But Eve was my very special friend. It was so good to be able to come really close to someone right outside the family, to admire and identify with another person's objectives. When she died at the age of 52 of a tumour on the brain at the height of her career as a wonderful GP and anaesthetist, I felt a sense of irreparable loss. Her courage during her short illness, just as one would have expected, was tremendous.

Music Comes into Its Own

Music was to prove a very important influence both at school and later. This was not only because it gave me such pleasure, but because through it I absorbed many important disciplines. I had learned piano from my mother starting when I was three. I loved it. Later I took it at school, also as an "extra". The teacher, a Miss MacNair, was ghastly. She wore high-necked blouses with a throttling velvet band round her neck, lace-up boots and frequently performed in a hat.

She slapped my fingers and indulged in a ridiculous set of marking cards on to which she stuck circles. **Red** − excellent, **blue** − good, **green** − fair, **blank** − bad. I had a lot of greens and blanks. I did not like all this, so of course I was stiff and tense and my fingers failed to perform. My mother, who knew I had some talent for music, told the Deputy Head that she would like me moved to the other Music Teacher.

A new era dawned. Dear Miss Tonge was a lovely person. She was old fashioned too, but so gentle and patient and a great musician. I leaped ahead, frequently played at the school concerts, and was taken at the age of about twelve to play before the famous Tobias Matthey, whose special "relaxed" technique had conquered the music world at that time. His greatest pupil was, of course, Myra Hess. He had a dome-like head, a slight stoop and a beard. He reminded me of some of the austere gentlemen who visited my aunt's home.

My audition with the great man was rather intimidating. Although he was in fact very courteous and gentle, and with a little joke wound up the music stool so that I could reach the keyboard. I don't think I played very well, but he praised me and then made one or two corrections in a very quiet voice. Miss Tonge was anxious for me, but very satisfied when at the end of the audition the verdict was, "She has potential". Unfortunately, Miss Tonge died very suddenly. I was deeply upset at this. It was the first time that anyone I had been closely associated with had died.

My next piano teacher was Ethel Dawes, whom I found delightful. I was then fourteen and she treated me as a grown up person. It was a wonderful experience to which I was able to make a very mature response.

She would take a phrase in the music, with which I was having difficulty, and we would analyse it in detail. I would then play it very slowly, each movement of my fingers being examined and controlled until the required technique to produce the right sound was achieved and committed to memory. After repeating this single phrase slowly several times, Miss Dawes would then say, "Now, please play it at the correct tempo" — and, of course, it went right. Then, smiling, she would say, "Now, you don't ever need to play that slowly again".

Very cleverly, she was, of course, helping me to break down the problem areas and discover where I was going wrong, but she was also showing me how to put them right — then having demonstrated exactly how to overcome the difficulty, she left me with the conviction that I know *how* to tackle not only this problem, but others I might encounter — my technique improved vastly, and more important, I gained confidence.

This analytical approach proved enormously helpful to me in all sorts of ways as my career developed. If an end result is unsatisfactory — very slowly examine it in detail and determine where the fault lies, experiment with ways of improving it or putting it right. This may perhaps take a long time, but if concentration is directed towards the task for as long as is necessary, it *will* come good. But one has to believe in one's capacity to do this. It was when I failed to do this that things went wrong.

Theatre Going and the Films

Alongside books, which today line most of the walls in my house, there was the fascination of films and the theatre.

My earliest recollections of the theatre go back to pantomines at the old Lyceum. In 1918, I was taken to see Cinderella and was completely transported into the fairytale world which was revealed.

I still have the book of the words which cost 3d!, but not the actual programme. Ninette de Valois and George Bass featured in the presentation, which I thought was unbelievably beautiful. To conclude the evening, I remember I missed my footing on the extra broad stairs and fell down a complete flight. Presumably, because I was still floating on air, no harm was done!

The following Christmas on 24 December 1919 — it was Dick Whittington. The beautiful impersonation of Dick Whittington's cat stayed long in my memory.

These visits were only the beginning of my lifelong romance with the Play. I have on file I suppose nearly 1000 programmes, ranging from Shakespeare at the Greyhound Theatre Croydon through every type of presentation in most London Theatres — comedy — drama — ballet — spectacle — ancient performances such as the Garden of Allah; Fred Terry and Julia Neilson in the Scarlet Pimpernel; Matheson Lang in the Wandering Jew; John Gielgud and Edna Best in the Constant Nymph, and so on and so on. The programmes are all there, priced from 3d in the 1920's to the current 50p or £1.

Some of the fashions illustrated in the early programmes, from Liberty's, Swan & Edgar, Debenham & Freebody, appear hilarious today. I particularly like the Milanese silk swimming outfit, voluminous and revealing nothing of the plump form underneath, priced at 49/6d. The low-waisted, cloche-hatted ladies of the 20's are a delight.

The exciting performances these programmes announced, filled my mind for weeks afterwards with images of fascinating people, inspiring emotions and noble sentiments, lovely clothes, gracious gestures, beautifully produced voices and real drama or humour. I even remember absurd lines from long forgotten comedies, such as Mrs Patrick Campbell, poised on a ladder outside a house and saying with exquisite timing and inflection, "I always wondered why men wanted to be firemen!" Pointless, perhaps out of context, but reminiscent to me of an evening of real artistry.

There were comical incidents too, such as in a performance of Julius Caesar came the moment when Charles Doran playing Brutus had been stabbed and collapsed, presumably dead, on the stage. At which point, unfortunately, his wig fell off, revealing a rather bald head. Rapidly, his "dead" hand reached out and popped the wig back on again! C'est la vie, or perhaps in this case, le mort!! But the sound of the slight sizzle which the curtain makes as it goes up on Act 1, still enchants me and fills me with a joyous excitement. This ranks second only to the keyed up anticipation which builds, as the violins and cellos give out their first trial notes before the conductor mounts the rostrum − a most poignant and expectant sound.

Films too played a major part in my development. Charlie Chaplin in "Shoulder Arms" and the "Keystone" comedies when the screen looked slightly pink and the movements were incredibly jerky. but, oh, what delight!

Then Hollywood Greats took over and one built heroes and heroines for all kinds of different reasons. The daring of Douglas Fairbank, Senior, the saccharine sweetness of Janet Gaynor and Charles Farrel, the dashing heroism of Ramon Novarro, the bluff humour of Marie Dressler, and dozens of others.

Going frequently to the theatre and cinema, one developed a fairly critical eye, so although I was prepared to enter right into the fairytale mythology of the silver screen, I also perceived the beautiful camera work, the fabulous realism of sets such as the Chariot Arena in Ben Hur and the exquisite costumes and dancing of the Fred Astaire comedies.

Becoming Aware

This, I believe, is an aspect of that awareness which we all need to build up if life is to be an in-depth experience, not just a superficial quickly forgotten triviality which leaves no impression. The point I think, however, has to be made, that to gain lasting impressions, which can in memory be re-lived and from which comparisons can be made, it is necessary to give something of oneself to each occasion. This, I believe, is at the very heart of communication.

No comedian, however talented, can make me laugh if my attitude is stony and projects, "Oh, so you're the funny man, then make me laugh. " No book can reveal its secrets if there is no willingness to follow the author's mind.

All communication is an act of sharing and if I can't or won't break down the barrier and go towards the other person — playwright — actor — musician — I will not get the message. Even husbands and wives will become remote aliens if there is no wish for both parties to reach towards the other. The outgoing hand gesture, the head tilted forward, the eyes directed and receptive, a willingness to pay attention and concentrate, and the message has a chance of getting over. Sadly, however, it is not always possible to overcome these inbuilt barriers. I, for example, have to say that many of Picasso's paintings say absolutely nothing to me — try as I will.

So, yes, we all are wrapped up in our prejudices, which are so very difficult to break down.

Animals

There are many threads which weave into the pattern of a normal home life, all of which contribute something to a person's make- up and character. One of these for me has undoubtedly been my interest in and love for animals. I find them utterly fascinating and love to have them for pets, and have always wished to see them respected and properly cared for in the wild. All the family were animal lovers, my father less than the rest of us, but we always had cats and dogs and I greatly regretted not being able to have a horse and ride.

It is, I think, important for human beings to have contact with animals. They teach us to use our power and strength more gently. The instinct to bully and get our way at whatever cost to others, which I suspect is present in everyone, can be overcome when we realise how defenceless animals are. They depend on us totally for care and understanding and provide a way for us to learn to control the bully instinct and exercise compassion. They teach us also to take trouble even when it is inconvenient for us. The devotion that animals show to us and which, if we have any sensitivity we must return, makes us a little less selfish and egotistical.

Cruelty in any form nauseates me and the fact that it often springs from ignorance, rather than intent, seems to me no excuse. I fear that long experience has taught me to distrust many people's attitudes to animals and birds. They are so often a profit or an amusement source and can be abused behind closed doors, as children can be, in a shameless way.

Bullfighting, trapping and shooting for the sake of it, or to bolster the "strut" tendency, which is perhaps more present in men than women, is so pernicious, and is to me disgusting. Equally, I think to sentimentalise over animals is in reality self-indulgence, which benefits neither human beings nor the creatures themselves.

One of my early dogs was Jack, a wire-haired Terrier, a ferocious fighter, which got me into all kinds of fracas. He usually attracted dogs twice his size, and then I found myself in the midst of flying fur and tangled leads.

There were memorable cats — Winky — Tabby and Snooky etc, but as I love birds and always feed them in the garden, there have been sad episodes and many bird graves. We never had caged birds which would have made me feel very unhappy because freedom, so precious to me, seems of the essence for creatures created to fly.

Religion

From the time I was very small, church played an important part in our lives. We went every Sunday, and after I was Confirmed I went very often to early Communion. This I liked. It seemed to me that the quietness and the flow of the familiar words, was both soothing and inspiring.

Ian and I were, I am sure, pretty badly behaved in church at times, but the comical always seemed to set us off giggling. Women in absurd hats, men who had large stomachs and looked pompous, clergy who droned on unintelligibly, and one woman who thought she had an impressive soprano and sang loudly and always slightly off key. It was no use, reverence went through the window and muffled laughter took over. My mother scolded us, but I am sure also saw the funny aspect too.

My aunts were much involved in church work, and when they returned from services and argued very bitterly about church feuds or trivial things, such as which pepper pot should be used, I found it contradictory, raising in my mind a considerable degree of scepticism. It seemed, even when I was small, that there was something hypocritical about the sanctimonious trappings of formal religion, which appeared to ignore the truly inspiring concept of the Christian faith.

This was the early beginnings of an ambivalence, which has remained with me always, and has entered into many areas of my life, not only religion. I like the formality, the rich trappings, the glorious music echoing round a vaulted roof, but I want to feel assured that all this does not cover humbug and time serving, a sort of whited sepulchre, which amounts to dishonesty. I recognise that human beings need ritual. It is a symbol which denotes respect whether for the Queen or God. It summons up reverence without which violence and cruelty can quickly develop.

My doubts that pomp and circumstance can become a cover up of deceit encourages another thought which forces me to say to myself, "And who are you to be so arrogant as not to recognise and sympathise with human frailty. When the prize is large, of course, people will manoeuvre to win it — you too perhaps!"

For me, deep convictions and a faith are essential, and I do not find such beliefs incompatible with logic. We cannot know everything. We, therefore, have to trust and from that trust comes a deep optimistic conviction that there is good in this world which, if we work at it hard enough, can dominate evil which sadly I believe is also a potent force.

Such philosophies and faith did not all come together at once, but grew and lapsed and grew again, as rich experiences and encounters with people, some priests, whom I could admire and trust, occurred. That from faith and belief comes a great inner serenity is certain, and for this I am intensely grateful. For those whose doubts or emptiness of conviction are predominant, I feel truly sorry.

Ian Goes to Work

By the time I was 14 years, great changes were happening in my life. First of these was that Ian left Whitgift School.

Early on he had shown great interest in mechanical and electrical things and wanted to be an engineer. However, that was not to be. The Head Master of Whitgift gave him an introduction to the Principal of the Crystal Palace School of Technology (I'm not sure whether that was the exact title), but it was then an important Engineering College. By this time, the war was over. In his interview with the Principal, Ian told of his wish to be an engineer and this "genius" said, "Forget it my boy, we've got too many engineers as it is who are all out of work. Whatever you do, don't waste your time on that. "

It was a knockdown blow to Ian. He was reticent as a teenager and did not reveal his inner thoughts and hurts, particularly to my father whose often sarcastic, though well-intentioned, remarks robbed Ian of confidence. He just did not know what to do. He had pinned his faith to engineering and now there seemed no outlet. As a young school girl, I was not sensitive enought at fourteen to realise what a shock this was to him.

My father, through a business friend, obtained an office job for him — Ian hated it. The routine was utterly boring to him and the monotony was just something from which he longed to escape. He stuck it out for a year or so and then the other great interest which my mother, Ian and I had always shared, the theatre and films, seemed to take over.

I was still at school and took a great interest in school drama. Our Elocution Mistress, Gwen Lally, was a tremendous character, who was at the time a well-known Pageant Mistress. She insisted on good diction and the Woodford School Drama Productions became quite famous, partly because of Gwen Lally, but also because of the veritable plethora of talent with which the School was blessed. A few years my senior were Peggy Ashcroft and Diana Wynyard! In later years, Peggy and Diana repeated the roles of Brutus and Cassius they had played in our School production of Julius Caesar, for Green-Room Charity Days.

The Stage

So when Ian's detestation of office life became unbearable, we talked of the stage as a possible outlet for his imaginative and artistic gifts. Gwen Lally accepted him as a drama student. Using the money he had saved from his office work, he took the plunge.

After a year's hard study, he got a job on tour and then progressed to the Old Regent Rep Theatre at King's Cross, where he played every kind of role — comedy — drama — juvenile leads, character parts. In the pattern of small reps, the Company rehearsed all day for the next week's production, and played at night the play prepared the week before. Terribly hardwork and all for the princely sum of £10 a week!

Ian loved it and acquired a great deal of skill and confidence. Good-looking and vigorous he gathered quite a fan following. Paying 6d in the Gods, I saw most of the plays — the Green Hat by Michael Arlen — the Brothers Karamazov — the Ghost Train! — delighting in hearing Ian's rich strong voice fill the theatre. After the shows we would talk and I would comment and criticise the production, Ian's own performance too, and the other characters in the show — often very stringently.

His wonderful gift for mimicry, which in later life could turn the most boring situation into a giggle, stood him in good stead. There followed the usual actor's pattern; in work, out of work.

However, he did have strokes of luck, working with Sir John Marten Harvey as juvenile lead, in films with Matheson Lang and in a very elaborate (for those days) production of Madame Guillotine where he ended at the guillotine, and for which he got excellent notices.

The Start of Fencing

Part of Ian's training for the stage had required that he learn fencing and very soon as the age of sixteen I took lessons also. We went to the Salle of Professor Felix Gravé in Cornwall Gardens. Felix Gravé was almost a caricature of a Frenchman, small, with a waxed moustache, an erect figure and flamboyant gestures. He had a precise, almost snappy temperament. He also wrote in the most perfect copperplate handwriting, as quickly as I take to produce my appalling scribble. He was generous with praise when one met his very high standards. He was a magnificent classical fencer of the old school, who valued style as much as winning matches.

It was great fun and I enjoyed every minute of the lessons and matches, showing some ability in the sport. After a year I took the English Fencing Diploma. But I learned much more than fencing from these lessons. I acquired co-ordination of body and mind. I became much more physically and mentally disciplined, and just as it was essential to direct my concentration if I was to gain points and defeat the opponent's strategy, I also grasped the importance of evaluating the opponent − and so observation and determination were developed. I think I had a natural body symmetry, but the magical quality about fencing is the combination of precision and strength, which have to be developed in the weapon hand, left or right, and the total relaxation and balance given by the other hand, which is carried loosely at shoulder height.

The capacity to control your body in this way while using your mind to the full, makes it in my view one of the most exciting and valuable sports. It gave me a sense of harmony and in tough situations later in life I could remain relaxed, although exerting myself mentally, and perhaps physically to the full.

Special Lessons in French

In addition, in the friendly atmosphere of the Fencing Salle, I made lots of new friends.

About this time, I also took special lessons in French conversation. A Parisian lady, Madame de la Bruyère, who lived in a tiny flat in West London and whom I visited once a week, laid an excellent foundation of my understanding of French. She was something of a tyrant, demanding that I read a book in French every week, commit to memory a passage of Racine or Corneille and also write an essay. No small order when this was just a part of my studies.

If these tasks were not completed to her satisfaction, she would say in strong tones, "It is no use your mother paying me for lessons, if you're not going to work. You ought to be ashamed of yourself. "

She could bring tears to my eyes which was a pretty unusual happening — but I learned French! and although I am still not satisfied with my knowledge of this beautiful language, Madame did give me a good accent, so that I pass today as more versed in French than in reality I probably am.

Madame de la Bruyère's appearance and style of dressing was to me unique, but typical I suspect of her era. Her hair was piled up on top of her head. She wore pince-nez glasses and, over lace jabots and collars, which covered the neckline of every dress, were draped gold chains caught up by brooches from which dangled a watch. She seemed to me to be very fussily dressed!

Other things which registered in my mind were the innumerable little religious pictures and crucifixes which were dotted round her poky room. I found the agonised expression of the saints, or the Virgin Mary, very depressing. The half-formed thought crossed my mind, that if adherence to the faith produced such misery, I wasn't sure that I wanted to join that band.

Years later, I learned of St Francis of Assissi's great message. He reproved his brothers if they had a sad face and urged them to cultivate, "Continual spiritual joy both inwardly and outwardly" and again "It becomes not the servant of God to show sadness or a troubled face" This I thought was the route for me, particularly when I found that the same thought was endorsed by my beloved R L Stevenson when he said, "There is no duty we so much under-rate as the duty of being happy".

I believe very much in this philosophy, because happiness brings optimism and believing confidently in the capacity to achieve; so achievement becomes possible. Vigour and energy are created and it is these which generate growth and destroy the negative. Adverse circumstance, even disaster can often in my experience be surmounted, if there is deep determination, linked with a joyous light-heartedness which does not allow gloom to smother hope.

So many experiences and opportunities made up my early life, not so elaborate and luxurious as would be demanded today; but expectations were set in a different mode. They did not relate so much to material things and so simplicity had a merit.

Perhaps it was this that made it possible for me to confront the difficulties which were to come without being totally devastated.

Here Ian is not quite seven and so I would be about one year old

At 3, life can be very serious

I inherited my rocking horse from Ian and I loved it even when its tail fell out

*My most prize possession was my teddy bear and Ian my constant
companion*

My mother was a very handsome woman who had great style

'Wait for it!'

My much loved Jack, who would fight anything on four legs

Ian as he was when preparing for the theatre

...m, featuring in Madame Guillotine with Madeleine Carroll and Brian Aherne

Fencing with Ian. He is lunging and I have failed to defend myself and so I am hit. The whippy blade of the foil bends nearly double. My left hand gives relaxation and balance. My right hand moved to late to protect me.

Chapter Two

Perceptions of the Outside World

My Father's Unemployment

In the mid 1920's, the disaster of my father losing his job hit us. The owner of the cigarette firm where he had worked for so long, died, leaving £75,000, a very considerable sum in those days. His legacy to my father, who had played a major role in the building up of the Company, was £500! The son sold the business and, sadly embittered, my father started to look for other jobs — he went to Malta for a while, which he disliked, and then to Liverpool where he did have friends — he worked as a Manager for two different cigarette firms in these two locations, but it was the time of the great mergers.

The Imperial Tobacco and The British Americal Tobacco Company emerged as the dominant companies, having bought up many small organisations which were just swallowed up. The trade was changing, handmade cigarettes virtually disappeared and bigger and bigger machinery took over, altering the whole technique of manufacture.

Inevitably opportunities for a man of nearly 50 against this background were almost non-existent, and when the Liverpool Company was taken over, there was no hope of my father getting back into the tobacco business. He was unemployed! Though money had never been plentiful, there had always been a secure base and now there was almost nothing! My formal education ceased and, as there were no social security payments — doles and the like, a sort of desperation set in — there was no money and apparently nowhere to go.

My father found these violent changes impossible to manage. Never a tactful man, he lost his sense of fun, became very depressed and irritable, and was often rude to the few business friends who remained and might have helped him.

He scoured the newspapers for jobs — nothing ever appeared at the management level, and sinking his pride he went for innumerable interviews for clerks, warehousemen or salesmen jobs. The advertisements and the interviews disgusted him. They included such phrases as "men of grit and guts required". He took this as an undesirable sign of the times. The old conventions and the dignity of commerce had, in his view, given way to discourtesy and aggressiveness. Things became really desperate, reflecting the disastrous situation which prevailed throughout the country. Thousands upon thousands of people were unemployed and the apparently insoluble national problems meant disaster for many individuals and families.

The Mood of the Country

The whole mood of the country was one of despair and cynicism. Less than ten years after the end of the war — the war which was to end all wars — many of the men who had been feted as heroes, were tramping the streets without work, or languishing with the effects of mustard gas or horrific wounds in homes like the Star & Garter. It was pretty depressing.

Women who had rallied and performed all sorts of difficult tasks during the war, from working in munition factories, handling TNT, which stained their fingers bright orange, to nursing, were pushed back into the domestic situation, and because there was so little money and opportunity, the less fortunate ones, even if well educated, frequently ended up doing cleaning, cooking or waiting jobs.

I felt desperately sorry for my father, whose whole character altered, and also for my mother who had to bear the brunt of the domestic difficulties. One of the most awful moments came when my father, to get some money, had to cash in his insurance policies long before they had matured. At that time, safeguards for the individual subscriber were very inadequate and it was perfectly legal for insurance companies to make a totally unfair return to people who wished to claim back their money before their policies had matured.

Vulnerability

So instead of my father receiving a few thousands as he had anticipated, the amount refunded was a few hundreds, not as much as he had paid in for contributions! Later, legislation was introduced to correct this unfairness, but at that time there was no redress. My mother, normally very shrewd and intelligent about business matters, had never liked or understood insurance and there was, therefore, criticism and some dissension over my father's choice of investment, which turned out so badly.

It is at times of strain and anxiety that differences between people fester. The atmosphere at home was often sad and tense. It is astonishing also, with no money spent on maintaining a home, how quickly things deteriorate. With stringent economies there was enough to eat, but anything like repairing a broken chair leg, or buying a bunch of flowers or a new dress, were out of the question − a truly spartan existence. I noted that my mother, who was very beautiful, aged markedly at this time. Her anxiety was obvious.

Family Possessions are Sold

To gain much needed money my father's signet ring and watch chain, a Cameo brooch of my mother's and other treasured possessions were, one by one, sold for miserable sums of money, because so many, many people were all in the same boat and there was, therefore, a glut of trinkets in jewellers' shops.

It was very bad also for Ian, as these oppressive difficulties came at a time when he needed backing for his career. Psychologically, as well as practically, it was damaging for him. When he should have been at a high point of vigour, projecting his very positive personality, he felt guilty that he could not make a financial contribution to the family finances, and when going for interviews or auditions, he was very nervous.

When one is at a low ebb of resources, a feeling of isolation settles over everything. The family closed in; we felt ashamed of our poverty and perhaps even more of our lack of significance, unaware that hundreds of other people were in just the same plight, through no fault of their own.

This was not, in fact, a time to withdraw with feelings of shame or guilt, but rather to step out and share with others. But that attitude, particularly with the social norms which prevailed at that time, did not seem possible. This led me to the conclusion that solutions would come, not by seeking help from others, but by my personal endeavour.

I felt I could not just sit still taking lessons in French, Piano, Singing. I knew that somehow I *had* to make a contribution.

The Fencing School

And so in 1928, I started a Fencing School, using my only asset, my Fencing Diploma. With my father's help, who understood about printing, I put together a little brochure, explaining what was on offer. I found a hall in Wellesley Road, Croydon, which now lies buried deep under the Whitgift Shopping Complex just about where Marks & Spencer Stores is situated.

We chose the typefaces and the paper for the leaflet very carefully, addressed 250 envelopes by hand and posted them, waiting expectantly for results. To my joy, five girls from my old school joined and so we were away. It was a tiny venture, of course, but I felt it could grow. The girls were very keen and I found myself learning to teach — to develop and control others. I enjoyed it very much and it proved successful and it did grow.

This inevitably, however, did not provide the money which was so desperately needed, so as well as the Fencing, which took place in the evening, I took on a jumble of penny-earning work activities — writing — modelling — advertising — using whatever resources I had, eg: my capacity for seeing the essential connection between disparate things, my imagination and a capacity for hard work. I became very highly motivated, developing a drive, determination and a sense of urgency which has remained with me always.

Fleet Street — Learning to Think

At that stage, my lack of Higher Education and formal training was a great handicap. However, I wrote articles, initially on fencing, but gradually on all sorts of topics, working for a sarcastic old devil of a literary agent on Fleet Street, who sharpened my wits and helped me to "come alive a little". He used to say, "If you cannot see the potential or the possibility of an extension of thinking behind a single news item, you're no journalist". It took me a long time to comprehend what he meant, which was, of course, that quick, shallow acceptance of events — happenings — ideas — without probing or questioning means inevitably that one's way of working is superficial and lacks creativity. One has to probe, question oneself as well as others. Not to accept, but to investigate, and then propositions enlarge. One adds something and so more is revealed.

From the bald statement, "man fell off the pier at Brighton and was drowned" — comes — Why did he fall off? Was he drunk? Was the balustrade broken? How many people have fallen off this or other piers throughout the British Isles? How much money do the Council spend on maintenance of the pier? etc. Then having asked the questions, **you go and find the answers.**

It is a technique which I shall refer to many times, because as my career developed it helped enormously. I was coming to realise that things do not happen by chance, they result from the perception of causes and sequences — in other words, there is a pattern, but one has to develop the acute awareness to enable one to see it.

Then having directed one's thinking to the problem in depth, the missing link is gradually revealed. Is this something which one could provide? Is this the entry gate which is going to lead to the solution? Almost certainly more thought is required and probably some practical endeavour in the shape of a written draft or diagram, or a model, which may, or may not succeed the first time round, must follow — then and only then do results start to emerge. Determination and perseverance are essential. Sometimes the process is quick, sometimes slow, but it will only come to a fruitful conclusion with concentration. We have the solutions, but like gold, they have to be dug out of our minds.

In many conventional jobs, this thinking is done for one, and the individual carries out other people's ideas, does not generate them. I was forced out of this mould. **There is, of course, a need in every job for technical and administrative skills as well as conceptual thinking.**

Brilliant ides that are not properly carried out with logical systems and detailed "follow through" frequently flounder and come to nothing. Some people are better at creative work and others at systematic detailed work, but I believe that eveyone has to have a modicum of both.

I made good friends and gained some credibility with several Fleet Street personalities, some of whom, particularly the Editors of the major women's magazines, were very interesting people. They were highly professional and could gauge their readers' tastes with great accuracy. From the point of view of a sophisticated reader, several of these journals were very low key and did not aim for, or attain, high literary standards. But they met the needs of their large readership very precisely; so that both in advertising revenue and circulation, they were money spinners.

Such publications brought high returns for a comparatively modest investment, and so the women who controlled them were highly respected and very powerful. They were of two types, some plumpish almost dowdy; others were very elegant, somewhat fanciful personalities, but they had great expertise and high moral standards.

The style of such magazines could be rated as "mushy", but no-one who read either the articles or the stories could ever have been corrupted by them. I admired their professionalism, although some people sneered at them.

My contributions were either factual articles on fencing initially, and then on such things as novel merchandise which I ferreted out, or ideas for home decoration. Sometimes I placed what I most liked writing, contributions which were called "think pieces". These were mildly philosophical articles aimed at helping women to think more positively about themselves. It has been my recurring life theme and credits me with at least one virtue — consistency.

I thought then, as I do now, although a little less clearly, that many women's expectations of themselves are so low as to be insulting to any human being.

The way I saw them then, perhaps even more than today, was that — usually quite unjustifiably, they were prepared to play second fiddle to men, to accept any criticism, justified or not, believing that they must be wrong and, that everyone else, particularly the male of the species, must be right, cleverer, more worthy of recognition. It made me deeply angry. This "I am worthless — I can only serve — not lead" syndrome is so patently inaccurate and generates such waste of ability, that I longed then as I do now to redress the situation. I was not anti-men, except when they gloried in their stupidities, I was just pro- women.

My journalism did not, however, attain great heights, because I lacked direction and so instead of developing a consistent writing style, I dissipated my energies and turned to writing copy for advertisments, or putting together publicity leaflets and such like, as opportunities offered. In retrospect, this was a mistake — one should get a line and stick to it, at least until it has been given a fair run. Hopping in desperation from one thing to another, however, tempting, is never a right course — one has to make a plan — trust in one's judgement and sit it out. I felt I could not do this.

Using Imagination

One of the most fruitful approaches which I adopted was to make contact with a number of manufacturers or suppliers of interesting fashion merchandise. I would study their current ranges and make a selection of those items which I thought were novel and interesting. I wrote about them, had them attractively photographed and I would then try to interest one of the women's magazines in the feature. If I was lucky, the article and photographs would appear, a credit being given to the supplier.

This was of course for them, excellent publicity. Following on the article, I put up to the supplier different follow-up ideas — using the photographs which I had already paid for, and writing punchy copy, I would create a leaflet which I sold to the suppliers as a sales aid to help them to sell into their retailers. Alternately, I created counter show cards which featured the merchandise. One such card showed a picture of an elegant, stylised hand. Two small holes at the wrist made it possible for the retailer to slot in a bracelet, which hung on the card and so created a most effective display.

I dreamed up these ideas and working closely with one or two supportive printers, I learned how to commission artwork which appeared very glossy, but which in fact used only one or two colours. In this way, costs were reduced to a minimum. It was a blend of artistic and practical skills.

I was, in effect, offering a marketing service which sold many hundreds of pounds of merchandise for the firms I worked with. In keeping with the times, however, my earnings were minute.

A Plethora of Jobs

These activities attracted the attention of Harry, a dynamic young advertising man, who had come to London from Bristol. He rushed about, talked somewhat boastfully of his achievements and aspirations — nevertheless, he was quick-witted and creative. I could see he had something to offer me. He suggested I work for him on a part-time basis and so, still keeping the fencing going in the evenings, I entered the advertising world, not only writing copy, but also making contact visits with prospective clients. I learned about block making, layout and space booking and a whole new set of techniques.

It was all very interesting and to begin with Harry's little company did well, but then the need for capital overtook him, the cashflow situation became dangerous and he was forced into doing things which I felt were risky, if not downright dishonest. I sympathised with his predicament, but I did not believe he was right to creep into dishonest practices, diverting money which had been paid to him for one purpose into other channels. This upset me, particularly as these shady deals affected one of the clients, a man I liked and found very sincere, who had been very generous to Harry when he first set up.

Reluctantly, as the sums involved were not insubstantial, the client brought a case against Harry. I had by this time severed my connection with the firm, because I did not like the way things were going. But when the case came up, I was called as a witness. It was the first time that my loyalty and my sense of justice had been in real conflict. I did not like the situation at all. Not to have given evidence would have been very unfair for the very honourable client, yet Harry had helped me and taught me a great deal, so I felt grateful to him. In the end, the case was settled out of court and my fear of giving evidence was removed. Harry, like so many mercurial people who have talent but not always good judgement, got involved in the cheaper aspects of advertising, drank heavily and, although I had not seen him for a long time, I was not surprised to read a year or so later that he had died suddenly of a heart attack.

Modelling

Another activity I was caught up in was modelling. Being photographed for fencing took me into many different studios where I was asked to pose for all sorts of illustrations and advertisements. I hasten to add that modelling then was not the luxury business it is today. One was paid a guinea, the old £1 and 1 shilling, for a morning or an afternoon's work, or £1 and 10 shillings perhaps, if one was lucky.

I posed for hats, clothes, cosmetics, foam baths, etc, etc. I thought the job was absurd. I did it as well as I could, but I felt it was pointless and would not lead me anywhere — which was only partially true. it taught me how to groom myself better, by picking up make-up techniques; how to move slowly until the camera man had discovered the right angle, and then how to develop the control to stand still in front of the camera without looking stiff and rigid. Later, of course, when I became involved in advertising — I was able to evaluate photographs, knowing what happened on both sides of the camera — but, I could not perceive all that at the time. I totally lacked an overall plan or objective; I was just moving from point to point hoping to earn money.

To add to the melee, with Ian's help, I played "bit" parts in the theatre and also did days as a film extra. On one occasion, the young Assistant Director on the Gaumont set was David Lean, then, of course, quite unknown, but always very polite and helpful to us extras, very much the "also rans".

In one of the productions, I met Kathryn Brook, an older woman who had made quite a name for herself in New York as the clergyman's wife in the original production of Somerset Maugham's "Rain". She told me a great deal about the American theatre, which prompted me to think about how marvellous it would be to go to the States.

Although all this mass of activities seemed shapeless and of no real significance it was, in fact, forcing me to get rid of my shyness and to present myself much more positively. I suffered agonies of nerves, and often felt totally inadequate, not least because my clothes were so meagre, but I learned a great deal about communication, written and spoken, and this, as I have said, was to prove invaluable later. All the time I was pushed into using initiative and determination and whatever the setbacks — I couldn't give up so I pressed on.

An Audition

On many occasions I failed from ignorance or anxiety, or both. Once, for example, through a friend, I was given an introduction to the BBC. I took myself off with high expectations to Savoy Hill, the old 2LO Station, for an audition in a play. I had never been in a sound studio before and hadn't any idea what went on.

Various people, whose functions were not explained to me, were wandering about; one was wearing a set of headphones. I was not introduced to anyone, and stood rather disconsolately until I was handed a script and told to read it through by a person who was, of course, the Producer.

He then went out of the felt-lined soundproof room and I continued to study the script by myself standing in front of a microphone. Then I was told to read it out loud. I tried to enter into the character of the passage, but out of context it really did not mean very much to me. I thought about all my lessons in voice production. I tried to breathe deeply and form my words clearly. I expect it sounded very stilted.

When I had finished the passage, which only took a very few minutes, presumably following the Producer's wishes, the man in the earphones gave me various instructions — raise your voice here — drop your voice there — etc, etc. I took in what was being said, but because I did not realise that, although the Producer gave me instructions through the sound man, I could reply to the Producer directly through the microphone, which I thought was reserved for "the performance" only, I said nothing.

There was a pause, and then the man in the earphones said impatiently, in much the same tone as we have come to recognise in the programme, "Does she like sugar? Do you understand what is wanted?". Realising I was doing something wrong, quickly and apologetically I replied, "Yes I do". "Then you'd better do it again", said the sound man. Which I did, but by this time I was confused and very nervous.

I finished the passage and then stood waiting. The sound man eventually said, "Well, thank you very much. We'll get in touch when we've made a decision", or words to that effect. Of course, I knew I had failed. I felt awful and crept down the stairs, bitterly disappointed, wondering what I was going to say to my friend, Leslie, who had given me the introduction and worked at the BBC as a pianist. He was very kind and said, "I guess you were nervous — you really shouldn't have been — but better luck next time".

Leslie also played the Wurlitzer organ at the Tivoli cinema in the Strand. I often used to slip into the back of the stalls to watch him rise up out of the organ pit, become visible to the audience and roll out the rich tones of the organ, which he played very well. Then, while the film was showing, we would have coffee together. He was always encouraging and tried to think of ways which would help me to make progress with my work. To have someone slightly older, kind and friendly, to pick up one's spirits at the down points, was great — Leslie also took my mind off such setbacks by talking music. He introduced me to the music of Edward Elgar — up to then a blind spot in my musical education. I thought the Enigma Variations were delightful and seemed to catch the mood of my up and down feelings of the period.

Outside Events

Social and political events did not touch me very deeply at this period, I was too pre-occupied with my own affairs — struggling to make progress.

Going back in time, the General Strike of 1926, for instance, hit everyone. Ian drove a train, but I don't think I did anything very much — certainly the true significance of the event did not reach me.

I was much more excited by Lindbergh's flight across the Atlantic — he seemed so young and it was such an act of courage and daring. The words, "Spirit of St Louis" seemed to say it all.

We had always had a great feeling for the United States of America. My mother had been taken by an uncle and aunt to stay for about two years in Dover, New Hampshire, at the turn of the Century, and I believe the more open and liberal way of life which she experienced there freed her, and in consequence us, from some of the snobby stuffiness which was all to common in England right up to the Second World War.

This more open attitude linked very closely with her views about women's careers and their position in society. So when in 1928 women were given the vote, my mother, *and* my father too, enthusiastically endorsed it as right and just. They both agreed that there was a great deal of unfairness towards women, and comment on the suffragette movement was always made in very sympathetic terms.

My mother was also very keen that I should develop a career and it distressed her that I could not continue my education and develop a clear work plan. She would sympathise and help with every new idea I dreamed up, in whatever way was possible, saying not pushily, but supportively, "What will you do now?" I never ever remember her saying, "Who will you marry?", which was so very different from many mothers of the time. Somehow, although the pattern of my life was so ill-defined, there always seemed the possibility of high endeavour which would one day materialise. It was a great inspiration.

The Wall Street Crash of 1929 was another blow to the wobbly world economies and, although I did not understand the faintest thing about it, I knew that it was disastrous.

Finding my Feet

About this time, when I was in my early twenties, little by little, I started to find my feet in the social world. There was always Eve and her warm friendship, but I also seemed to get invitations from young men whom I met in the course of my many jobs. I was taken out to dinner, or on occasions to tea at the old Trocadero, which was in those days very elegant, discreet waiters serving tiny triangular sandwiches and mini eclairs to the background of Palm Court music!

I was beginning to feel that, although I was still very uncertain and insecure on the money and career fronts, my personality did seem sometimes to register with people with whom I was in sympathy.

Initially, to my surprise, people, men and women, began to take notice of what I said and did. If I wore a new dress or a pair of high heeled shoes, people turned to look at me, I felt, approvingly. In other words, I became conscious little by little that I was a person in my own right which both pleased and frightened me a little. But I was too diffident to take proper account of this, because I did not realise the influence I had on people and sometimes at a down turn of confidence, I would become gauche and hesitant again and blush painfully.

Men and Romance

So when from the world of music a man twice my age, not Leslie, suggested we should live together, I was astonished. I had been acquainted with him for quite some time through lessons and concerts, but we rarely met out of the company of other people, so I did not think I knew him as a man at all. His proposition, therefore, came as a bolt from the blue. I don't remember exactly what I said, but I thanked him politely and explained that I did not wish to accept his offer, as I was not in love with him and, in any case, I was too involved with family affairs. I don't think he really minded, although I was aware that he was a very lonely person.

Another young man who was really devoted to me and whom I liked very much took me about a great deal, to the theatre and into the country walking. We dined and danced every week and we had a great feel for non-stop variety — which today, I fear, would bore me to tears, but which at the time we thought was great fun. It was a very happy association, more serious for him, I fear, than for me. His well-off parents were very kind to me, but when he proposed, and talked about putting our engagement in the Times and Telegraph, I took fright.

I thought to myself — I don't want to become a social person, a housewife like his mother and sister, however, well to-do. Without knowing what I was trying to attain, I knew I wanted freedom and an independence which I wouldn't have if I followed Frank's pattern. So I retreated rapidly and, probably not very kindly, I broke everything off. Frank just couldn't understand what I was talking about — he was puzzled and hurt and I saw in a flash that he was solid, not at all exciting and not very quick witted! When it was over — I felt tremendously relieved, as if I could fly again free and untrammelled.

Other young men appeared, but I was very careful to ride lightly over the surface, making sure that I did not lay down formal patterns of any kind. Young people living together as they do today, did not come into it. One would embrace very tenderly and, I think, I was affectionate and warm hearted, but as to leaping into bed with anyone — I would just as soon have jumped off Beachy Head! I am sure today it all sounds incredibly naive and simple, but there was courtesy, respect and no fear. Also, inspite of continued money problems and battling away with home difficulties, I know I laughed a great deal, so perhaps I was good company.

However, I was conscious that I had not really been anywhere much, nor done exciting things like Eve, for example, who went ski-ing every year. She invited me to go, of course, but I couldn't afford the outfit or the fare.

Shyness and Ignorance

So at some of the early dinner parties I went to, I was very shy and woefully conscious of my ignorance and inexperience. One very interesting naval man invited me home to dinner with his people in the Temple — his father was a judge and his mother was charming, but it was all a little intimidating, particularly when the conversation turned on Art and I was asked which of the Dutch Masters I preferred.

Bluffing it out, I said I liked them all which must have sounded absurd, but as I hard scarcely heard of Rubens, or Rembrandt, or Franz Hals, I had to say something and felt perfectly silly. But I vowed that never again would I be caught out quite so badly on Art. The stupid thing was that if I had had the skill to turn the conversation on to music, I could have talked quite intelligently about Mozart or Beethoven, but I had neither the social adroitness, nor the confidence, to do this. Also my excessive humility made me think that others chose the topics and I followed.

The very next day I went to the library and started to take out books on the Great Masters. I also visited the National Gallery and attended the free lectures which were available. I cannot be sure of this, but I believe that some, at least, of those lectures were given by Kenneth Clarke, later Sir Kenneth of "Civilisation" fame.

My Love of London

I found I loved pictures and on my way to a modelling session, I would slip into an exhibition or a City church. I adored London — something about the atmosphere gripped me and I was conscious of the history and romance which pervaded, particularly the City. I was always discovering exciting things and buildings like the Grinling Gibbons carving in St Martins on Ludgate Hill — or Soane's Clock Museum in Lincoln's Inn.

One of the things I subsequently regretted was that I did not make notes and attend more carefully to the information my father gave me when on rare occasions I walked with him through different parts of London. As a boy in the 1890's, he had roamed all over the city when it must have been a dirty, vicious, if exciting place.

We were walking up Kingsway one day and he told me that before it was made into a wide and handsome thoroughfare, terminating at Aldwych with Bush House, he had remembered it as a nest of filthy little courts and alleys, with every third building a gin shop or a pub. At night drunks festooned the pavements and it was not safe to walk because of pickpockets. Perhaps we have come full circle!

Eve's Wedding

In 1936 a lovely event occurred — Eve became engaged to a charming man — Harry Attkins, a dentist whose family had lived in Highgate for several generations. He was much older than Eve, but he was gentle and very kind and welcoming to me. He also had a most delicious sense of humour and could poke fun at people without a touch of venom.

I greatly enjoyed being with them and when, to please Mrs Forgan, Eve's mother, a rather grand wedding was planned, I was invited to be a bridesmaid. It was very exciting. I wore a dress of gold coloured satin with a little head-dress. The wedding took place on 9 February, Eve's twenty sixth birthday at All Soul's, Langham Place, and afterwards there was a wonderful reception. We danced modern dances, but also Scottish reels until late into the night — Eve and Harry went to Switzerland for their honeymoon — I felt, as always, totally relaxed and at home.

Holidays

The only holidays which came my way, apart from sandcastle paddling holidays in Kent when I was a little girl, were with my aunts.

All through the years, I had regularly visited dearest Auntie Norah, who lived in a terraced house with Great Aunt Emma in Leicester. Trams went up and down the road outside, and I would often go with Auntie Norah to the neighbouring Church School where she was the Headmistress, and sit in at a lesson, or look at Natural History exhibits.

The school was housed in a perfectly awful old building, where the roof leaked and the loos sometimes didn't work. But Auntie Noe, my pet name for her, was a tremendous teacher, who inspired her staff with enormous enthusiasm and produced some astonishing results, succeeding in getting at least two of her pupils to Oxbridge in the 20's. Her fascination with learning was infectious and she spurred everyone who came in contact with her to unimaginable heights.

When I hear of the elaborate equipment and the opportunities for study and travel which both teachers and pupils have today, and the often very limited results which are attained, I am filled with admiration at the truly amazing attainments which came from that little school.

My aunt's leadership — vision — love of people, young and old, were, of course, the key factors. It is my view that glossy equipment and elaborate apparatus are no substitute for these wonderful personal qualities with which people can truly identify. However big or small the organisation, human beings will always respond to sympathetic people, which they will not attempt to do for things, lists of instructions, not even material rewards.

This is no justification for poor buildings, inadequate libraries and inefficient equipment; it is a plea that everyone who plays the role of the mentor to a child at school, to an employee in a bank or factory, should recognise not only the enormous opportunity and excitement it brings, but also the grave responsibility it imposes. They should know that they have to understand their charges and give them the motivation and strength to rise to the highest level.

I believe that all leaders, managers or parents have to remind themselves continually that every task they permit to be done less well than it could be, every corner cut to save time or effort, gradually builds into a slovenly mass, which becomes a way of life without inspiration or satisfaction. Inevitably, this leads to a waste of abilities, shabby standards and either mediocrity or disaster, reflected all too clearly in such happenings today as Britain's two million illiterate people, or a Townsend Thoresen disaster.

Auntie Norah took great pleasure in helping both Ian and myself in all sorts of ways. She gave me, for example, many of my clothes, which were made by a little local dressmaker called Polly, who was quite an artist, always adding a little touch of embroidery, or a decorated belt to a dress or blouse, which, of course, I liked very much.

When I was staying with my auntie, I was often invited to tea and supper by her friends; some very old gentlemen, others younger women with whom I visited local beauty spots, Charnwood Forest, or Belvoir Castle. I was pleased to be such a cared for visitor, but I perceived that the scene was a very narrow one, which carried with it considerable restrictions. I often could not, for example, say what I had in my mind. I sensed that the rigid conventional thinking pattern of many of these people prevented this. I knew they would not have understood and would have been hurt or angry, so I left it, saying to myself ungratefully, perhaps, "It doesn't matter, I shall soon be home".

The red-brick buildings, with blue-grey slates, and the tiny double entry passages which led to two separate houses in many areas of the city, together with huge red chimneys were my mental picture of Leicester — a city which had never known the poverty of northern cities in the great depression. Hosiery and knitwear were the staple merchandise and it seemed there was always a market for them.

In addition to going to Leicester, I would often be invited to stay when my aunts went on their annual pilgrimage to Devon or the South Coast.

Part of me enjoyed these trips very much. I loved the countryside and in those days places like Dartmeet were exquisite — totally wild and unspoiled and *no* people. The clear peat streams and the smell of thyme on Woodbury Common with skylarks rising, trilling to the sun was to me a delight.

The Fascination of Light

It was about this time that I became very conscious of light — light on water, cloud shadows racing across the Downs — sunsets half glowing brilliance, but with dark and sinister patches, purple to black — the clarity of the atmosphere and the delicious fragrance of the countryside after rain, or again the captivating translucent light which occurs on certain evenings, when the sun has almost gone and colours take on a glorious intensity. There's also the crisp sparkling clarity of the atmosphere under an aquamarine sky, which I call "new moon" weather. All these things filled my mind with wonderful images.

If I found my aunts, with the exception of Auntie Norah, a bit old and frumpy, I could take myself off walking and dream about the future like every girl of the period who read the books of Ethel M Dell. I imagined myself drifting in a romantic haze with a handsome man, who gave me a lovely wardrobe composed of six, only six — no extravagance, please — exquisite outfits, for day and evening. In these day dreams, I saw myself mistress of a lovely Georgian house on Richmond Hill, with the silver Thames winding far below. Don't ask me why Richmond, unless perhaps it was because Sir Percy Blakeney of Scarlet Pimpernel fame, I believe, lived there!.

So it was not all hard work and problems, there were fairy tales and fantasy interludes too. A bit like my taste in the theatre and books — stark realism or Swan Lake delicacy.

A typical fencing photograph

Some modelling photographs were taken on location. Here the picture was advertising river holidays

*The results of one of my modelling jobs, advertising the effects of a beauty cream. The photographic technique of the time was to use thick filters on the camera and with heavy re-touching remove every expression line or mark of individuality. Such pictures were incredibly artificial but thought very **a la** mode*

Chapter Three

The Fencing Era and the French Influence

Little by little, in spite of all the other distractions, the Fencing School grew and became the dominant interest. The number of pupils who joined the School increased steadily — there were as many young men as women and this gave a new dimension to the Salle.

This was due to the fact that Ian began to take more and more interest in the School. It was very valuable for him as the theatre and film business slumped and the recession continued. The Jarrow March of 1936, when miners tramped all the way from the north-east to the House of Commons to complain of the terrible conditions and the lack of work, was a phenomenon of this period. It was small wonder, therefore, that many theatrical ventures either failed, or were often not even started for lack of capital. British films in particular were at a very low ebb.

I was delighted to have Ian work with me as a full partner. It was a disappointment for him that he could not progress in the theatre, but he accepted it as an inevitable part of the depression. It was no use grumbling, and he felt he was very fortunate to have something else to which he could turn his attention. He became a first class teacher — acting and teaching have much in common. He not only taught foil, but epée and sabre too.

These are the three weapons which comprise modern fencing. The character of each of them is quite different.

Hits in foil fencing are scored with the point, the movements are neat and exact and aimed at a restricted target. With the epée, hits are registered again only with the point, but the target is the entire body, including legs, arms and even the back. The sabre is a slightly heavier weapon with a guard to protect the hand. Both the point and the cutting edges are used, so movements are much wider.

Perhaps the fundamental principle of all fencing, which is "hit your opponent and remain untouched yourself", has much to recommend it!

Building up the Fencing School

We realised that if we were going to gain more pupils, we had to get publicity. Because of the finesse and speed of the point work, it is a difficult sport for the uninitiated to follow. Fencing is not, and has never become, a "spectator" sport. The way points are won or lost is too quick to be seen easily from a distance. The progress of the match is often not understood except by those with a knowledge of the game, so it lacks popular appeal.

Once people become involved with the sport, it has tremendous fascination, but until then it is almost incomprehensible. The task, therefore, was to attract people to fencing by stimulating their interest with a bolder more visible approach.

With this in mind, we put on displays and galas which not only presented the usual foil and epee matches and contests, but also always included an element of the spectacular. These presentations appealed to many more people and encouraged the Press to take notice of a sport they frequently ignored.

An account in The Queen magazine in 1933 reporting on one of our gala evenings made just this point — it read — "It is always with a pleasant feeling of anticipation that one attends the displays put on by Eleanor and Ian Macdonald, for apart from orthodox items of strictly fencing interest, this ingenious pair always produce something spectacular and sufficiently theatrical to appeal to the lay onlookers, while not outraging the rigid principles of modern swordsmanship, a unique combination".

This particular year, using Ian's knowledge of the theatre, the spectacle we devised was called the "Shadow of the Sword". With back lighting which threw up the opponents in silhouette, the history of combat was outlined from the Broadsword, through the era of Elizabethan rapier and dagger to the eighteenth century duelling sword and so to modern days.

Contrary to the article in The Queen, some conformists I am sure thought our approach over-theatrical. Fencers had been a very elite body;

our aim was to interest a much wider group of people in a sport which they previously had never heard of, let alone taken up.

The audience found the spectacle hightly entertaining and the extensive Press coverage obtained increased our members considerably.

For another display, we created a fencing "ballet", which was performed to Gershwin's "Rhapsody in Blue". The costumes, which were very "art nouveau", were made out of brilliantly coloured shiny material with a strong zigzag motif. Teams of fencers moved in harmony, creating colour patterns as they were grouped about the stage. In the end, the red team prevailed over the green troupe, who met an untimely end. It was great fun!

The following year, an article I had written on fencing was featured prominently in the Daily Mirror, then quite a serious paper. This resulted in a large post bag. People, mostly women office workers, wrote from all over the Home Counties. They wanted to learn fencing as a health exercise and a sport with a very romantic tradition. It was obvious they were not going to travel to Croydon, so with the support of the Daily Mirror we started a London Club.

As always, accommodation was the big problem, because so much space is required. Fencing is performed on a conventional narrow planche, the fencers moving back and forth, keeping within the prescribed width of approximately 6ft. A room which could accommodate the width of several of these planches was not difficult to find. The problem arose with the length of the planche, which has to be 40ft for foil, longer for epée and sabre. By approaching all sorts of people, both in the West End and the City, we eventually obtained the use of an untenanted top floor in Bush House. It required a great deal of persuasion to get people to help us, because we could not possibly have afforded standard London rentals. However, we managed it and the City Club, as it was called, started with 40 members.

Teaching in Different Locations

We divided the evenings of the week between the two locations, Croydon and Bush House. In addition, we were invited to teach fencing at other clubs. I was, for example, the first woman to teach fencing at the boys' City of London School. The LCC also became interested and, while Ian was going to instruct at an insurance company in the West End, I would trail off into the East End of London to give lessons at 8 o'clock at night to little girls who worked in the sweat shops of the rag trade off the Commercial Road.

Another East End class I ran was held in the Bernard Baron Institute, where I encountered that remarkable pair, Sir Basil and Lady Henriques.

They were famous figures in London, who performed a wonderful services for so many under-privileged people. During the day, Basil Henriques was a magistrate in a juvenile court, and Lady Henriques devoted her time to organising the Institute, which occupied a large five-floored building.

All kinds of sporting and leisure activities took place in the Institute to interest poor Jewish youngsters and help to keep them off the streets. As well as fencing, one of the activities offered was ballet, and I still have a mental picture of this dynamic middle-aged lady wearing a faded tutu, taking a ballet class. She marched about the room with great authority demonstrating entrechats, pliés and jetés which great determination, not forgetting occasionally to add such injuntions in her clear high-pitched voice as, "Keep the back straight and don't forget the deodorant powder, please, girls!"

I was very fond of the Jewish ladies in my class, some of whom showed considerable ability for fencing. They often brought me little gifts, although they were so poor; a packet of Matzos cakes, or a tiny hair ribbon from one of their workshops to express how grateful they were for the trouble I was taking in coming all the way to the Institute so late in the evening. I also felt very privileged when, as Liberal Jews, they occasionally allowed me to attend services in their synagogue in the basement. They would explain some of the ritual to me and I would join in the singing. It was a different world and I greatly admired the camaraderie and good humour which enabled these splendid people to rise above their poverty and problems.

It was certainly hard work, because as well as the teaching, I frequently had to carry quite heavy fencing equipment in a large bag, slung over my shoulder. It was all right on fine evenings, but when a heavy drizzle set in, or the fog rolled up from the Thames, which runs parallel to the Commercial Road, one felt pretty jaded having to face the late journey back to Croydon. But surprisingly, there was absolutely no danger. In all the years I gave these classes in one of the toughest areas of the City, I was never once accosted, nor threatened, and I felt perfectly safe. I feel so sad that the same discipline does not prevail today. I cannot believe that it is just poverty which has generated modern violence, because the East End people of that time were *really* poor.

As our pupils became more successful and won matches against often well-known clubs and carried off cups, we realised that if the School was to develop and enlarge its reputation, we ourselves must continually improve our skills; so we started to go regularly to Paris, which was the recognised centre of fencing in Europe. We had been given introductions to various fencing Salles in Paris by Professor Gravé.

Going to Paris — Fencing in Exclusive Clubs

In Paris we met one of the most charming and generous people I have ever known: Mâitre Alfred Bourdon. He was an excellent fencer and a brilliant teacher. He shared his tremendous knowledge and skill with us and refused to accept any fees for the long training he gave. We were astonished — we thought we would have to pay large fees and were very apprehensive that we would not be able to afford them, but he was adamant. I think he regarded working with us as an opportunity to pass on his knowledge and expertise to a new young School. He could also, I think, see that we were utterly genuine in our love of the sport and our desire to practise fencing in the best traditions. This I regard as one of the many generous gestures which have made possible my advancement.

We took our lessons in a little Salle just behind the Gare Lazare in the rue de Londres. We would have lessons and practise bouts for about two hours in the morning, usually with Mâitre Bourdon on our own.

Then we would walk down the rue de Londres and have a sandwich and a Moitié-Moitié (half Noilly Prat, half Cinzano) in a little bistro, where we would find other fencers, pupils of Mâitre Bourdon's evening groups.

The very demanding morning sessions were given with great care and enthusiasm. The finer points of technique were precisely demonstrated and carefully explained with never any sarcasm or superiority. Alfred also introduced us to most of the other well- known fencing Salles and Fencing Professors throughout the City. One of these clubs was a very chic establishment — the Cercle Hoche , not far from the Arc de Triomphe. The membership was very exclusive. The activities offered in addition to fencing were boxing and shooting. French women in the 1930's, with a few marked exceptions, did not take fencing as seriously as I was trying to do. So no provision was made for them to attend the Cercle in the evenings, they had two mornings set on one side for their participation.

Alfred, however, felt that I, as well as Ian, should go in the evening to gain the experience of meeting senior fencers. It was a very special concession, which he arranged with the distinguished Secretary of the Cercle, who on my first evening with great courtesy met us at the door. Bowing, he apologised, explaining that there was no ladies' changing room in the evenings; so would I mind using the Board Room on the first floor? I was quite happy, of course, just to be there.

With much trepidation, I mounted the wide staircase which, if I remember correctly, had marble pillars on either side. I found myself in a grand room with highbacked leather chairs and massive furniture. It was all pretty frightening.

I changed quickly, folding my street clothes carefully over the back of one of the chairs. My fencing kit was, of course, regulation white — shoes and stockings and a short heavily pleated or flared skirt and a tight-fitting jacket, the colours of our two clubs crossed on the left arm. Later breeches became standard wear. I chose my foils carefully and realising I had taken no time at all with this, I paused.

Ian, I felt sure, was being welcomed and would be chatting and talking to the many men, professionals and amateurs, in the large elaborately equipped changing room in the basement. I must not go down too soon, I said to myself, otherwise I would be the only woman in the room and the first to arrive.

So looking round to fill in the time, I saw a splendid set of leather-bound volumes on a shelf by the fireplace, records of all kinds of fencing successes I was sure, perhaps names and scores of past champions and other fascinating data. I felt I must look.

Feeling a little guilty for being nosey, I opened up the first volume and then I knew I was in Paris! No authentic records there, they were bound copies of the Folies Bergère programmes! Georgeous pictures of the glamorous be-feathered chorus and famous stars like Josephone Baker and Mistinguet doing their stuff. I chuckled ecstatically.

The men downstairs might be fencing champions and aristocrats taking their leisure, but they no longer intimidated me.

Almost jauntily, I went downstairs and I was, of course, treated royally with true French courtesy. All the attendant professors offered me lessons, and fencers, including many distinguished champions came forward with the traditional invitation, "Vous voudriez avoir cinque pointes, Mademoiselle?" It was tremendous – the graciousness, but the seriousness which prevailed, was delightful.

These visits to Paris were a major experience. Our fencing speed and style improved immeasurably. We fenced on an average 6-8 hours a day. Like anyone who has had such intense physical training, we were slim and lean and at a high pitch of mental alertness. often after a late dinner at a little bistro, costing next to nothing, not even thinking about being tired, we would go to a midnight film, perhaps Fred Astaire and Ginger Rogers, or a Roman Policier.

Mâitre Bourdon realised that our success in England depended on our professional standing, and after several years of his tuition, he organised a special evening at Cercle Hoche when most of the panel of Professors were to be present, and we were to fence in front of them. It was not a formal examination, but we were under the scrutiny of a very exacting body of people, who had great pride in their professional standards, so we knew we had to perform well.

We obviously did. Because as a result of this nerve-racking experience, we were judged as qualified to become Mâitre d'Armes de l'Academie d'Epée de Paris. There were very few foreign members of the Academie and I was the first woman to receive the award. We were thrilled. It was a most important step forward for us and we were always enormously grateful to Alfred Bourdon for having arranged it.

We came to know pre-war Paris very well using the old swaying buses or the Metro, with its inescapable smell of ozone and "gauloise bleue" cigarettes, to move from Salle to Salle carrying our heavy equipment over our shoulders.

La Famille Bourdon

The Bourdon family became great friends. Madame Bourdon, Alfred's sister, was very hospitable and we frequently visited her little Paris apartment and met her lovely daughter, Raymonde.

Raymonde was studying art at one of the Paris schools. She was a quiet, elegant, almost girlish person, and we felt that perhaps she was rather dominated by the very strong personality of her mother. Both Raymonde and Madame Bourdon were keen fencers, Madame having been a champion.

Mâitre Bourdon and Madame's father, who had died many years before, had run a Salle in Paris for several decades and so the whole family had been brought up in a fencing tradition, which we found most stimulating.

Some of the other fencing Professors whom we visited, had great reputations. There was the Salle Gardère, run by Gardère Père, whose two sons, Edouard and André, both became champions at different times.

Another little old fencer, a famous Professeur Remez, gave us lessons in a small oddly-shaped room at the back of Galeries Lafayette. He wore a sombre black outfit and little soft leather boots. These sessions were an experience. The delicacy and precision of his point work was astonishing. He could take the most effective counter parries with a mere twist of the wrist and, although he was probably 70 and was not able to move fast, he could still beat most people by sheer expertise, timing and accuracy. It was this kind of style we were trying to emulate.

We visited Paris every year, sometimes twice a year from 1932 until 1939 and I took part in various exhibition matches, one I remember in the Bois de Boulogne in 1935. We fenced out of doors and I recall the sun glinting through the chestnut trees which had come into full bloom almost overnight.

Knowing the Bourdon family so well, whenever we attended a competition or a match at such places as the Racing Club, we met all the well-known fencers and referees of the time.

I observed how dedicated people were to the sport, and also how sometimes this enthusiasm spilled over into points of temperament or temper! When something upset them, some competitors would stamp off the planche and even refused to come back to continue the match until they had been calmed down, or even worse very childishly, the score was adjusted!!

The Italians were formidable contenders for the various trophies and both they and the Czechs were unbeatable at sabre. I have never seen such rapid reflex actions as they were capable of.

This perfectionism was a splendid stimulus for both Ian and me. I came to see that co-ordination of mind and body was the key — to fence well, one had to observe, work out a strategy which one's physical technique could sustain, and then with determination carry it through.

Concentration and timing were of vital significance and when meeting a really strong fencer perhaps for the first time, one had always to maintain an element of surprise.

This mental training was invaluable to me in my later life, because all the skills I have referred to are all called for in management.

Maître Bourdon's private life was a little unpredictable. He was such an attractive person, tall, with a marvellous bearing, and a wonderful sense of humour. He obviously found women's company very agreeable, and they his. Eventually, he married a little lady with bright brown eyes and rather alarming yellow hair. We were introduced and she prepared a wonderful dinner for us. She was not, however, a fencer and we did not find a great deal in common with her. This marriage did not last.

Alfred Bourdon was to us always charming, generous and very amusing. We realised how lucky we were to have had his support and guidance.

Other French Friends

We also had other friends in Paris, Lucien Guitard for example, whom we met on our very first visit. He was a teacher of English and became a very distinguished Professor at the École Superieur de la Sorbonne, the senior teacher training establishment. Over the years, he published many excellent books on learning English for French speaking people. As one might expect, his English was impeccable. His knowledge of English literature was vast and our conversations were highly stimulating.

We went about the City together, the three of us, visiting famous buildings and historical monuments. One of my favourite places was the Musée Rodin, which was quite close to the tiny Left Bank Hotel where we used to stay.

Paris was incredibly cheap in those pre-war days and had great atmosphere; like thousands before us, both Ian and I felt very much at home in this lovely City and fell ready victims to its all-pervading charm.

Lucien married an actress Geneviève, who took us to the Comédie Française to see a play by Marivaux. In the interval, we visited the very elegant Green Room at the back of the stage, far more like a salon than any Green Room I have seen in a British theatre. We met several of the performers.

In accordance with tradition, we patted the bust of Molière on the head, shiny from many hands, as we came back into the theatre. Lucien and Geneviève lived in a large studio flat, which we sometimes visited. But I fear their personalities were not really compatible. Lucien had a totally different rhythm to Geneviève — he was slower, more reflective, and eventually they split up.

We were sorry for any unhappiness which may have occurred, but when later Lucien introduced us to Isabelle, whose clear blue eyes conveyed a quiet serenity, we were enormously happy, because we thought we perceived the tranquility which we believed Lucien was seeking.

They are still married and living together very happily, not in the rush and bustle of Paris, but in a quiet country town, Vannes in Brittany. I have never visited them there, although we correspond frequently, fifty years on!

Back to England

Returning to England, we worked very hard and became visiting professors to more schools and clubs. We often gave 150, 15- minute lessons in the course of the week, travelling considerable distances on public transport to reach the different clubs.

In addition, there were correspondence, books and accounts to be coped with and Ian learned to mount all the weapons we provided for the pupils — foils, epées and sabres.

We bought the whippy steel blades and string bound handles in France, the guards and pommels, the heavy piece of metal which holds the parts together and gives the right weight and structure to a weapon, coming from Birmingham.

Ian took great care to balance each foil perfectly, so that they were light and made possible the most exact movements.

Such finesse is not required today, because the electric judging machine has long come into its own, making more accurate judging possible, but the machine requires that weapons have wires running down the blade, attached to the fencer and then to a machine which enables the points scored to be registered by a system of lights which flash when a point is scored. This adds considerably to the weight of the weapons.

The precision of point work which we aimed for, and learned in Paris how to attain, had a quality and fascination of its own. Time, however, marches on and each generation demands different standards. This is not to say that fencing is not still a very precise and disciplined exercise — but the standards have altered.

Fencing — a Training for Management

Inspite of all this endeavour, financial rewards were not great, but I was learning some very valuable insights into methods of management, particularly the handling of people. Each pupil naturally had different abilities and a different temperament and needed to be handled with perception.

Some members developed considerable technical ability, but had little motivation and will to win, so that when in combat with others, they mentally gave up and lost, often when they need not have done so. Some expended all their energies in the first few minutes of a match, become tired and were overcome by not being able to stay the course. They could not measure and utilise their strengths correctly.

Yet again, some fencers were easily rattled if a particular strategy they had planned didn't work, as a result of which they lost their temper and their play became untidy, they let their guard down and their opponents slipped through. There were others who had such high goal orientation that they would beat more skilful and experienced fencers against all expectations.

Sometimes success went to people's heads. They became arrogant and would develop mannerisms when coming on to the planche, such as taking a long time to adjust their gloves or masks in an effort to discomfort their opponent. Inevitably a minority were just bad sports — shrugging their shoulders and turning away from their opponent sulkily if they thought a point had been wrongly scored against them, or pressing in on top of an opponent, which was not allowed.

The selection of fencers for a match could also be a tricky business. In the early days, Ian or I would make the selection, but as our teams' expertise increased we left this to the Captains. At times this generated a certain jealousy and we had to smooth down tempers.

One of the annoying aspects of the job was that because it was a leisure activity for the pupils, they would quite demandingly take us on one side in the middle of a busy evening of lessons, or ring up at any hour of the day or night to discuss often trivial personal concerns — virtually, our leisure time did not exist! This was quite hard to bear.

I did a great deal of judging at various matches. I found this exhilarating. One's role as President of the panel of four judges — two watching one fencer and two the other — was similar to that of a Chairman at a meeting or the presiding judge at Wimbledon, except that the President in fencing has to move up and down following the fencers. One had to register a casting vote if the judges disagreed, decide on timing and when a point had been awarded, or conversely declared null and void, bring the fencers together again to re-start play.

AUTOBIOGRAPHY OF A PIONEER BUSINESS WOMAN

It was vital that one not only knew the rules very thoroughly, but also that one did not hesitate or get into arguments over points, otherwise the match could drag on, the fencers become dispirited and irritated, causing the quality of the play to deteriorate.

Quickness of eye, alertness, concentration, impartiality and speed of judgement were all required. More difficult, was calling a fencer to order for bad behaviour or any violation of the rules — sometimes a sort of McEnroe situation would develop.

This again was all excellent training for management.

An aspect of team working which took me much longer to understand and to handle was the effect of one member on another in a crowd; in other words, the group dynamics. If one strong personality started to grumble about something — the state of the planche, the light or the heat, then inevitably several others would follow the lead. This was not easy to handle, because the facilities we were able to afford and offer we knew did not measure up to the standards we would have liked. There were no showers, and storage space for equipment was always limited, so we felt that there *were* causes for complaint.

We had, therefore, to act with a great deal of tact and patience but occasionally, with some of the pettiness which was shown, there had to be a little straight speaking.

The great reward was the enthusiastic loyalty which the large majority of the members showed. They stayed with us for years and often volunteered to provide refreshments, or transport and the like. Match and competition results of the Salle Macdonald were steadily improving, so a considerable esprit de corps developed.

There were many Challenge Cups and Annual Championships which took place in London every year. We always encouraged our people to enter for these as soon as they had reached a good enough standard. The experience which such events provided was a great fillip.

By 1937, we had pupils either from the Croydon or the City Clubs represented in the finals of such events as the Women's Foil Championships, the Coronation Cup and the Men's Foil Championship. Much later, Arthur Smith, a brilliant left-handed fencer, whom we regarded as our star pupil, became a member of the British Olympic Foil Team in 1948. Another girl, Gillian Sheen, who won the Girls' School Championship when I was teaching her at Queens College, Harley Street, again, after the war, became Women's Foil Champion.

It was not, however, only the top scorers we were trying to help. We wanted everyone who came to the Salle for exercise, for companionship, for slimming, to have a really good time and enjoy the sport to the full.

One of the ways we sought to publicise fencing was by writing an absolutely basic book about it. There were many volumes about swordplay, but they were highly detailed and intended for sophisticated readers. We felt there was a place for a "beginners" book, so we sought out a publisher and wrote a brief descriptive volume in the simplest language, with absolutely no frills.

The equipment, the techniques, the rules and conventions of the game were all carefully described and illustrated with action photos, which conveyed some understanding of the vitality and crispness of the play. It was published in Foulsham's Sports Library, a series of 1/- sports books, which were intended to introduce wrestling, golf, fishing or table tennis to larger audiences. Like all "How To" books, in spite of its brevity, it was very difficult to write. Brief precis work always requires a lot of patience and effort. It proved very popular; the edition quickly sold out, but there was little profit from it.

Coaching duels for Stage and Screen

The historical background of fencing was, of course, linked in the public mind with such characters as the Count of Monte Cristo, d'Artagnan, the Three Musketeers and the like, versions of whose activities were always being dramatised. When duelling was featured in such a play or film, to make the sword play look professional, Ian or I were frequently asked to produce these duels. We had learned a rapier and dagger routine when we first started to fence, and had purchased some antique weapons, often performing colourful duels in full Elizabethan costume. The moves were carefully rehearsed rather like a dance routine and included accurately timed strokes, which made it appear that, for example, I narrowly missed having my head cut off, or Ian losing a hand. Finally, one or other of us would be disarmed and the dagger plunged into the defeated opponent's chest. The audience always found these presentations quite exciting, because with a great deal of practice and rehearsal the different strokes could be performed very quickly and made to look both realistic and dangerous.

Ian developed various versions of the rapier and dagger routine and frequently trained actors, playing Mercutio, Tybalt, and Romeo in Romeo and Juliet, to carry out the famous duels.

I was invited once to go to the film studios at Elstree, where a nineteenth century drama was being filmed. The two actors playing the leading parts had only a very elementary knowledge of fencing, so I was asked to train them very quickly to perform a duel in which one of them was to be killed.

Before that happened, the script required that the villain narrowly missed killing the hero. The actors were wearing elegant shirts with lace ruffles at the neck and wrist, and the Producer wanted the villain's sword to pierce the shirt, but miss the hero. No masks could be worn, so when this quite dangerous little sequence was ready to be filmed, I doubled for the villain, and with my back to the camera, so that my face could not be seen, I lunged at the hero, tore his shirt, but thank goodness did avoid touching his body, which was what was required. I breathed a sigh of relief, but, of course, in the manner of filming, the whole sequence had to be re-done! Fortunately, the second time also my sword ripped the shirt, but didn't damage the wearer!

Another sortie into the film world came when we persuaded Pathé Films to make a short film on fencing for their Gazette programme, stressing the health and beauty angles of the sport. To open the sequence, we presented about twelve pupils in a formal routine called the Grand Salute. It was a frequent practice to use this as a starting item at championships or galas. It comprises a most elegant set of movements which demonstrates the various positions used in fencing, and stresses the courtesy and style which is an essential part of the sport. Even today, every assaut, however informal, always finishes with a salute.

Various other matches were included in the film which created quite an amount of short-lived interest.

The Lord Mayor's Show

In 1938, the concept of physical fitness captured the country. A National Fitness Council had been formed and as far as possible we worked with this Body to promote fencing.

A splendid opportunity arose when it was decided to make the Lord Mayor's Procession for the year a sports event. The pageant was called "Physical Fitness Through the Ages". Every kind of sport was represented, either in period or modern costume.

We were asked to organise the fencing section. We decided that it should comprise two aspects, the first was a group of about 20 or 30 men and women fencers, marching along four abreast with their foils at salute. They looked very smart in spotless white jackets and skirts or trousers. We draw these "marchers" from our various schools and clubs. It was quite difficult to find sufficient members who could devote a whole day to this, as well as all the many rehearsals and preparation that was needed.

The other part of the presentation was a series of tableaux of period sword play, including Richard the Lionheart broadswords and Elizabethan rapier duels up to modern epée, sabre and foil bouts. These were performed on a platform that was driven slowly along the city streets, the usual Lord Mayor's crowds lining the streets, clapping and cheering.

The quality of the fencing was pretty shaky as the moving platform jerked every now and then, but it didn't matter — the impression was realistic and that was what was required.

The then new Lord Mayor, Sir Harry Twyford, was highly praised for the novel presentation which was rated the jolliest Lord Mayor's show ever.

Domestic and World Events

All these work activities took place against a background of highly significant national events. I have to confess that at this time I was so involved and caught up with my own business and interests, that I did not make the time to read newspapers carefully and so my knowledge of both national and international affairs was very sketchy.

The abdication of Edward VIII was a major happening, which registered with everyone. I had always admired the young King as a person with sympathy and understanding. I, with thousands of other people, felt very let down, therefore, when he rejected the country, and all it represented, for someone who many saw as just a socialite.

While some people regarded the event as a tragic love affair, it seemed to me a terrible thing for Edward to desert his duty and lump his responsibilities on to someone who had not been fully trained for the throne and who was known to be rather frail in health. For the marvellous way they responded, I admired both George VI and his lovely Queen enormously, an admiration which has never faded.

Another event which puzzled us was the Spanish Civil War and all the brutality and bloodshed that it entailed. It was obvious that it was not just a domestic affair so there was much speculation as to what its real significance was and also what Germany's role was in the whole episode. There was great distrust concerning Germany's lust for power, and the growing strength of Facism made Neville Chamberlain's appeasement policy seem totally unrealistic.

Some people felt the need to make some preparation against possible disaster and joined organisations like The Royal British Legion, or St John Ambulance. I did not have the time for this and felt slightly uncomfortable that I was doing nothing. I did, however, start to learn German.

My Father's Changing Fortunes

Domestic matters had by this time improved somewhat. My father had in a measure re-established himself. He worked first at the Oxford and Cambridge Club, where Brigadier Jeffries was the Secretary. He was very good to my father, and when he moved to the Junior Carlton Club he took my father with him. He could see that Daddy had both technical and administrative abilities. He put him initially in charge of the cigars, cigarettes and wine cellars. Daddy had a very refined palate for these things and his ability to taste and purchase this merchandise, often at very advantageous prices, was very important to the successful running of the Club.

Then, resulting from his knowledge and love of books, he undertook a survey and valuation of the books in the library, most of which were never even looked at by the members. It was an important collection and valuable volumes had simply accumulated dust, and in some cases had deteriorated badly. Daddy realised that the library was a considerable asset to the Club and it distressed him to see rare and lovely volumes totally neglected. Some of the more valuable books he had restored, and a complete catalogue of the whole library was set up. He added up-to-date books on political and social affairs, which were of interest to the members and made recommendations for some of the really precious, but little used folio volumes, to be sold to boost the shrinking coffers of the Club.

One of these beautiful books was the masterpiece, Gould's British Birds, which, of course, found a ready market, but at that time if I remember correctly, was sold for only a few thousand pounds, a sum which today would be regarded as absurd. This initiative and its resulting success persuaded Brigadier Jeffries to recommend that my father be made the Librarian.

As 1939 moved on, the Summer recess came — as was customary, fencing finished and people went away to the country or abroad. As usual we cleared up all outstanding paperwork and equipment, and went off for a much needed holiday in Devon. This was the last time we were to go through this end of term rigmarole.

War is Declared

On our return, Poland was invaded and the Second World War began. I remember we sat and listened to the solemn announcement of the declaration of War on an ancient cat's whisker radio. The full impact of this devastating news did not at first hit us. From a personal point of view, what it meant was the immediate end of both the fencing schools. Ten year's work just disappeared over- night. As the days went by, mobilisation began in earnest and we knew that it was the end of an era.

I often ask myself what I learned from the fencing years — I have highlighted certain points as they appeared to me, but over and above the actual events, I think the most important thing which I learned was sticking at things, however remote and obscure the goal may appear to be.

Later in my life, I compared this kind of situation to climbing a mountain range. Halfway up the first mountain, very depressingly, the distant summit, the true goal, is completely obscured by the mists of doubt and the intervening peaks. That is the moment when one is tempted to give up, because it seems one is on the wrong track. But if one can keep going on the basis of trust and confidence, the mists do clear and one can achieve, not always perhaps as well as one would like, but it becomes possible to reach the first summit, and gain sight once again of the far peak the ultimate goal and so go on again.

I think I was just coming to the point of the first summit when the War started.

The Shadow of the Sword — a representation of the History of the Sword.
Here the Roman era is depicted showing the net, trident and dagger which
were the weapons of the period

A Fencing Ballet — The fencers carried imitation weapons and moved in harmony to Gershwin's 'Rhapsody in Blue'. The lunge, the attack, the parry were all included in a stylised mass duel

The start of the City Fencing Club. I give a foil lesson to a member. The panorama of the city forms a backdrop

The en garde position, the foil held in one of the eight hand positions which become parries to the oppponent's attack. The flexed knees enable the fencer to advance or retreat very rapidly and the loosely carried left hand balances the tension and precision of the weapon hand

*Ian Macdonald in the lunge which carries the point of the foil to the target,
but keeps the attacker's body as far out of reach of the defendant as possible*

Ian and I perform an Elizabethan rapier and dagger duel in costume. Each movement was exactly timed and carefully rehearsed. Without masks there was an element of danger

Here I am leading a team of fencers into the Grand Salute, rehearsing for a fencing interlude presented on Pathe Gazette

*The Lord Mayor's Show in 1938. A modern fencing demonstration
performed on a float that was driven through the City streets as part of the
"Physical Fitness through the Ages" pageant*

Chapter Four

The War Years

After the first shock of the declaration of war, everyone's feelings were in a turmoil; there was great excitement involved in such a tremendous undertaking, but there was also a sort of numbness, because we didn't really know where we were heading. Were we going to be bombed out of existence or invaded? Could we be starved out if the shipping lanes were closed by German U-Boats? I remembered vividly what a menace they had been in the First World War. The German use of the devastating Blitzkrieg techniques which over-ran Poland in about two days obviously made everyone think hard as to what could happen here.

We blessed the English Channel as so often before in our history.

The weather in Autumn 1939 was absolutely beautiful — bright blue skies and golden sunshine — perfect September weather, which somehow seemed incongruous. Very soon soldiers and volunteers appeared in quite large numbers on the streets, digging holes to form barricades and filling bags with sand, which were packed against buildings to act as shock absorbers against possible bombing. In spite of the darkening mood, the spectacle of men's dishevelled heads popping out of holes in the ground seemed utterly hilarious.

The Paraphernalia of War

Leaflets and announcements in the newspapers instructed everyone to black out their windows. The theory was that even a glint of light from inside houses or offices after dark could alert enemy aircraft.

So everyone rushed out and bought yards of black fabric or black paper to gum on to windows and fanlights, and as the Air Raid Precaution Officers were mobilised, they came round to check how efficient these precautions were. Anyone who showed a chink of light after dark was either reprimanded or fined.

We also had to collect gas masks which came in little square boxes, for which we bought pouches so that they could be slung over the shoulder, as we were never supposed to go out without them.

Later on, the masks, having been left on the tops of radiators or on window ledges in the sun, when they were extracted from the boxes they were often nothing more than a glutinous mass of rubber — and therefore totally useless. But people still carried them around. Identity cards were issued, everyone was allocated a number and later ration books had to be claimed. These were to ensure that everyone got an equal opportunity to obtain a fair share of essential foods, when supplies started to run short. Tiny amounts of butter, fat, bacon, eggs, sugar and that loathsome stuff, egg powder were obtained in the shops in exchange for the coupons, which were snipped out of the books. What a grotesque performance! But by people showing incredible patience — it worked.

Of course, a small minority of people cheated, but for the most part people put up with these meagre rations with a good grace. Although standing in long queues to get these things was very infuriating. Offal and fish were never on ration and so when one saw a crowd collecting at the butchers or fishmongers, one rushed to make a purchase, even without knowing what was on offer and perhaps not particularly wanting anything.

All these tasks took an incredible amount of time, which I suppose was not a bad thing as our attention was taken away from worrying about the war.

Joining the Censorship Department

Ian had immediately volunteered for the Forces, but was rejected on health grounds. Although he had amazingly maintained drive and stamina in the very hard work of fencing, he was not robust. A wobbly heart and very uncertain digestion made him totally unacceptable for the armed forces. Naturally we both wanted to make a contribution to the war effort, because excitement was at fever heat. We also needed to earn money.

Ethel Dawes, my dear friend from school days, had already been recruited for the Censorship Department as she was bi-lingual, German and English. She suggested that we also volunteer for the Department, which we did. Ethel could both read and write Schrift, the ancient Gothic script which was still then widely used in Germany by all well-educated people. She went off to Liverpool to examine and censor prisoners-of-war mail. Later, letters from high-ranking German Officer prisoners, who deliberately mangled their writing in order to disguise important messages, came through. Miss Dawes was able to decipher most of these almost illegible letters and so valuable information was revealed.

Following Miss Dawes' advice, I went off to the War Office and was interviewed by a very pleasant officer, a Major Bevan. He examined my credentials and I was recruited at once. I immediately signed the Official Secrets Act. Major Bevan then instructed me to report to an office, which surprisingly had been located in the Wormwood Scrubs Prison.

Office space was difficult to find at that time, because civilian activities had not as yet wound down and war activities, such as the gas mask and identity card business, were mushrooming. Because prisoners with a reasonable record were released to join the Forces, many of the prisons were emptied providing quite soon, much needed accommodation for Government use.

I do "Time"

I set off for Wormwood Scrubs at the appointed time, and was kept standing around for simply ages, very much like the interminable hanging about on a film set. Other people were rushing about looking important with piles of papers. But never looking in my direction. Finally, I was allocated to a Section called the Information and Records Branch. Several men were already established there, and although they were not attached to any regiment, they had resuscitated their military ranks from the 14-18 War — they wore uniforms and we called them Captain or Major.

No-one really knew what we were supposed to be doing — for several days no instructions were given and I had not the slightest idea what I was about. I was put in a cell about 6 feet wide and 8–9 feet long with a little window high up in the wall, a trestle table and a chair. The keys in the locks of all the cell doors had been turned, so no doors could slam or be completely shut, and therefore we could not be imprisoned. My cell in "B" Block was on the first gallery, which was made of metal. We could look down into a well or across to the other galleries where people were working. A few prisoners were still in the prison, but they were carefully segregated and soon transferred. Every now and then the heating vents released a few bugs on the unsuspecting occupants of the cell. But a great cleaning operation took place and this state of affairs was soon rectified, thank goodness!

One could not help speculating about the sterile lives which had been endured in this hideous building. One indication of the terrifying lack of privacy was revealed by the ex-prisoners' loos which we had to use. The doors only came down as far as people's knees so that both the legs and the feet of the occupant of each cubicle could be observed. Very soon the doors were taken down to the floor, but the horrid initial impression remained.

In my cell I found myself confronted by a whole mass of intercepted mail — the messages were mostly quite unintelligible to me, so all I could do was to sort them into some kind of order — places of origin or dates. As it turned out, this was exactly what was required to be done, although I had no idea then what was wanted.

Gradually the department took shape. I learned that we were to allocate data to various Government Departments according to a schedule of requirements.

More people joined the Section. Two girls, Jane Farmer and Mary Wise who arrived at this time were to become very close friends; indeed it was the start of two lifelong friendships. Some time before the war started, Jane and Mary had served as members of The Royal British Legion, so they reported every day for work wearing the neat khaki uniform of The Legion. I and most other people wore civilian dress. We were not members of the Services — we were temporary Civil Servants. I found the senior people in our Section somewhat aloof and I hesitated a long time before I went to them to ask a question. I think this was due much more to my approach than to theirs. The whole experience was so completely strange to me that ridiculously, I discounted all my previous achievements and allowed myself to feel nervous and insignificant. The pomposity of some of my colleagues added to this.

By contrast in another Section which I had sometimes to contact was a delightful, very friendly man, Dr David Bannerman, the famous ornithologist. Later I was to work with him very closely. He was always very jolly and had a friendly word for everyone.

Personnel Increase

The recruitment of personnel at this stage was quite haphazard. People either knew someone who knew someone who recommended them, or they were Civil Servants from such establishments as the British Museum, where peace-time work came to an abrupt end, and the staff were seconded to various War Departments.

The people whom I found myself working alongside were for the most part very well educated; they often had degrees or two or three languages, but many of them had little experience in administrative jobs. So, looking back, I can see that things took an inordinate time to get organised. Everything took ages and quite frequently when initial systems didn't work, jobs had to be done all over again.

The facilities at the prison were of course very poor, except for an excellent canteen service which was quickly established. A marquee was erected in the open ground by the prison and fortunately as the fine, warm weather continued into the Autumn, until such time as a building could be found, we ate mostly out of doors. I couldn't help thinking that it was very comical and very British putting up marquees in Wormwood Scrubs.

I was still living at home with my parents in Croydon, so the journey to and from the prison was a very long one for me. I had to walk or bus to an Underground Station and then to Victoria Station and then an ordinary train to Croydon. However it worked well enough, because at this stage there were no bombings, indeed nothing very much in the way of warfare occurred for several months. It was the period known as the "phoney war".

As the weeks passed, more recruits joined the Section. It was very pleasant to be working for the most part with such agreeable people. Inevitably, one or two members of the Department developed an air of great importance, acting, I felt as if they were members of the "inner cabinet" or something. They did not tell me, as small fry, any more than they possibly could, making it seem that only they were privileged to be trusted with important information. So I had to pick up data as best I could — which I thought was rather silly.

Just across from my cell the so-called Editorial Section was established. It was run by a very well known author, who had collected round him a group of his socialite friends. They came to the prison in large cars, looking very stylish. If they were going off to parties in the evening, they positively glittered with diamonds. Most people thought this was overdoing it somewhat.

This element quickly disappeared. They really did not have much to contribute and so they went on their way. It was a sort of settling down period.

Bit by bit I began to get the hang of the job and also to learn something of the Civil Service methods under which we were working. Gradually the systems became more formalised and I could see the purpose of what we were about. We were grouped according to the Ministries we were serving, and so I learned about the British administrative "machine" which was adapting slowly and reluctantly to the war situation. It was completely new ground for me. I found it fascinating.

I also enjoyed the new acquaintances and friendships I was making. There were informal coffee and lunch breaks and a good deal of laughter, because we were all quite young.

We saw a great deal of members of the Translation Division, where about thirty languages were represented, including Greek, Finnish, Japanese and Chinese. These translators were specialists and again were drawn largely from the British Museum staff.

A New Pattern of Life

Within two weeks of the start of the war, Ian, who had also been accepted for the Censorship Department, was sent to a Division in Liverpool, not the Prisoner of War Section where Ethel Dawes was working, but one dealing with a different category of mail.

He found digs in a typical Victorian cotton merchant's house where the landlady was very kind and helpful. Little by little he transferred his belongings up to the north. My father decided to spend the weeks in Town at the Club, coming home only at weekends, so Moppett and I were very much together.

She quickly got organised to a new pattern of life, engaging in the awful shopping routines, and by clever cooking she made the food rations work well for us.

Fears of a German attack on the country did not materialise, but the U-Boat Warfare soon began to have an effect — vessels were sunk and the North Atlantic passage became very hazardous. British soldiers were sent to France to serve alongside the French army. There was enormous confidence in the Maginot Line, the vast fortification which went along the Franco-German border. it was fitted with every known device to assist with the defence of France. It was regarded as impregnable. What misplaced confidence that proved to be!

After a stagnation period of six months, in April 1940 things began to happen very rapidly. First the Germans invaded Denmark and Norway; a little later Holland and Belgium were over-run. The meagre information about these attacks which did filter through was terrifying in its brutality.

Before this war, we had never heard of troops landed by parachute, and we all began to wonder whether the Blitzkrieg technique would work here; so tension mounted.

The Fall of France

After Belgium, France was attacked by the simple strategy of circumventing the Maginot Line. The hoards of German troops which poured into France divided the allied forces; the French were forced south, the British north and west. This lead to the fall of France and the invasion of Paris.

One of the most poignant memories I have of this period was of the actual day that the Germans entered Paris. I suppose because of all the fond memories that I had of the city, to think of her as vanquished and trampled over by brutish troops was unbearable. To make it all the more tragically memorable, the weather took on an almost sinister appearance and feel. It was like an impending thunder storm, only instead of the sky just being black or grey, it had an almost copper coloured glaze; a threatening, brazen darkness settled over the whole landscape. It pressed in on us inescapably.

This sinister pall seemed to typify the horror of the current happenings. I personally was deeply grieved. Something that I loved was being despoiled.

Part of the French Navy managed to escape from the German High Command and sail to Britain. One day, to my utter amazement, Lucien Guitard telephoned me at home. Now a Naval Lieutenant, he explained what had happened to him and that he was in London. We met and had dinner together. There was an unreality about this perfectly normal social activity; but to be eating food in a quietly civilised way, when the rest of the world was crashing into ruins seemed bizarre. Nevertheless, it was a wonderful feeling to have contact with a French person whom I knew.

One's imagination, which always run riot at moments of great disaster, had made me think that after the fall of France, hardly a single person had been left alive in the country. Ridiculous, of course, but one always dramatises things. So actually to sit with dear Lucien and hear how he had fared and to learn that some resemblance of real life was going on in France, was wonderfully reassuring. Within a couple of days he was summoned to re-join his ship. I just hoped that he and all the French convoy would be safe.

Shortly after he had left, I was delighted to receive two cables from Lucien in Oran, where the French navy had sought shelter. I knew that at least for a while he was safe. At long intervals Lucien wrote letters and cards to tell us they were all right and implored me to reply, but as France was enemy occupied territory, I could not do so.

Dunkirk

There then followed the famous evacuation of the British Forces from Dunkirk. This together with the fall of France forced our spirits to a very low ebb. We seemed to be surrounded by disaster.

Yet the incredible episode of Dunkirk generated enormous pride at the sheer guts which were displayed. For example, not only were larger ships rescuing and transporting British soldiers across the Channel, skippers o tiny little craft, running the gauntlet of blistering enemy air attack, brought back perhaps just a few wounded soldiers.

The unselfishness, the bravery and the determination were inspiring, but there was great anguish too at the terrible loss of life and enormity of the set-back to the allied cause.

The sustaining presence in all this was Churchill. His wonderful speeches, realistic but inspiring hope, determination and the will to triumph against any odds, put heart into every person. He made it possible for ordinary people to build their courage and enthusiasm. We all felt that we had a purpose, a task to fulfil and, as a result, everyone re-doubled their efforts.

After Dunkirk and Pétain's shameful Treaty with the Germans, the bombing of our airfields started. Biggin Hill in Kent, Kenley in Surrey and the other air stations round London were all subjected to repeated aerial attack by the Luftwaffe. It was obvious that the enemy was trying to break down the air defences of London. The air-raid sirens sounded very frequently.

The RAF, still woefully ill-equipped, retaliated and brought down hundreds of enemy planes. We had our losses too. One of the really distressing happenings at this time was the sight of an airman, perhaps limping down a street on crutches, his face scarred and distorted as a result of the terrible burns he had sustained, when his plane had probably been brought down in flames. As one passed, trying not to stare, one just had to say "thank you" under one's breath.

The Battle of Britain

Worse was of course to come; we were on the eve of the Battle of Britain.

My experience of the very first day of this terrifying period was quite dramatic. I had finished work one Saturday afternoon and was making my way home, when the wailing sirens sounded warning of an enemy attack. As I looked towards the river, I could see in the sky, coming up the estuary of the Thames, flight after flight of German bombers. Within seconds came the sound of the distant thud of exploding bombs, flames leapt into the air and soon great clouds of thick black smoke were billowing upwards. The bombs had hit the oil installations down at the Docks. I could see that it was very serious. Soon the Spitfires were up and the crackle of machine guns told that aerial "dog fights" were in progress.

Home-going trains were quickly knocked out of service, so I had to find some other way to get back. Picking up a lift or grabbing a place on one of the few remaining buses, I made a roundabout way towards Croydon. At one point when the shrapnel was starting to fall, the wardens cleared the streets. I spent a couple of hours in a huge air-raid shelter with all kinds of people — women with shopping baskets — service personnel, men and women — frightened little children who were a bit weepy, or others like myself returning from work. By this time darkness had come and then the all-clear signal sounded. I set off to walk the remainder of the way home. One had to grope along the darkened streets trying to pick out familiar landmarks. Sometimes I walked with someone who was going the same way, a civilian or a soldier; sometimes I was on my own.

Then the sirens sounded again, another raid had started; the shrapnel soon began to fly about, aircraft were overhead. There were no shelters at that point, so I just crept on keeping as close to the walls as possible.

By this time I had linked up with a soldier, who was making his way to his barracks at Caterham. A warden directed us how to complete the last mile or so of the journey, and eventually we reached home. It was my first experience of real danger.

My father and mother were overwhelmed with delight at seeing me, and soon there was hot tea and good things to eat for both the soldier and me. The German raiders were still humming overhead, but we knew that the Spitfires were also there attacking. There was an occasional boom of the anti-aircraft guns that were placed strategically all around. Peeping through the black-out curtains, but showing no light, we could see that in the direction of the river, the sky was glowing with a harsh, orange light, surrounded by the black smoke. The oil installations were obviously still burning.

Then the all-clear sounded again. The soldier went on his way and we crept into uncomfortable make-shift beds under the stairs, which was said to be the safest part of any house.

I was working the next day, Sunday, and so I set off at the usual time to make my way to the office, which by now had been moved from Wormwood Scrubs Prison to a building just off Holborn.

The air-raids of the previous evening had wreaked havoc. The trains only went a very little way; then all the passengers piled out and took whatever buses were running, walked or picked up a lift. Because of all the damage of the night before, roads were blocked and we had to make frequent diversions. As we got close to London the real devastation hit us. Fleet Street, for example, was hardly recognisable.

It was a mass of battered buildings, broken glass inches thick was strewn all over the road and huge beams torn out of the buildings lay smouldering in the gutter.

The firemen were sitting, grimed and exhausted on the edge of the pavements, and although buildings were still burning, they could do nothing about it because their hoses were dry, the water supply exhausted. Lulled into complacency by the "phoney war", we had been caught totally unprepared.

The deluge, not only of high explosives, but also incendiary bombs which had been poured on to the city that Saturday night was horrifying.

There was a public outcry against the inadequacy of the water supply. Little by little this was completely re-organised and huge excess water tanks were constructed on bombed-out sites. But it all took time.

There then followed ninety days of non-stop bombing on the Capital. It became a nightly ritual to get home, if possible before dusk, have supper and then when the sirens sounded creep into one's safety spot — for us, under the stairs; for others, a shelter in the garden, which, because they were often cold and damp, gave people bad colds. It seemed one took one's choice, bombs or pneumonia!

People kept their nerve and miraculously, even the unlucky ones who had their houses bombed at night, mostly turned up for work the next morning. People just did not grumble — they got on with things.

More shelters were erected and the Underground was opened at nights and people in central London slept and almost lived in the squalor, but safety, of the labyrinth of passages and tunnels which lay under the city.

My Responsibilities are Enlarged

It was against this background of what was I suppose, considerable tension, but which we largely came to accept, that work at the office continued.

The Department was re-organised and Dr Bannerman was put in charge. I became his Deputy and my responsibilities were greatly enlarged. Because of his deafness, Dr Bannerman did not always fully hear and understand what was being said, so he got into the habit of taking me to policy meetings. This was invaluable for me. Further, he took an intense dislike to one of the senior men, whom he did not trust. Often overcome by impatience he walked out of the meetings and left me to complete negotiations.

During this period, my personal development was tremendous. I met very senior people in all the Services and was exposed to very different influences, important decisions being left to me. I found that if I worked at jobs steadily, whatever my initial doubts about my ability, I was able to tackle them. I became aware, to my surprise and I hope without conceit, that I was the mental equal, sometimes the superior of the people I was dealing with, both men and women. I had never before evaluated myself.

Up to then, I think it is true to say that I had always worked with enthusiasm, but that mere survival had been a large part of the objective. Now for the first time, I began to develop a completely different approach.

I began to view myself as a total participant, able to initiate many of the ideas and systems which were required. A few months later, Dr Bannerman decided to leave. He had always found it difficult to fit into the administrative pattern of the Department. He became impatient as he did not always see the significance of what we were being asked to do.

The skill that I most admired about his work was his beautifully written memos and reports. His clear flowing style, succinct and very readable, was a model which I tried to copy. Needless to say, the verbose, muddled letters which often came to him aroused his disgust. His comments on these were unprintable, but very comical.

Having made up his mind to go, he recommended that I take over the Department, which now numbered about twenty. This was fully endorsed by the Departmental Heads and I got promotion. In just a year — I had come a long way.

I found administrative and staff management work came easily to me; I think because I paid attention to detail and could concentrate. The skills and authority I had gained from running my own business gave me confidence and credibility as a Manager.

New initiatives were required and the changing war scene called for different responses. I seemed able to think creatively and logically and apply resources to objectives.

The Department's activities were rated as Secret and, as I have already mentioned, I had signed the *Official Secrets Act* when I first joined the Department. I therefore said absolutely nothing outside about the things I did in the office. Indeed, we were so security-minded that when I came to search my war-time diaries for items of interest, they were almost empty; there was nothing about the information I learned at my desk, not even references as to where bombs had fallen, just stupid little notes about lunch or hair appointments or rare visits to the ballet or theatre!

Managing Staff

I was becoming more skilled at handling people. Many of my staff, who were all women, were very able — they all had one or more languages and were tremendously keen and co-operative. To make sure everyone was fully informed of what was going on, I held regular meetings and encouraged people to express their views and voice ideas.

One woman was very elegant and had lived quite a moneyed existence. She had never needed to work, but she buckled down splendidly to the rather dull routine and, provided I set out the guidelines clearly, she did her work very well.

Another young woman was an extremely hard worker, very good-looking and with a really responsible attitude. She got through the mountains of paper which confronted us very rapidly. She rarely made a mistake, was also very observant and quick to spot something unusual which might require investigation. Whenever I asked her to research something, she always took her enquiries one step further than I had requested and frequently turned up most valuable material. In the post-war world, I often wished I could convince staff of the value of this meticulous kind of work.

Another absolutely gorgeous girl was called Bridget. Indeed, when Dr Bannerman was running the Department, because there were so many attractive young women in the Section and because his initials were D A, we were called DAB's lovelies; but that didn't stop us turning in very useful work.

To return to Bridget — she was a titled person, who had enormous charm, but not many brains. Bridget lived a very full social life and, although she never bragged about it, she frequently dined out with people like Lord Beaverbrook and even Churchill. She could be maddening. She would arrive late, make mistakes because she did not concentrate and chattered both on the phone and to her companions.

Mostly I ignored this irritating behaviour, because it would have been very difficult to dismiss her and she was quite harmless. Just occasionally my patience gave out, when I felt she was interrupting others, and I would call her to order. Bridget would then cry, saying, "Yes, Mac", which was what everyone called me, "I know I'm hopeless, but I will do better. I'm very sorry." Large tears, which did not so much as disturb an eyelash, would then trickle down her cheeks.

I think that annoyed me too, because whereas had I wept, I would have ended up snuffling with a pink nose and blotchy eyes; Bridget when she cried looked even lovelier. In terms of the constructive work of the Department, I'm afraid I rather dismissed her. I gave her just dull routine jobs which she did cheerfully and willingly. Until one day when the air-raid sirens had sounded, and the actual raid started very quickly, a bomb crashed down not far away before we could even get down to the shelter in the basement. In her little girl voice, Bridget said, with complete serenity, when other people were beginning to panic, "That one was really rather close, wasn't it?" Everyone laughed, tension was relieved and we continued to trot down the stairs in an orderly way.

I thought to myself, we all have qualities and strengths. Not everyone is clever, but we do have a contribution to make — serenity, composure, dignity — they all count. I felt a little ashamed of my previous, perhaps somewhat dismissive behaviour, towards Bridget.

On these descents to the basement shelter, it had been our practice to gather up our work in filing baskets very quickly, so that we could carry on working in the shelter until the "all clear" sounded. Unless we did this, so much time was wasted just sitting and waiting; taking papers with us, therefore, seemed a good idea.

Unfortunately as we were going down the stairs one day, a breeze from an open window caught up a single paper, stamped all over "most secret", and wafted it into the street below. It was picked up by a passer-by who took it to the reception.

It arrived on the Director General's desk and filtering down through the complete hierarchy, Deputy Director General, Controller, etc, etc, it finally reached my Boss, whereupon I was asked to explain the presence of the offending SECRET!! document in the street. The paper contained a totally meaningless message, but great principles were at stake. So I was severely reprimanded and from then on we were forbidden to take our work to the shelter — a pity, because this procedure had saved a lot of time.

A large part of the work of the whole Branch related to Trade. This Section was manned by about 20 or 30 older men, who had been engaged in some sort of commercial work before the war. They were a pleasant enough and I am sure a very knowledgeable crowd, but they were middle-aged and rather dreary, and my attractive and gay (this word has now acquired a different connotation) little group thought them incredibly boring.

When an exchange of documents was found necessary, one of my girls would trot over with them and receive a long lecture on the significance of oil, or magnesium, or cobalt, to the war effort. One impish girl, after one such encounter, returned to the Department and said, "I feel I shall never impress Mr D — you see I've never travelled in brushes in the Far East!"

Meeting Senior Officials

Work now included many meetings with senior officials in the Services, Government Ministries and the Intelligence Department. I had to report on what we were doing. Some of these personalitites were very impressive. I think they were a little surprised at having a young woman talk to them on quite important matters. I tried not to let their sometimes imposing appearances, and rather haughty voices, put me off. I would say to myself, "If that's the way they've been taught to behave, there's nothing I can do about it." So I just got on with what I had gone to discuss. I confess, however, it was not always easy. The upsetting attitude was when such people appeared to look down on me and made me feel stupid. The answer was always to prepare before going to such meetings, have my facts absolutely clear and always to be armed with back up papers to support expressions of opinion.

The Controller of the Division, le Tournet, taught me a great deal. To begin with I found him irritating. He was wealthy, had been everywhere and done everything. I made a practice of being available to any member of my Department during the day and then in the evening I would clear up the paper work. Le Tournet often wandered through the Department in his nonchalant way and finding me working would ask how things were going. He also talked a great deal, not indiscreetly revealing secret data, but in terms of general procedures and personalities. He told me about members of the Inner Cabinet he had been at school with, explained how X had moved to a particular Ministry, and why, and what degrees or qualities of character had won that person success — or why someone else hadn't made it. He made such comments as, "Unstable chap — even at University he would fly into violent tempers; able, of course, but couldn't be trusted with responsibility under stress." I came to see how highly qualities of character were valued.

Churchill had introduced some unusual people into the Government. Beaverbrook, for example, whose dynamism really got the Air Ministry cracking and Brendan Bracken to whom our Department now reported and who was a very unusual type of Civil Servant.

If le Tournet approved any of these moves, he would tell me why. Equally he rather gloated over the demise of some starchy old Etonian, who had become atrophied in a senior job, from which he thought no-one could dislodge him.

I came to see that things are accomplished, not only by personal application, but through people, and that I had, therefore, to learn to link *with* people. Up to then, I had just never entertained the idea that this was the way things were worked. Le Tournet was giving me insights into what we have come to call, "The Old Boys' Network".

Gaining Recognition

Obviously I was not part of the Network, but as my work became more valued, I was beginning to be recognised. I perceived how to play situations, when to speak and act, and, more important, when *not* to. I observed people making disastrous mistakes in meetings and being written off and I also perceived that such difficulties rarely arose from lack of skill or knowledge, but from poor judgement on timing and a desire to show off.

There was one very able young woman in the Division who had a very sharp mind and, unfortunately, sometimes a tongue to match it. She practised a technique which I certainly benefitted from. After a meeting in which she had participated very cogently, she would come out and on her own battered old typewriter she would immediately type up her recommendations for the solution of a problem. She was not the official minute-taker, but she quickly got down on paper the important reasoning and conclusions which had been arrived at in the meeting.

Others who had attended usually did not think about it in depth, perhaps for several days, so when action was taken it was her version, clear and definitive, which was followed. She got the decisions she wanted, which fortunately were usually the right ones. It was a very commanding tactic.

I kept in close touch with Ian throughout the war. It was marvellous that we could contact each other by phone when there had been air raids. The blitzes on major British cities were very distressing — although allegedly aimed at factories and docks, the cathedral at Coventry, for example was destroyed and in Liverpool and Bristol, innumerable hits were scored on domestic property and many people were killed, maimed or rendered homeless.

As a family, we were incredibly lucky. The most which happened to our home was that part of a garden fence and some bushes were set alight by an incendiary bomb. My mother and I put out this little fire with a few buckets of sand.

I Take Over Another Department

Another re-organisation took place in the office and the Reports Section was added to my responsibilities. It was the first time that I had encountered any resentment of my management position.

The previous Head of Reports had been a rather conventional person whom I scarcely knew. He died suddenly of a heart attack and le Tournet, who had not liked his style of editorship, saw this as a splendid opportunity to break up what had become a rather enclosed little group.

The woman who had acted as the Deputy Editor, a Mrs Craig, felt sure she was going to get the job. When, therefore, le Tournet put me in charge, she was annoyed, hurt and critical of my ability. Mrs Craig was a rather cold personality with a very precise way of talking and thinking. I was convinced that having done this job for a long time, she knew far more about it than I did. I was also conscious that my education was not as formal as hers. Mrs Craig was an academic and the staff which comprised her Section were very much cast in her mould.

I could see that the reports were well researched and factual, but I thought they were too long and rather dull. The No 1 Department on the circulation list for these weekly documents was the War Cabinet.

When le Tournet put me in charge of the Section in his casual way he said, "The reports are too long — too stuffy — liven them up a bit".

I realised I would have to go carefully if I was not going to generate a lot of antagonism from Mrs Craig and her staff, but to satisfy le Tournet I couldn't wait for ever to make adjustments.

We had a number of rather frosty meetings. I tried very hard to identify with Mrs Craig's views, but she continually pointed out that cutting items short would lead to ambiguity and misinterpretation. It seemed useless for me to say, "But very senior people haven't got time to read pages and pages of material and remember they do have other sources. Part of the function of this document is that it is corroborative".

Until she could take this message, I think what I was trying to do deeply offended her. However, I ploughed on, and eventually succeeded in reducing the length of the reports and enlivening the style. In the end, we became good friends and while I think my often racy manner rather shocked her, I think she came to enjoy being associated with someone who was prepared to take risks. The work of the Section did receive commendation from the Prime Minister, so all was forgiven.

About this time, I had what was initially a rather nasty shock. On to my desk one morning came a large official envelope from Downing Street.

I caught my breath. It must be a complaint from the War Cabinet, I thought — had we made some ghastly mistake in one of those wretched Reports? I groaned. Then very hesitantly I opened the envelope, only to discover that I was being offered a Decoration for my work in the Department. I was astonished, but very pleased and excited. I went to le Tournet and thanked him for having put my name forward. He just grinned.

I realised, of course, that the Award was in recognition of the work of the whole team, not just for my efforts. The Department was, after all, 70 strong by then.

It intrigued me that although I was in charge of both the Information and Reports Section, and tried very hard to bring them together, the two groups never really merged. DAB's lovelies didn't want to know about the staid academic ladies in Reports, and the Reports personnel adopted a rather long suffering tolerance towards the "young things" across the corridor.

Later in post-war management situations, I saw these same divisions, which never quite healed. The esprit de corps which makes the initial group successful, can so easily turn into a disdainful élitism towards the newcomers, which is expressed by such phrases as "those were the days!". Neither side seems able to identify completely with the other.

Inter-Departmental Difficulties

Another staff situation which took me by surprise concerned the Records Department. This section had the responsibility to file the many thousands of documents we handled. This they did with great efficiency. I had known the woman who was Head of this Section since it was created. She was a jolly, happy-go-lucky person. It was a difficult job in that the work was repetitive and monotonous. She had about 30 clerical staff, who I am sure at times found the work rather boring. She handled them splendidly.

Because the heavy demands which were made on the Section came irregularly, there were from time to time bottle necks. My staff used the Records Section all the time. When they were compiling a case they had need sometimes to get past documents quickly.

At one point, several of the girls came to me and complained that their work was being seriously held up, because they had to wait for documentation. At the very same time, the Head of Records came up to my desk in an absolute fury. She claimed my people had been rude to her clerks — that their requests were unreasonable and that they frequently came down into her department pressuring people.

I was very shocked at this — but of course I had no means of knowing whether the complaint was truthful or exaggerated. I said I would investigate at once and find out exactly what the problem was. My people denied that they had been rude, rather that the Records girls were unco-operative and that requests were not promptly attended to.

I insisted that the situation be carefully monitored and the length of time documents took to arrive recorded. I also said that we must show great courtesy and tolerance with the Records staff as they did not have the exciting jobs we had. I pointed out that the boring character of the work of the Records clerks must be pretty hard to take day after day, and that everyone must be specially helpful and polite. The outcome of the survey showed that there were delays, but also that the work in our Section was growing and that the number of requests was therefore on the increase.

We resolved the situation by getting a better request system organised, but I fear the old warm friendly feeling with the Records Head was never quite recaptured, for which I was very sorry.

Work Most Secret

About this time, a most fascinating discovery was made, curiously enough in the Department which Ian controlled up in Liverpool. For years and years I never ever said a word about this development — the *Official Secrets Act*, contrary to many people's view today, to us meant silence. However, some five years ago a book entitled *A Man Called Intrepid* was published. To my disgust, because I still think the less said about sensitive matters the better, most of what we were doing was revealed in the book.

Briefly what happened was that through keen observation and a great deal of painstaking research, networks of German agents in North and South America were unearthed. The information that was being passed by them back to Germany was discovered by us in intercepted mail and handed to our Intelligence people. The mail was then released and sent on its way. Although the Germans knew that mail was liable to interception, they did not know for a very long time that we had cracked their coding device, which was the use of micro dots.

Handling this very sensitive material took a great deal of planning and organising. A special section was set up headed by a marvellous woman, Peggy Evans, who with two or three others hived off from my Department, worked exclusively on this most important project.

We continued to liaise very closely, but Peggy took over the whole unit and handled it brilliantly.

Lectures at Provincial Branches

As a HQ Branch, we were, of course, dependent on the efficient working of all the outlying censorship posts. These were based in different cities throughout the country, not only Liverpool but Glasgow and Bristol too.

I was conscious that the staff in these different centres were very remote from the HQ, and that instruction memos were not always clear and explicit. As a result, we sometimes received rather critical phone calls from these centres which revealed disappointment, because the staff there felt neglected and out on a limb. I thought it was vital that morale should be kept high and that the very loyal staff in these centres were better informed and encouraged. So I proposed to le Tournet that I should go to the provincial posts and give a talk on how HQ worked, explaining how valuable the material the out-of-London offices sent to us was, and what use was made of it.

The suggestion was warmly welcomed by the Officers in charge of the Provincial Units and by le Tournet, so I set off. I planned my presentations carefully, collecting plenty of practical examples to illustrate the talks. I also answered any questions which were posed, and I think the scheme did serve a good purpose. It left people feeling as if they belonged a little more.

I had never been to Scotland before, so I linked the visit to Glasgow with some leave that was due to me and took Moppett for a lovely little holiday at Hunter's Quay on the West Coast of Scotland. The peace and quiet after the hustle and bustle of London and the anxiety of the air raids was wonderful. All the people in the hotel were warm and friendly and being close to the country, where chickens and ducks and fish were readily available, the meals were a delight.

The only other holidays we had managed were short breaks at Gomshall in the heart of Surrey and a little village called Pishill in Oxfordshire. We always went to the country and never to the coast, of course, where there was a much greater risk of bombing.

Doodlebugs and VIIs

The next aerial onslaught which we had to face was the doodlebug attack, as the flying bombs were called. These ghastly contraptions were in effect enormous remotely controlled aerial rockets. They were released from launch pads in Northern Europe and whirred over the Channel to land sometimes harmlessly in a field, but more often on houses and buildings, creating absolute havoc. When they first arrived people were really frightened, because they came actually out of blue and being unmanned, had a mysterious quality. One report, I remember, spoke of a flying telephone kiosk!

The counter move to defeat these missiles was the erection of enormous nets, which were slung from tethered barrage balloons that floated high above the ground. The nets were strategically placed to cover the known "lanes" that the doodlebugs followed and formed a trap round the outskirts of the city covering Surrey and Kent. The nets entangled the doodlebugs as they flew in, which then fell in open ground comparatively harmlessly. The system was not wholly effective, and some of these rockets reached their targets in the suburbs and central London causing great devastation. Later the Germans improved on these missiles. The second version, which were known as the V IIs were even more deadly and accurate in their aim. They roared in overhead and then the engine carried in the missile cut out and after a pause the horrible thing crashed. We learned to gauge this waiting period. If there was an interval of a minute or so, we knew we weren't underneath it, and so we carried on with our work. It seemed very callous, but in high emergencies we just had to ignore those things which were not our direct concern — heartless, perhaps, because under the distant thump we knew there were probably dead bodies.

The number of near misses which one experienced was amazing. One lunch time I had to take a document to the other side of London. I took a bus and proceeded peacefully on my way. Having delivered the letter, I heard a V II come over, and then the landing thump. I heaved a sigh of relief that I had escaped and got on to my bus to return to the office. On the way back I arrived at the Aldwych. The whole place was in confusion, this was where the V II had landed. There was wreckage and bodies were lying all over the place. The rescue services were already at work and so my bus just proceeded on its way.

The sickening thought came to me, that a mere quarter of an hour before I had been at the disaster point, and here I was going on unscathed. Back at the office, I just had to put the whole thing out of my mind and attend to the papers on my desk. With all these bizarre experiences, I, together with everyone else, matured very much.

Allied Liaison Officers

Another intriguing element to the job was the Allied Liaison Officers with whom we had to work. There was a permanent contingent of Americans who all wore Naval uniform. They were very pleasant and easy to work with.

Periodically, we were also visited by members of the Free Norwegian, Free French, Free Dutch and Danish forces. I say "Free" because there were pro-German puppet governments in all the over-run countries. The forces that had escaped, set up governments here in order to prepare for the ultimate invasion of the Continent — they were the HQ's of the Free forces.

We shared everything but "Top Secret" documents with them. This category of information had to be passed through different channels. This sometimes gave rise to some tricky situations, like rapidly stuffing papers under blotting pads when unexpected "visitors" walked into our "open plan" office.

All these Officers, many of whom were very young, were most co-operative to liaise with. They occasionally took me out for a meal and we talked about the day when the Allied Forces would invade and they would be free people once again. They all had such different cultures and attitudes, I found it fascinating.

There were also permanent groups of Army, Air Force and Navy Officers in different parts of the building. However serious the matters were before us, there was always time for a joke and a laugh.

One night a bomb fell on part of the office. It cut an almost exact round hole through the roof and the ceilings of the three floors below. Without exploding, it embedded itself in the concrete on the ground floor, so no-one was hurt. Word quickly got round the next morning about what had happened and in two's and three's we went to investigate, only to find that the Navy boys, on whose offices the bomb had fallen, had put a mouse trap by one of the neatly cut ceiling holes!

Inevitably with so many attractive girls and fellows around, romances blossomed. Some took them very seriously and when there were transfers and people went away, there were tears and gloom for a while.

My romantic involvement was right outside the office, which was I think good, because I was in charge of a large staff and it would have been quite difficult if my boy friend had been sitting in the next office — there was enough gossip as it was!

I had met Patrick years before on Fleet Street. He was great fun, a very good companion and incredibly courteous to my mother. (He was a Captain in the Signals). I liked him very much but I soon perceived that his transfers overseas which occurred from time to time provided him with a convenient excuse to elude any commitment, sometimes even keeping a date. He was equally charming to everyone and I saw that any serious feelings I might entertain would be at risk from his somewhat unreliable approach. In sight dedicated — out of sight, who could tell! I took this rather badly.

However, my life was very full. I had for some time turned my attention to some serious study. As early as 1941, when working with Dr Bannerman, I discovered that I had some ability to be creative, but I had also realised that I lacked the sharpened thinking processes which would convert these quite good conceptual ideas into high achievement. I need more mental discipline, more precision of thought. To me that meant working for a degree — so that's what I decided to do.

On holiday with my mother in Oxfordshire

Chapter Five

Taking my Degree — Early Post-War Jobs

When I left school, the thought of a degree did not enter my head. It was not that I considered and rejected the idea, I just didn't think about it, because I was carried by force of circumstances into the practical world of earning my living. I had never regarded myself as an academic, although I was competent at school and always got high grades — but the range of studies at Woodford was limited, although what we did was done thoroughly.

Inevitably, therefore, I was largely ignorant of the vast bodies of knowledge which exist in the world, and also their practical application to human activities. I had learned a little about business from my father's affairs. I knew something about teaching, advertising and publicity from first-hand experience, but I did not comprehend the structure of world affairs and commerce, or the range of academic and scientific studies. I could not, therefore, aim for any precise vocation or career, say accountancy or the law, because these disciplines were not realities to me. I had no real comprehension of engineering or the production function, and subjects such as economics and statistics, were empty, little comprehended words.

In later life when I came to do career counselling, I could identify very closely with young people who came to me knowing what they wanted to do. From the classroom to, say, the Financial Analyst's Department in a Bank, was to them and also to me at this time, an incomprehensible leap in the dark. How could you be expected to know what lay beyond the school walls and how to choose a career, if you didn't know what people did?

When, therefore, in my war time job I dealt closely with the well qualified people and had reports come across my desk touching on all kinds of world activities, the enormity of my ignorance really hit me. I realised I could never begin to hold my own unless I could come to grips with at least some aspects of these hitherto unexplored realms.

Preliminaries

So I made enquiries from London University about how to approach the business of taking a degree, because this seemed to me the route I should take if I was to develop. The first data I was given was very disappointing; I learned that if I wanted to gain a place at London University I would need to have Matriculated with Latin. It was one of the obligatory subjects.

The subjects which had comprised my passing out examination from school, the Junior Cambridge as it was then called, did not include Latin and did not entitle me to Matric exemption; so if I wanted to take a degree, I learned I would have to start at the very beginning. Initially a 3-year degree course had not seemed all that difficult, but to add at least one to two years' study in basics, seemed a pretty daunting prospect. Was I taking on more than I could sustain? Would I be able to keep up my enthusiasm? I did a lot of hard thinking. A further aggravation was that another obligatory subject for the Matric was either Maths or Logic. I had not enjoyed Maths very much at school, so I felt I could not go back to that again. I decided on Logic, which I found very interesting.

The only way to get up to the required standard for these pre- degree exams, after so long away from school, was to get special tuition, which I did. I had for many years taught Fencing at Queen's College, Harley Street; Miss Kynaston, the very able Head, was delighted to help and obtained coaching time for me from two tutors. One, Miss Chaplin, a charming and most dedicated classicist, became a great friend. She built up my knowledge in Latin and general studies so that at the end of six months I sat the Matric exemption exam and passed.

Then I had to tackle the Higher or A Level exam. This was obviously at a more advanced standard, but the syllabus was more flexible, so I dropped Logic and substituted History. I chose a very Arts orientated programme! I did not talk about my study activities much outside the family. I wasn't sure whether people would find it a little absurd and as I wasn't at all sure that I was going to succeed, I thought that until I had proved myself a little, better to say nothing.

One of the causes of this hesitancy, I think, derived from the attitude to University education which prevailed in this country. It was, and up to a point still is, surrounded by a kind of élitism, which took the shape of a conviction that if you were not a product of a senior Public School and Oxbridge, you weren't really in the running. More modest patterns of education, described by such phrases as *minor* Public Schools and red brick Universities, tended to be dismissed.

I have a tremendous respect and admiration for our ancient seats of learning and all that they stand for in the pursuit of excellence, but I cannot, because of that, denigrate other forms of education. Nevertheless, I had to go through a process of personal rationalisation to come to the conclusion that knowledge is knowledge, however acquired, and that it is our own attitude and behaviour which make experience, wherever gained, valid and fruitful or the reverse.

However, by the time I had passed the Matric and was well on the way to the Higher, I met one or two people through the work at the office whom I felt I could talk to.

Degree Choice

One was Professor David Mitrany, an Economist, but with strong political and sociological interests. He was at that time an Adviser to the Royal Institute of International Affairs. I had to liaise with him as part of my job. When very hesitantly I told him what I was doing, he could not have been more supportive. He reassured me that if I could find the time and the energy, taking a degree was absolutely the right course and now was the time to do it. We also discussed what discipline I should follow for my finals. After reviewing my abilities, considering the various options and reading a number of introductory books on different subjects, I decided that I would go for sociology.

It seemed to me that the subjects which formed the sociology syllabus were ones that would give me valuable skills for whatever post-war job I was going to try for. Indeed, when applying for my University place I was asked on my application form what were my reasons for taking the degree. I wrote "To widen understanding of social problems, so that I can make a more valuable contribution in whatever work I undertake in post-war reconstruction". I was perhaps unconsciously fixing my goals. Among the subjects were Social Philosophy and History, Methodology, Political science, Law, something on Comparative Religion and Sociology itself. It seemed to me that all of these would provide an understanding of social relationships, human interaction and collective behaviour, which I felt all had relevance to the way I saw myself developing, although I was not sure then what I was ultimately going to do. The thought process I was going through is perhaps one which everyone who is working for a degree should follow. Without turning education into a vocational study, one has to consider where the qualification is going to lead.

In 1944 I enrolled for the degree and started a course of evening and Saturday lectures. Facilities for study in London were very limited at this time; the London School of Economics, the natural home for Sociological studies, had moved out of the Capital because of the bombing and only Birkbeck was struggling to keep going. David Mitrany undertook to supervise a special course for me. He introduced me to Professor Ginsberg, who, when LSE would eventually return to London, was to be in charge of my studies.

In spite of all the war-time difficulties, my study plan was taking shape. As I have found so often, one has only to ask for help and show some real dedication and the response from people is more often than not overwhelming. I was deeply grateful for all this assistance and was absolutely determined to make a success of the venture. I was thrilled to be starting on this really significant part of my studies.

There were, of course, no grants for study at this time. My initial coaching was quite expensive in my terms, although my teachers' charges were modest enough. Then there were books and the actual lecturing charges at Birkbeck and later at LSE. These were not great, but there were always enrolment fees and exam entry charges, all of which added up. At that time one had to devote personal money as well as time to such a study project. It was a squeeze, but I knew that would be the case when I started and I didn't begrudge it. I just didn't expect to be subsidised by anybody, which of course is not today's pattern. I have a tiny black book in which I recorded all these expenses. This little tome is a source of some satisfaction to me.

Working extramurally, one does not get the feeling of belonging to an institution in the same way that full-time students do, but I did make quite close relationships with several of the professors.

The University

Without any doubt, my favourite tutor was Professor Ginsberg. A small, gentle-mannered man with a quiet studious approach, he impressed me with his tremendous knowledge and his willingness to share it. His own work was meticulous and his example called for the same high standard from all his students.

Another of my lecturers was Professor Joad, a much more flamboyant character, with a very amusing turn of speech. I enjoyed his sessions very much. He debated with us freely in a very thought provoking way and opened up new and challenging ideas for me. Probably quite inaccurately, I did not judge him a very profound thinker, but I found him an excellent tutor. He certainly taught me a great deal.Inevitably I was just not on the same wave-length with all lecturers, one or two of whom I thought were politically biased with a tendency to play to the facile response they could always get from the younger full-time members of the group by making trite, clever comments.

I found these kinds of lectures, because I was very pressured, not the most advantageous way of spending my time; so I did not attend them. In-depth reading, careful note-taking and discussion with other students, I discovered, was a more productive method. Fortunately, when the final exam took place, I passed those subjects without the lectures, but it was a decision which took a bit of courage.

This may sound arrogant and perhaps my listening, rather than these tutors' lecturing, was at fault, but by this time life at the office was so hectic that I had my work cut out to attend lectures, do the necessary reading, study and essay preparation. I just knew I had to plan my time very carefully, otherwise I would never cover the syllabus.

To illustrate the pressure which war time conditions imposed, on a particular evening in one of Professor Ginsberg's lecture sessions, which I always enjoyed, I was so tired that my eyes closed — not for long I suspect, but when I opened them again, dear old Ginsberg was looking straight at me. I thought, "Horrors — what have I done? He won't put up with this, he'll kick me out of the course". I felt terrible, and particularly unhappy, because here was my favourite tutor, who was always so polite and I had shown him, of all people, this incredible discourtesy. At the end of the evening, Professor Ginsberg called me over — my heart sank. I thought it was the end of the story — not a bit of it. With a very gentle smile, he said in his small voice, "You are very tired — I think you should put your books away and go home and have a very good sleep!" I apologised, but he simply smiled again and that was that!

Students who do their studies extramurally in their own time I think for the most part are very dedicated and quite a number of my group were really hard workers. Two of my fellow students I liked very much. One was Mary Grieves, who had been terribly disabled by polio when a little girl and had to go everywhere in a self-propelled wheelchair. I so admired her determination. She made no fuss about things which were obviously so much more effort and exhausting for her than for the rest of us — a tremendous person.

My other colleague was Olive Wareham, who was much more of an academic than I was. In the final months of the last year, we made a little syndicate and worked together, going through old papers, discussing and comparing notes and possible answers. I always said that it was Olive who got me through the exam. When I, in my usual imaginative way, would propose an answer to a question according to the 'Macdonald Theory', Olive would say, "All very well, but don't you think we're supposed to be quoting Marshall here!" Of course she was right! With her help, I learned to eliminate some of my flights of fancy and work along more conventional, academic lines.

The Practical Approach

One approach which I did adopt, which no-one else in my year did, and which I am sure was right for me, was to get as much first- hand experience of the different topics we were studying, as possible. To read about disturbed people or methods of scientific and social research was all very well, but for me to comprehend the full significance of such studies, I felt I needed to see the theory as it applied in real life. So with the help of several friends, notably Captain Edwin Boyd, more of whom later, and Professor Mitrany, I was able to get permits to visit the Law Courts to hear civil, criminal and divorce cases. I also went to Juvenile Courts and heard Basil Henriques preside. In addition I visited nursery schools, mental hospitals and VD clinics. I found this first-hand observation absorbing.

The study of human beings at all levels and in widely differing circumstances broadened my understanding and greatly increased my sympathy for people. Sociology is sometimes described as the science of society. It has the function of discovering general laws or tendencies by the comparative study of the behaviour and attitudes of both individuals and groups of people. By linking the theory which I was trying to learn with the observation of actual social practice, I felt I was doing just that.

Sociology is a comparatively new discipline and is not, indeed cannot be, as precise as some other studies. In, for example, chemical research, it is possible to vary one factor at a time in order to prove causation. Social phenomena are immensely complex and the human factors which make up this complexity cannot be tampered with and experimented on to suit the researcher. It is, therefore, extremely difficult to draw conclusions as exactly as one would like.

From time to time, it has been fashionable to deride sociology as an inexact science which has let loose on to society a lot of muddle-minded theorists, the do-gooder brigade who lack discipline and precision of thought.

This was not a true interpretation of sociology for me. It opened up whole new perspectives and because of the breadth of study, showed me the connection between things which up to then had seemed totally dissociated. As a mature student, deeply involved with a very demanding job for which I had to do a great deal of tight thinking, I did not swallow or follow every concept or theory which the course presented to me. I was learning to be selective. I am absolutely sure, however, that the whole experience was enormously beneficial, and the acceptance or rejection of the ideas which came my way was making me think much more constructively.

All this challenging personal work was done against the background of demanding office activities, and in addition the continuous bombing and the need to take up valuable time chasing round half empty shops looking for things in order to make the most of our very limited food and clothes coupons, was tedious. Dear Jane Farmer, who two years earlier had volunteered to go to Rhodesia, as Zimbabwe was then called, and work in the Censorship Department which was established there, came home on leave.

Quite where she had got hold of them I don't know, but she had brought back some beautiful things which were incredible luxuries to us — nylon stockings and some very pretty underwear. With characteristic generosity she gave a little party and allowed her eight or ten guests to buy these goodies at, I am sure, much less than she had paid for them. We were thrilled at this lovely surprise.

D-Day

But the great joy in the early days of 1944 was the wonderful news of the Allied successes. By the papers which came across our desks, we knew that war supplies, guns, bombs, aircraft were at last building up to a point when a final offensive would be possible. Then, a closely guarded secret, the news of D-Day, 6 June 1944, burst on us. Our spirits soared and as mile by mile the Germans fell back, we knew that victory, in Europe at least, was in sight.

The joy and the relief were intense, yet strangely enough my recollection of the victory celebrations is not nearly so clear as many of the war incidents themselves. It was almost as if so much emotion and nervous energy had been used up by the struggle itself, in which one felt so closely involved, that the day of success left a feeling of remoteness and unreality, almost an anti-climax. I have never discussed this with other people, so I do not know whether this was just a personal reaction or whether others felt the same way.

Very soon our work in the Department, which related largely to the European, not the Far Eastern, theatre of war, started to slow down. It became largely a matter of co-ordinating papers and leaving records adequately documented, so that they were comprehensible if ever they were needed.

Several of the girls had married mostly men in the forces and they went where their husbands were posted. It was very much a winding-down operation.

I started to turn my attention to what I intended to do.

Personnel Work

Originally I had thought that my degree studies in sociology and the fact that for some time I had managed a staff of 70 people, would lead me to do Personnel work. Accordingly, in mid 1945 I sought an introduction to Elizabeth Buckley Sharp, who was the Head of the developing Personnel Management Association. Personnel work, which up to the War had limited recognition as an organisational function, was beginning to develop into a properly structured activity. Betty Buckley Sharp gave me a lot of time; up-dating me on the latest developments in the area and also assessing my potential for staff work.

At this time, she was one of the most knowledgeable people in the whole field. Incidentally, I feel that Betty has never been adequately rewarded for her splendid pioneering work in the Personnel field. Due to her organising ability and tremendously hard work, the foundations of the present Institute of Personnel Management were laid. I would have liked her major contribution to Personnel work in this country to have been much more generously recognised.

She sent me for several interviews. Two I did not get, and I never knew whether my work experience was inappropriate or whether my interviewing skills were inadequate. I was offered another position and, perversely perhaps, turned it down, because I thought the organisation was old-fashioned.

Then a splendid opportunity arose, Selfridges, the big departmental store, was beginning to structure its post-war plans. Miss Harvey, the woman who had been Women's Staff Controller since the days when Gordon Selfridge founded the store in 1911, was retiring. She was in charge of 2,500 women and was a very influential figure in the Store.

She interviewed me and we got on very well. I was than seen by the Chairman, Mr. Holmes, The Managing Director and two other Directors. I did not find these interviews quite so daunting as earlier ones; I suppose I was getting used to the performance. So although I was nervous, my confidence in my capacity to present myself better was growing. Miss Harvey wanted me; both the Chairman and the Managing Director approved of me, but said that they felt I was too young to be given such a big responsibility. I was very disappointed. I was, after all, 35. I felt I had come so close to success.

However, Mr. Holmes, the Chairman, said that if ever I wanted at some later stage to discuss openings which might occur as Selfridges' plans developed, he would always be pleased to see me — the Managing Director, Dickson Scott, confirmed this. I was greatly encouraged.

Another position came up; this time in a Government Department. I wasn't too keen to remain a Civil Servant; however it seemed an interesting opening and the woman Controller of the Department, a Mrs. Thomson, outlined the advantages of the job adding she saw it as a position of national importance and one which would develop.

It was a smaller department than I was used to, but I found Mrs. Thomson agreeable and her Deputy, Evelyn Page Roberts, absolutely delightful. I accepted the job.

Back at the office, le Tournet was prepared to release me quickly, as my work had virtually come to an end in the Department, so I was all set.

There were many farewell parties and lovely gifts; then I went off to the country for a week's holiday, returning in early August to take up my duties — I was so looking forward to this new experience.

My First Post-War Job

I had learned how to read Government files quite expertly, whipping through the verbiage and getting to the heart of the matter quickly. I started on a thorough examination of all the back-up material I could find in my new office. The further I delved, the more disappointed I became. It was plain that the Department had been highly significant during the war, but that its activities were beginning to shrink and I even came across references suggesting that the whole undertaking might be wound up in a year or so. It was far from the glamourous development opportunity that the job had been described to me. I realised that it was a very limited and, what was worse, a shrinking field. At the interview, I had not probed the conditions carefully enough — I had wanted the job and allowed myself to be misled — it was an important lesson for the future.

Mrs. Thomson was out of the office a great deal, so I had little contact with her. On the third day, I sought out Evelyn and expressed my doubts. She was, of course, very discreet, but when I said that the changing character of the work had not been properly described to me, that it was not the growth position I wanted and that I felt I had made a great mistake, she nodded and had to agree with me.

The real problem I could see was going to be Mrs. Thomson, who was an ambitious woman. She had obviously wanted to enlarge the size of her Department in order to increase her own importance by adding a senior member to her staff. How she succeeded in getting the vacancy approved initially, I could not imagine. But my problem was how to get out of the job.

The major stumbling block, as I saw it, was a piece of legislation, the "Control of Engagements Order", which had been imposed in the early days of the War, to prevent people with essential skills hopping from job to job. It made it possible to hold civilian employees where they could to the most good and maintain continuity. In other words, you could not change jobs without the permission of your Head of Department, whether in Government or a commercial undertaking, because everything was directed to the War effort. The Japanese conflict was still going on; the legislation had not, therefore, been repealed.

Quite obviously my Controller lady, having got me in her Department, was not going to admit that she had misrepresented the job to me and, as she had the powers to hold me where I was, I feared I was going to have a real battle if I was to get away.

I went back to my office and did more research into the files and had discussion with other members of the Department. A mere week after my arrival I knew my assessment was correct — the job was not what had been described to me, it was withering and would offer me no challenge. Just at a time in my career when I had to get really significant experience, this was a dead end.

Fearing what her reaction would be, I made an appointment to see Mrs. Thomson. She was furious — I could see her anger mounting her brown eyes flashing, her chubby cheeks went red with rage and seemed to swell up. Feeling rather like jelly inside, I pressed my case with determination. She told me I was wrong — had totally misinterpreted the situation, that I was arrogant and finally said she would not release me. I said my mind was made up and I would be pleased if she would pass my letter of resignation to the Director, when I had written it.

The interview ended; it was the most unpleasant experience that had occurred to date and and I felt very apprehensive about the future. I wrote my resignation letter as carefully and tactfully as I could and put it on her desk. Nothing happened. I waited several days and then saw her again. I confirmed my intention to leave one month after the date of my letter, which was a piece of pure bluff. I said to her there was not enough work to keep me busy and that it was not in her interests to hold a disgruntled individual in her Department. This seemed to strike some chord. She could see I was adamant and something made her hesitate. I perceived this and continued to press my point. What in fact I was doing without being totally aware of it, was to play a power game with someone who by wrongly asking for a senior staff member was herself in a very vulnerable position with her seniors. Quite suddenly, she agreed to pass on my resignation.

Escaping to a New Opportunity

My next consideration was the future. If I was going to get out of this tangle, I needed another job and quickly, so I immediately sought an interview with Mr. Holmes at Selfridges. I explained what had happened, that I was determined to leave and could he help. He explained that he could not be involved with obtaining my release, but if I succeeded in freeing myself he would probably be able to suggest something.

Back in Mrs. Thomson's Department, I tried to fill in the almost empty days and then one morning an older, rather dignified man arrived in the office and asked for Mrs. Thomson. I happened to be in the outer office and explained she was not in, but that I would give her a message when she returned. He was about to leave, when he said, "Are you by any chance the lady who wishes to leave the Department?" It was the Director. We had a brief, very courteous, conversation, his only query was — didn't I think it was a very quick decision to make after only a few weeks. I expressed my reasons firmly, but as circumspectly as possible. He left.

In a very few days, Mrs. Thomson told me that I could leave in two weeks. She was positively benign and asked what I was going to do. I innocently explained about my contact with Mr. Holmes and she expressed interest and pleasure and hoped I would get an interesting job.

I heaved a sigh of relief — by the time I left, the whole episode would have lasted a month. I counted myself very lucky to have escaped and went back to Selfridges.

I found Mr. Holmes in a very quizzical mood. Rather to my surprise, he asked me the name of my Departmental Head. I told him, Mrs. Thomson, and he laughed. I was puzzled. "You may be interested", he said. "She has been to see me to ask for a job." I was amazed.

"Did you know her?", I asked. He shook his head wisely. "No, indirectly as you might say, you effected the introduction!" I had never before encountered such devious manoeuvring. I realised that I was still something of an innocent abroad.

Mr. Holmes called in Dickson Scott and they jointly outlined what they could at that moment offer. "Not a very marvellous job", he said, "But I suggest you think about it carefully. The proposal is for you to edit our Staff Magazine with the help of our Advertising Manager. As that will no be a full-time occupation, you will at the same time be attached for one or two weeks to as many departments as possible, not only on the sales floor but in administration, stores, production." He explained that post-war plans were not far enough advanced to have a precise position at my level to offer, but he said that if I took this assignment, I would learn about store business and be in a prime position to be considered when Management jobs did develop.

I went away and this time thought about the proposal very carefully. I trusted the people I had met; I liked the feel of the whole place, vibrant and challenging and most important I would be learning something. I accepted I was to report to Dickson Scott and could start as soon as the other job finished. I felt it was an excellent opportunity.

I had the run of the Store and Dickson Scott, a very shrewd Scotsman, was very supportive. I had some problems, of course. The Advertising Manager, my co-editor on the house magazine, who had been in the Store for years, thought I was superfluous, but I did not worry and went quietly on with my work, noting and observing and making a lot of friends with the very outgoing people in the Store, Buyers, Managers and Sales Staff. They were not as academically educated as the people I had dealt with during the war, but they were professionals. They knew their jobs and had a tremendous pride in the way things were done. War time problems meant that standards had slipped disastrously and they were all desperately keen to get back to the right level, both of merchandise and service. It was going to take time. I felt if I did my apprenticeship in the way Mr. Holmes had outlined, I could make a contribution.

Not very long afterwards, a very unexpected thing happened. The woman who had been selected for the Staff Controller's position did not prove a great success and she left. I was offered the job, which I accepted with enormous pleasure. This was what I had wanted. I could not resist pointing out rather mischievously that I was only a few months older than when I was interviewed for the post before and considered then to be too junior!

So as to give me every assistance, it was suggested that if I would like it, an invitation could be extended to Miss Harvey to come back from retirement to work with me for a month. I was delighted; it was just the help I needed and to my great joy, Miss Harvey accepted the invitation and was marvellous.

I found myself in a spacious office which, if a bomb had not blown in the enormous windows which made up the whole of one side of it, would have been very attractive. As it was, it was drafty and unsightly, the window was a patchwork of bits of wood and hardboard. However, I had a splendid desk, a secretary and lots of facilities, like lunching in the best dining room in the house. I felt I was in clover.

Miss Harvey again was no academic, but she knew the Store backwards — the systems — the personalities — the weak links in the structure. She guided, advised, warned and chivvied me into working fast and accurately.

She sat in when I interviewed people. She did not interrupt while applicants were present, but when they'd gone she would evaluate my interviewing techniques, quickly, adroitly, objectively. I didn't mind the very direct criticism and I valued the praise.

Why didn't you ask about that? — do you really have an understanding of that woman's intentions? — why did you waste all that time asking that and that question? — what you needed to know was — It was first class! There was no malice; she was entirely frank. She insisted that I keep the paperwork in order after each interview, and was direct and critical of other members of the Staff Department who did not bring me the right documentation or data quickly.

"You haven't got time to put up with slow, slovenly work from your Support Staff", she said, "You must keep them up to scratch. *You're* in the firing line in this job, if things go wrong you will get heavy criticism — you must, therefore, have maximum support from your own staff. They've been allowed to get undisciplined."

The Staff Office was somewhat removed from the hurly-burly of the shop floor, but the excitement and immediacy of the operation reached even this quieter domain. Store events governed our lives — Sales —. Special Promotions — Christmas — they had repercussions in the Staff Office as they all called for additional staff, often of a specialist type and because we were building up our post war personnel, the work never stopped.

Buckingham Palace

Just before Miss Harvey left, came the great excitement of going to Buckingham Palace to collect my "gong", as decorations were laughingly called. My mother and Ian accompanied me. I did not have enough clothes coupons to buy a new outfit so I purchased a new hat, which looks absurd in the light of today's fashions.

The whole ceremony was beautifully organised from the very start. We crossed the courtyard and entered the Palace where meticulously dressed attendants guided us into pre-arranged groups.

We were ushered along the wide corridors, hung with many impressive portraits, to the throne room. A military band played and the tension mounted. At last the King entered and took his place. The senior awards were given first. Eventually my turn came. I just hoped I was not going to stumble with my curtsey. Fortunately I didn't and I accurately observed the protocol of not raising my eyes until the King spoke. The medals and ribbons were handed to the King by equerries and at last my award was pinned onto my lapel and I retreated. The King looked very pale, I thought, but he was very gracious and found a word to say to everyone.

Because it was such a wonderful occasion, I failed to notice many of the things I afterwards questioned myself about, but the lasting impression was, as with all British ceremonial events, that the organisation was superb, correctly timed, beautifully presented, the acme of dignified discipline.

There are many today who sneer at these ceremonies, calling them unnecessary and valueless. I cannot agree. They make even shaggy people behave with a poise and courtesy which adds to everyone's dignity and sense of pride — paying respect builds each person's self respect. I felt very honoured.

Making the Job My Own

With Miss Harvey's departure I was on my own. I had learned a great deal, and would be eternally grateful to her for her help, but I could not agree with just everything which this very dear lady had said. She was of the old school, somewhat authoritarian, and I knew that newer ideas would have to be introduced in some areas, indeed this is what the Chairman and Dickson Scott told me they expected of me.

By being selective, I was exercising that personal judgement which had initially practised rather hesitantly with my Censorship job and then later with my studies. I was happy to take guidance, but I had learned to stand by my own decisions, not aggressively, but with a measure of confidence I knew that when dealing with certain things I had to draw my own conclusions and act on them, otherwise I wouldn't be me, but a pale copy of someone else. I realised that inevitably there was the attendant risk of being wrong and making mistakes, but I reckoned that if, and when, that happened, I'd learn more quickly and more comprehendingly from such errors — at least they would be *my* mistakes and *my* corrections.

Little by little, I made changes. One thing, however, which Miss Harvey taught me, which, whatever my workload — and it was pretty crushing at times — I always did for an hour or so every day, I went into the store, because that was the place where the action was going on. I would walk around and talk to everyone; I found out where discontent was brewing, noted the performance of people both senior and junior first-hand and got the feel of what was happening. It was an invaluable piece of advice she had given me, which I believe personnel people today could well follow.

Negotiating and Making Things Work

It meant that when people came to the Staff Office, very frequently I had a good idea of the problem I was going to be asked to address, and the staff really got the feeling that I was interested and cared about them.

Some things, however, did take me by surprise. For example, one afternoon the very nice motherly woman, Mrs. Dowling, who ran our inexpensive restaurant very successfully by real skill and firm dealings with her staff, came into my office in great distress.. "They're all going to walk out", she wailed.

The events which had produced this drastic situation were not all that terrible and were certainly very comical. Salads were washed and prepared on plates for the waitresses to pick up to meet customers' orders, as they passed the salad counter. One very pretty Irish waitress on this particularly busy day had been kept waiting once or twice, because when she got to the counter there were no salads ready. So she started to tease and provoke a little old salad preparer who was getting behind with her work.

Eventually, the salad lady could stand this jibing no longer, so she picked up a plate of beetroot and threw it with good aim at the Irish waitress! Pandemonium broke out. The restaurant staff immediately divided into two camps, taking sides for the waitress or for the little old lady. Neither group would give way and they all threatened a walk out which would, of course, benefit no-one. I asked to see the two culprits. The mere fact of having to come all the way up to the Staff Office and be interviewed by me, cooled tempers down and I was able to listen to the stories separately and then try to restore order.

Salad lady: Too much work, cheeky waitress, always asking too much too quickly — let them come and have a hand at being in and out of water all the time —

But wiping beetroot over people's faces is no way to behave and Mrs. Dowling is a very good Boss and you're not helping her, are you?"

I know — I know — I'm sorry.

Pretty waitress with delightful Irish brogue: My commission depends on quick turn round — don't you want the customers to have good service? — they take too long fiddling about in that kitchen.

Maybe, but what about respecting other people's problems — salad washing is a dirty, tedious job and she's not all that young — not very fair was it? — nor to Mrs. Dowling who has her figures to make too. She's a very fair Boss, isn't she? -

Yes, she is that.

Coming together there was sheepish hesitation and then a reluctant handshake and work was resumed, Mrs. Dowling and I heaving huge sighs of relief. It was not high level diplomacy perhaps, but very practical negotiations, which saved a lot of profit and the reputation of Selfridges, which would certainly have become a little tarnished if orders having been taken and a long queue of customers waiting for service had been greeted with no food and the restaurant shutting down!

There was another case which brought home to me the necessity to act with absolute integrity when dealing with people and never make promises which cannot be fulfilled. During the war supplies being very limited, the costume jewellery department, run by an elderly Head of Department, had just kept ticking over with an Under Buyer who had long service in the Store, but not high potential for a smart fashion section.

The Head of Department retired, having, quite improperly, promised his Deputy his job. He had no authority to do this and had, therefore, very unkindly, falsely raised her expectations of promotion.

It was my responsibility to tell this woman that she was not in the running for the Buyer's job. Her happy expectant face as she had come into my office told me everything and made me feel awful. I knew what she was expecting. So when I told her the position, I was not surprised that she broke down, lost her temper, called me and the Company very unfair, adding, "So my long service counts for nothing then? and don't expect me to stay in the Department and work for some new person, I won't". She ended by threatening to resign. I tried to explain that it was our intention, as really good merchandise became available, to build up the Department to double its present size. It would be an enormous task which would put a very unfair strain on her — as to resigning within two years of retirement and so losing pension rights, it was not very sensible.

The outburst continued, but eventually I got this poor little person to trust me for just a week or so before handing in her resignation. "You will see", I said, "The Company is not unfair. Good things will come out of this." Wanting to believe me, but still very upset and distrustful, she left my office.

What was I going to do? If only I could find a position somewhere in the Store where her steady, reliable, if uninspired, work could be of value. My luck was in. Within two days, one of the really charming and efficient Buyers, a Mr. Wing, who was Head of the China Department, came to ask me for someone whom he could train to develop an idea he had dreamed up. He cleverly pointed out that the public was sick and tired of the drab, white china which was all that could be manufactured in the austerity days of the war.

People had to have cups and saucers and plates, but the raw materials for decorating china had been diverted to war purposes and all the skilled decorators and artists who make our gorgeous English porcelain had been serving in the armed forces and were only then coming back. Mr. Wing was of the opinion that many people had tucked away in cupboards, or perhaps even in attics, tea and dinner services; perhaps surplus wedding presents that had never been used. His idea was as a stop gap, until the porcelain factories got going again with real china, as he called it, for Selfridges to buy in this second-hand merchandise, and sell it in the store. Customers, fully aware that it was not new, would, he felt, be very happy to purchase it. So what he wanted was someone who could learn to recognise the well-known pre-war tea and dinner services and purchase them at a price which would give the Store a modest profit.

"I will teach her the job and I will back her all the way." Here was the very job I had been hoping for, for my costume jewellery lady. I explained to Mr. Wing who I had in mind and the problems which had confronted this person. Mr. Wing was interested and I persuaded my problem lady to see Mr. Wing. His courtesy, enthusiasm and quiet appreciation of her long service — dispelled her bitterness and with some hesitation, she accepted the position and made a great success of it.

There is a sequel to this, but it comes later — enough to say that Serendipity had once again enabled me to mend a very sad situation.

Continued Study

Of course while all this was in progress I was still carrying on with my studies. As the final exam was not due to take place till the following year, I felt at times as if I had a split personality — divided in more ways than just the store and studies.

The first winter I was in the staff office was a very severe one — ice, snow, bitter winds and very little fuel; they all contrived to make life into a real misery. The high windows in my office had still not been replaced, as plate glass was virtually unobtainable, so I sat at my desk wearing a coat, scarf and mittens with a rug around my feet and a miserable little one-bar electric stove which hardly kept the temperature above freezing. Trying to look efficient, dressed as if one was on an Arctic trek was a bit incongruous. However, grumbling was certainly not the remedy.

One domestic job which caused me to curse and giggle in turns was the way I tried to cope with the shortage of fuel at home. There was very little coal, so we hauled out of the roof an old fashioned oil stove which created as much smell as heat, as it burned paraffin. That also was in short supply. The local shops were either sold out or shut by the time I could get to them and my mother, who was not at all well, could not possibly carry cans of oil. I prowled around the narrow streets at the back of the store and discovered a little oil shop which did have supplies of paraffin, so I would trundle up to town with an empty oil can, purchase as much paraffin as I was allowed, and trundle home with this load, which seemed to get heavier and heavier as I progressed. Carrying an oil can with an absolutely stupid metal handle designed, it seemed, to cut one's fingers in half, was not my idea of fun.

I think it was the restrictions and continued shortages of food and essentials *after* the war had finished, which were so hard to take. We'd won the war, but we learned that in many other countries all the things we still lacked were in plentiful supply. It seemed that standing against the Nazi threat didn't win us Brownie points. I didn't mind too much for myself, but I felt very sorry for older people like my mother.

Store Personalities

There were many personalities in the store whom I liked very much —
some I did not. Perhaps the ones whom I found very unacceptable were
some of the tough Buyers, who were very demanding and often quite
ruthless and unfair with their staff. Good, certainly experienced, assistants
were difficult to find and sometimes the poor treatment that these
conceited, ill- tempered heads of department handed out caused a great
many unnecessary upsets, frequently resulting in good staff resigning.

The Queen Bees or King Pins would then either phone down or come
to the staff office to complain that they couldn't do their job unless I
provided them with good staff. They were very powerful figures and I
remembered the warnings that Miss Harvey had given me — "Don't take
them on, because they are the money spinners in this business and if they
go to town on you, you'll get no support from top Management!"

There was more than a vestige of truth in this and I found it
exasperating. Other managers of departments were just the opposite —
co-operative with the staff office and good with the assistants.

A very happy department was the Display Department. Selfridges
windows had long been famous for their exquisite taste and great
originality. The department was headed by a most talented designer, Inge
Sonsthagen, whose white blonde hair, blue eyes and exquisite complexion,
confirmed her Norwegian nationality. I had had very happy associations
with Norwegians during the war and so we had much in common.

I had been in the staff office for quite a while when, fresh from the
RAF, in 1946 Bill Fowles was appointed men's staff controller. He had
modern, forward looking ideas, like me, and so we worked together very
co-operatively and, happy to tell, Bill is still one of my very special friends.

I Become Uneasy

But somehow I was not wholly at ease. The lack of personal decision
making, occasioned by the attitude of some department heads which I have
described, was very frustrating. I felt I had to accede to people who did not
understand the real meaning of good personal practice. Furthermore,
since the work tempo of my immediate Head did not inspire me, and
because of some uncertain moves on the Board, I became fidgety. There
was, I am sure, some in-fighting going on and I wasn't sure whether the old
brigade with their rigid authoritarian approaches would win supremacy, or
whether the Chairman's faction with more consultative policies would hold
their ground. Dickson Scott was himself somewhat restive and I saw Mr.
Holmes very rarely.

I knew I had gained the confidence of the staff and that I was spelling out progressive policies which were supposed to be implemented as soon as the immediate post-war difficulties had been surmounted, but I had doubts. I felt that perhaps I was promising people things which would never materialise. I did not want to mislead people who had come to trust me. I felt confused.

About this time David Mitrany, who had by now become Adviser on International Affairs to Unilever, introduced me to Ambrose Addis, the Chairman of Atkinsons, one of Unilever's subsidiary companies which was famous for its perfumes and cosmetics. Ambrose was getting together his team as they came out of the forces and decided that a week-end conference to establish post- war objectives and rebuild civilian skills would be valuable.

He asked me if I would contribute to the programme and I spoke on the skills of communication. The talk went down well and then I forgot about it.

Some months later, in 1947, Ambrose asked me to lunch and outlined a new job he had in mind for a woman manager in the Company, to study the cosmetics market and make recommendations to him and his fellow Directors as to the kind of merchandise which would be acceptable to the retail trade. He offered me the job.

I explained that I knew nothing about perfume and cosmetics and that my experience lay in a totally different direction. But he said that training would be given so that I could acquire the purely technical aspects which the job would demand. He wanted me to join the Company for my knowledge of women and my capacity for communication.

I hesitated — I so much liked the majority of the work I was doing at Selfridges and the atmosphere of the Store, pulsating with life. I was also tremendously grateful for the splendid opportunities which both Mr. Holmes and Dickson Scott had initially given me. I knew that within two years I had carved out a position for myself — that people liked and trusted me and that I was still learning the retail trade and store business. Was it right to forfeit all this?

On the other hand, Unilever was a huge company. I knew the opportunities that such an organisation could offer must be greater than those available in a single department store, however large. Further, I wanted to move from the Personnel field which, contrary to my original thinking, I perceived might be becoming a side step activity, not leading to really senior jobs. One of the problems seemed to be that Personnel entailed a great deal of responsibility, but not much authority. A situation which I think still sometimes confronts particularly women in many areas. The Unilever position carried management status which I felt would open up many more opportunities. I would be progressing both in level and salary.

Nevertheless, I was uncertain about the job at Atkinsons. It was not what I had trained for and was a strange, unknown sphere.

However, after I met Ambrose again and also his two Directors, I began to feel that perhaps a real challenge awaited me. Before the job was conclusively offered to me, I had to meet a Senior Executive of Unilever, who in the layered structure of the organisation was the reporting point for Atkinsons' Board.

I was asked to go for an interview with this man. I had anticipated an impressive management figure, another W.H. Holmes. My interviewer was not this. It was obvious that my rather attractive dress and little straw hat, which I wore tilted to one side, dumbfounded him. If I thought I was going to be nervous, the shoe was on the other foot! I really felt very sorry for him, because it was plain that I, perhaps all women, terrified him and that he knew nothing about interviewing at which, by this time, I had some skill.

The interview started with an awkward and what seemed in interminable pause. The Unilever Executive said absolutely nothing. Realising that he was completely tongue-tied, I said smiling, "Would you like me to tell you a little about my experience?" "Oh yes" he said thankfully, "I would". So I rambled on as helpfully as I could, explaining my war job, my present position, my wish to get into line management, etc. Even then this Senior Executive still said nothing, until quite suddenly he blurted out, "Are you going to get married?" I nearly burst out laughing, but managing to keep a straight face, I said "I have absolutely no plans in that direction at the moment. I wish to consolidate my career!" The interview virtually finished at that point and I stepped out into the bright sunlight of Howard Street off The Strand, saying to myself, "Well, I shall never hear any more of that".

But I was wrong. Within a week an offer was made. I discussed this with several friends whose judgement I felt I could trust: David Mitrany, who was of course all in favour, also Don Bliss, the American husband of Gabrielle, one of my very close Censorship friends. Gabrielle had never been in my department but we did have a lot of contact and her delightful manner and exquisite style — she was a Spaniard — were an education for me. She was highly sophisticated in the nicest sense of that word. Don was Second Secretary at the American Embassy and was closely concerned with economic affairs and business. He strongly recommended that I take the job. "You must make it work for you", he said. So I accepted.

Then came the awful job of breaking the news to Mr. Holmes, Dickson Scott and, of course, Bill. The Chairman and Dickson Scott were astonished and offered to make changes in my position. But my mind was made up — I talked it over with Bill and told him I felt thoroughly mean, but that the offer was too big for me to miss. He, I think, was as surprised as the others.

Parties and luncheons and all kinds of friendly, sad little gestures followed, and feeling more and more miserable I finally left, with two taxi loads of flowers and presents. The euphoria did not last!

I take up my job as Women's Staff Controller at Selfridge's

Outside Buckingham Palace with my brother when I collected my decoration

Chapter Six

Unilever — a New World

Several of the interviews I had with the Directors before I actually joined Atkinsons were conducted at the Company's showroom in Old Bond Street. It was a most attractive establishment. There was a shop at street level, a graciously proportioned room which still exists on the corner of Old Bond Street and Burlington Gardens, although it looks very different today. Then it had a very Art Deco appearance with mirrored walls and gilded furniture. Later, I was responsible for having it re- decorated in a more modern softer style.

In the basement which was the Board Room, a large beautifully polished table filled the centre of the room and was surrounded by period chairs. It had a very imposing appearance.

The building was surmounted by a little tower in which hung an eleven bell carillon which we used to have played for special occasions, such as Christmas carols. The exterior architecture was neo-Gothic and still has a fantastic, highly ornate appearance.

The whole establishment had a great air of luxury, a fitting background for the exclusive merchandise which had made Atkinsons famous ever since it was established in 1810. It had been brought into the Unilever complex of companies in 1929 and was a surprising type of business to be within the fold of a very down- to-earth company, whose basic product was mass-produced soap for a mass market.

I don't believe that Unilever ever really felt comfortable with its ill matched associate. I was to discover later that the whole idea of being linked with up-market beauty products and fragrances rather embarrassed the tough business executives who operated in Unilever House, but I did not know that then.

I started work at Isleworth — the factory and research establishment where many Unilever toiletries were made. It was a cheerless, unwelcoming ugly building which began life as Pears Soap Factory, but many years ago had become another Unilever subsidiary.

Ambrose greeted me courteously and kindly, but he had, in these surroundings, playing the role of Chairman, I thought, a rather formal manner. The other two Directors were very pleasant, but pre-occupied with their own affairs. One of them, the Marketing Director, to whom I was to report, had laid out a splendid induction programme for me with planned visits to other Unilever establishments. I was to spend time in the Old Bond Street Show Room and also several days at Port Sunlight in Cheshire, the manufacturing base of Unilever's huge soap business.

I was tremendously impressed with Port Sunlight. The original Lord Leverhulme had, away back in 1880, turned a pretty derelict swamp into a huge factory and, in order to house his work people, he had created one of the earliest residential model villages. It was a wonderful social concept — paternalistic perhaps, but genuinely caring. No two houses were the same and were, according to the standards of the day, well equipped. The village still exists today, complete with churches, a library, and an art gallery, which contains some rare treasures, clocks, pictures and furniture. The factory area is extensive. It includes huge soaperies, as the enormous vats in which the soap is still made are called, storage areas for raw materials and finished goods and a very large accounts or banking hall. The whole site, which re-vitalised a pretty derelict area and gave work to hundreds of people, was a wonderful testimony to the vigour, imagination and skill of the Company's founder. I thought it was tremendous.

Another part of my induction programme was a prolonged visit to the Atkinsons Factory in Bermondsey, where all the perfumes were blended and manufactured. It was not a large factory, but the perfume laboratory was a most fascinating place presided over by our Head Perfumer, Laurie Dalton. He had blended perfumes all his life but far from being a sophisticated city gent, he wore rough tweeds, was round and chubby and looked rather like an elderly farmer.

The Director who was in charge of the production side at Bermondsey was Jack White. He was to prove a great ally later on. Even at this early visit he was particularly helpful — he had a gift for clear explanation of technical details to non- technical people and he answered all my questions, many of them probably very naive, meticulously and explicitly.

I was also scheduled to accompany two or three of the Atkinsons Salesmen on their visits to retail shops and stores. I was seeing the other side of commerce. Selfridges had revealed the retail aspects of business, the end of the chain, so to speak, where the customer was king. Now I was one degree further back and involved in the production and marketing aspects. I could see the need for sound management here because of the large sums of capital which were involved. I had observed that there was a long lead time in the store business between the purchase of goods and the money being handed over by the customer, never less than six months; but in manufacturing it was even longer.

Everywhere I went I was received in a most helpful and polite way — people seemed happy and involved in their work and very ready to share information with me. I was beginning to be conscious of a very purposeful atmosphere.

I did not realise that my title of Manager made my entry into this new world very much easier. This is a point which is sometimes overlooked, particularly by women as they build their careers. Titles in themselves are of no significance, yet they do give a recognisable status, particularly for newcomers. They are, in other words, a useful shorthand which people can comprehend and know how to respond to. They are essential in a hierarchical situation.

Yet contradictorily, title and rank hunters and worshippers are a great nuisance in an organisation. Nevertheless, the right title gives an entry gate and an authority, just as the right level of salary, pitched at the market level of the job, is recognition as well as reward. Status should, in my opinion, never be over-played and always backed by sound knowledge and hard work, which regrettably is not always the case.

Knowing one's own value and, if necessary, insisting on an appropriate title, were things I had not yet learned to do consciously. It was my good fortune rather than my tactics that brought me the Unilever offer at the right level. I did, however, by this time have a sense of confidence. I had a feeling that I could tackle things if I really wanted to, which I think was reflected in my attitude and made me a credible figure as I moved round the Company. I think it is also important to add that I was not conscious of any patronising behaviour from the men I met, although some of them, I think, were surprised that I acted with assurance. There were virtually no women in Management positions, so it was very much a male orientated company, but I was very involved in learning my job and, without exception, they all assisted me.

Getting to Know the Company

My induction trip completed, I returned to my drab little office at Isleworth and started work to create my job. A large number of Atkinsons staff worked there, mostly Sales Personnel and back-up people such as order and invoice supervisors and accounts clerks.

They looked at me as if I had come from outer space. My manner was different; my clothes were different. In some strange way, I felt I had no affiliation with any of them — the disciplined formality of the Government Office was lacking, the zest and drive of Selfridges was not present either. Many of the junior staff, with whom later I was to work with very happily, initially appeared to me mouselike, uninspired people. Some of the Sales Control people I found crude and unattractive. I felt like an alien soul.

I believe this was due to the fact that I did not at that time have specific duties to fulfil, so there were no particular relationships with these people — they did not know what to make of me, nor I them.

It took me nine months to acclimatise to this totally new environment. For a greater part of this time I didn't enjoy the work. Many times I felt that I had made a very wrong decision in leaving Selfridges. There seemed to me an incomprehensible lack of pace. Few decisions were made and no-one seemed to be concerned to direct my activities.

What I failed to appreciate was that the Company was still only just getting back into a positive pattern of business after the war. Many of the staff were trickling back into their jobs as they were released from the Services. Rationing was still in force and the raw materials required for manufacture only very gradually became available — this applied to the packaging and containers as well as the products themselves. This meant that the pace of the whole operation was in my terms painfully slow.

Further, the whole scale of the Company was totally different from anything I had experienced. I just didn't understand the structure. I came to realise also that there were differences of opinion among the three Directors. Added to this, the Chairman found decision making very difficult, so events took shape rather slowly. Ambrose did not appear to be a fast thinker. He spoke in an extremely measured way and tended to use long pedantic words which I often felt were unnecessary. He seemed unsure as to how plans should be laid. There was an air of masterly inactivity.

I Take My Exam

Up to a point this suited me quite well, because I had to take some leave to sit the final of my exam. The various papers I had to take could very fortunately be contained within a week. I do not consider myself a good examination candidate; at least in those days I allowed myself to get too worked up about them. However, I did not think the papers were too awful and the week soon passed.

The exam completed, whatever anxieties I had about failing or passing were masked, because there were many preoccupations at the office.

Fortunately I learned in due course that I had passed. I was, of course, delighted and felt a great step forward had been achieved — the result of nearly five years hard work.

A new line of fragrances which were called Daytime Perfumes were being prepared for launching. I sat in at the discussions, although these products were not my concern. I felt an inordinate amount of time was spent on selecting the perfumes from samples that Laurie Dalton from Bermondsey submitted. Similarly the designs for the bottles and packaging were gone over and over. Sketches were rejected and miniscule alterations called for and the advertising platform was changed several times. Alister Morison, the Sales Director, and John Mann, the Advertising Director, became somewhat impatient with this procrastination which Ambrose claimed was necessary if the products were to be of the superb quality he felt was essential.

Still no-one gave me any lead on the cosmetics side. I was, of course, learning all the time, if unconsciously, about the Company, its history and philosophy and about marketing, distribution and advertising. So I took matters into my own hands and made as thorough a study of the cosmetic products which were on the market as possible.

I visited shops and stores — studied cosmetic trade journals — obtained price lists and purchased the products of all the well known houses, comparing quality, texture, fragrance, performance and price.

I talked with Jack White about the methods of manufacture of these different products and also had discussions with the Research Chemists at Port Sunlight. I discovered that the range of cosmetic products that Atkinsons had manufactured pre-war was very unsophisticated by comparison with the merchandise which the major houses were then presenting. During the war, because of the shortage of raw materials, particularly of oils and fats, only one cosmetic cream had been manufactured. It was called Skin Deep and was an all-purpose cream which had a high market share, but it was not a sophisticated cosmetic product.

So I came to the conclusion if we were going to enter the highly competitive beauty market, the Company needed to learn a whole range of new techniques.

A Paris Visit

About this time Unilever purchased the Harriet Hubbard Ayer Company, an American cosmetic firm, which had a base in Paris. They were about to launch some new products and so senior people from Unilever wished to see this event. Ambrose Addis and I were included in the party.

We were to fly from Northolt, the predecessor or Heathrow, and were travelling by Air France. The whole event took on a slightly comical air. Our plane developed a fault and would not take off. Waiting lounges at this time were flimsy, temporary buildings, inadequately equipped with a few, very uncomfortable chairs. It was all pretty unsophisticated as passenger travel had hardly developed. It was my first air flight and therefore quite an adventure.

The important Unilever Executives, however, got very cross that their precious time was being wasted and stomped about expressing grave displeasure — to no avail. The plane couldn't be adjusted and so another one had to be flown over from France. This performance took approximately five hours — by which time the authorities had been repeatedly informed what these very grand people thought of this inefficiency.

The final bizzare touch was when we were all seated in the second plane, an Air France official walked nonchalantly across the tarmac swinging an enormous spanner and proceeded to adjust something on one of the wings.

I couldn't help smiling and saying to myself "how to win clients and reassure passengers!"

The Harriet Hubbard Ayer Salon in Paris was the height of luxury. The Manager of the Company and the Directors of the Salon received this important London party with great civility and we watched the elaborate presentation of the products with deep interest.

Naturally I was particularly fascinated because I could see that there was a great deal to be noted and learned. After work there were several receptions and we met the senior Directors of the main Unilever Paris Office.

The trip was a delight. The restaurants were beautiful and the food out of this world. I couldn't believe that France had recovered so quickly from war-time privation.

It was arranged that I stayed over for a couple of days again to obtain ideas for packaging, presentation and products. This left me free one evening which I spent with Alfred Bourdon and lots of our old fencing buddies at a little bar restaurant in the rue de Londres, which we had so often frequented in the 30's. I remember I wore a 'New Look' Dior type outfit in pale blue, softly gathered calf length skirt and neat little jacket top fastened with about twenty imitation pearl buttons, finished with a small crunchy straw hat which was swathed with black veiling. After the severity of the war, Dior's 'New Look' revitalised women — one felt quite different. To obtain this treasure, I used most of my own clothing coupons and some of my mother's and father's too!

Needless to say, coming from London in a Dior style was a source of comment and delight to my fencing friends. Now my fortunes were very different from the old penniless early Paris visits. I was on an expense account and instead of staying in an obscure little 'rive gauche' pension, I was at the George V.

One could see that Paris was scarred by the war and many faces showed fatigue and anxiety, but the chestnut trees blossomed just as beautifully and places I had known and loved before the war — the Musée Rodin and the little Auberge Coucou in the shadow of Sacré Coeur Montmartre, which I also had time to visit with Alfred — had all the old appeal and fascination they had always had.

Great cities all have different characters but they are exciting places. They may in parts be dirty and unkempt, but they still represent the combined endeavours, hopes and fears of the hundreds of people who have tramped their streets and lived in either luxury apartments or squalor. So one cannot but respond to, and be moved by, this kaleidoscope of humanity past and present. In spite of their widely different characteristics, London, Rome, Dublin, New York and Paris all exercise a great fascination for me.

The Experimental Salon

Back in London, refreshed and stimulated by the Paris trip, I decided that what I needed to do was to set up a small experimental beauty salon in which the few existing Atkinson cosmetics, and as many competitors' products as possible, could be tested.

I drew up a complete plan, including details of how a test panel could be formed, the recruitment of assistants, who could apply the products and observe and record performance. It was an original plan and was going to cost several thousand pounds, but I estimated that at the end of six months we would know a great deal about the market we were aiming to enter and I would then be in a position to brief our research chemists.

Having laid out these ideas very carefully and costed them, indicating the length of time the experiment would take and what we could hope to learn from them, I presented the brief to Alister Morison. Would anyone accept such a scheme?

When I came to describe it I began to have my doubts but, as so often happens when innovative ideas are thoroughly worked through and well presented, and with enthusiasm and conviction, agreement often comes more speedily than one dares hope. Alister probed my reasoning and the budget. He then agreed it and told me to get ahead with the plan.

I knew I could not carry out such work in the drab office atmosphere at Isleworth so I asked for a few improvements to be made to a small basement area behind the Board Room at Bond Street. There was only artificial light and very little air but I didn't mind — the location was right.

I recruited two staff, explaining to them that the effort was purely experimental and that the working conditions couldn't be improved until such time as we could report on our findings and make some recommendations as to how to proceed.

In other words, we had to prove ourselves. They accepted the posts with alacrity. Initially, the test Salon was a very simplistic operation, but little by little our methods became more and more professional and our carefully documented experiments soon showed very interesting results.

The kind of tests which we conducted were neither chemically, nor dermatologically scientific. They were empirical tests in which, from the consumer's angle, we could assess product types and qualities, observe the different properties and types of skin and relate the performance of the various categories of creams, lotions and powder on these different skins.

We categorised skins into such groups as very dry and scaly, dry, normal, greasy and very greasy, noting such points as size of pores, the presence of acne or pimples. With reference to skin textures, we noted tendencies such as firm and pliant, spongy, harsh etc, and then with our creams, lotions etc, grouped into light, heavy, oily, quickly absorbent, we paired the skin type with the product which performed the best and were able to draw conclusions.

As I remember, some of these conclusions were — when the skin was taut and dry, its capacity to absorb products was low, whereas we found that a heavier type of product which had to be left on the skin for a period of time before it would penetrate, was eventually absorbed. By contrast, heavy oily creams when applied to fine grained or normal skins had a clogging effect, which felt disagreeable and was ineffective.

Ageing patterns were also carefully noted. We discovered that people with very soft spongy skins which seemed to have little support from either the underlying bony structure or a resilient muscle base, aged the most quickly of all — wrinkles formed and the jaw line and throat muscles sagged.

The reaction of skin tones to cosmetic shades was also an area which had to be studied carefully — some people darken powder shades, others emphasise the yellow or red tones, in an unacceptable way. It was essential that we made these tests on the largest number of people possible, if they were to have validity. We did not, of course, have a great problem in persuading women to have what was virtually a free beauty treatment while we noted reactions, which of course were treated entirely confidentially.

I began to see where we were heading and I was able to reassure the Chairman that within a few months I would be able to give him some recommendations.

Social Activities

After the restrictive atmosphere of the war my personal life changed a great deal. I was a frequent visitor to Gabrielle and Don Bliss's London flat, for quiet lunches or quite elaborate dinner parties where I met a number of contemporary politicians such as Hugh Gaitskell and also many American diplomatic officials. These occasions were great fun.

Jane Farmer immediately after the war had married Colonel Campbell whom she had met in Rhodesia. Noel was a charming man with many different facets to his personality. Half Spanish by birth, he had served in the 7th Hussars as a Cavalry Officer until the regiment was disbanded many years before. Then, surprisingly perhaps, he got involved with the theatre and worked as business manager for stars such as Sir John Martin Harvey and Matheson Lang.

His first wife died in the early days of the war and then he and Jane married and settled in a charming old house in Addison Road where they entertained frequently. Ian and I both enjoyed these lovely evenings.

Noel was short, dapper, a magnificent horseman and had a warm outgoing personality and although very dignified he had a great sense of humour. Jane and Noel were very different personalities but they were tremendously happy together.

I also went to Scotland to stay with Captain Boyd, who had helped me with introductions at the time of my early degree studies, and his charming American wife. They were marvellous hosts. They lived in Ayr and we went on visits to many of their friends in the surrounding countryside. I was enchanted with the courteous and polished way of Scottish country life, the gentle pace of things, serene and unruffled − so very different from London. And the scenery was gorgeous − the sunsets, for example, over the Heads of Ayr were breathtaking.

Eve, my old school friend, and Harry, her husband, were of course frequent companions. I have always felt that friends were terribly important − giving me enormous pleasure and a feeling of security. But of course, like everything else in this life, I believe friendships have to be worked at − they don't just happen − phone calls made, letters written and anniversaries remembered. I wonder sometimes whether ultimate loneliness is not the result of continued disregard and forgetfulness of others, or over-preoccupation with self. If you wish people to concern themselves with you, you have to care for them. Nevertheless, I feel I have been especially fortunate with the people who have been kind enough to bother with me.

Friendship does not, of course, call for agreement on every viewpoint, nor approval of every action. It is a feeling of close companionship, the concept of two travellers journeying together who respect each other and wish to share, not all, but at least some of their hopes, joys or aspirations, together with a growing understanding of where the other is coming from.

It was about now, late in 1949, that I was distressed that both my mother and my favourite Auntie Noe became ill and at the same time my old music friend, Ethel Dawes, died. I have noticed so often that when one unhappy event occurs it is often followed with others — both sorrow and sadness rarely come singly. One just has to wait patiently for the tide to turn.

Working on the cosmetic range

Plans at the office were developing fast. My two staff, however, married and left. I needed others. One of the newcomers was a most attractive girl, April Hunt. She was only nineteen and did not have any qualifications. Her father, a well known journalist, had died suddenly and April needed a job. She was so willing to learn, was genuinely interested and had real style, so I felt she had much to offer us and could be trained. I also recruited two other fully qualified beauty experts.

My tests were drawing to a close. I wrote my report on the experiments and concluded it with my suggestions as to what products should be included in the new Atkinson range. After lengthy discussions my recommendations, which included alternatives in each category of products, were tentatively agreed.

I went off to Port Sunlight to brief the product research people. I explained what was required and asked to have samples made up and submitted for user testing.

The first samples were not as refined as I felt was required and we had to work very hard and very tactfully to get the consistency and the properties we required. By now we had a large consumer panel and a little shop further down Burlington Gardens which was owned by the Company fell vacant and we were able to move from our dungeon premises to daylight and space. It was a great relief. Yet at no stage did anyone grumble at the poor conditions — they were all so keen to prove our experiment. It was a true team effort. I felt delighted at the enthusiasm I had generated.

When later I came to talk about management techniques, I knew from personal experience how important it is to set goals, offer a challenge and have each member of a team clear about their responsibilities. I had insisted on all these things. So the pretty shaggy conditions did not seem important. People were too interested and got on with their work.

By 1949 the cosmetic products began to take shape and the salon tests enabled us, on performance, to select some of the experimental samples and reject others. I realised that as well as straight advertising there would be need for a great deal of PR work when the range was launched, so I felt I had to anticipate this aspect of the work.

I was fortunate in that I met Anita Christopherson, who was a very able journalist working on 'Women & Beauty', one of the attractive glossy magazines of the time. We found ourselves very much on the same wave length and realising that I was trying to create a new modern image for Atkinsons, she very kindly introduced me to many of her colleagues on different papers and women's magazines. Gradually I built up a network of Press contacts, who learned what Atkinsons were doing and how, before long, we were going to have interesting information to give them. These women wielded a great deal of influence and I found I got on with them very well. I knew that when we were ready they would give us a lot of support, because they approved of the thorough way we were approaching the creation of the range. I was gradually building their confidence in our expertise, which is the only way that PR can be effective.

I also made contacts with the fashion world through Lilian Hyder, whom I greatly admired for her style and skill and who always made me laugh. She has a most droll sense of humour. She was Secretary to the Incorporated Society of British Fashion Designers, and dealt with her sometimes highly temperamental principals with great skill. Hartnell, Hardy Amies, Mattli — were the Houses then at the top of the fashion scene. I realised that if I was to harmonise cosmetic shades with current colour trends, I needed to have a feel for haute couture, so I visited the fashion shows and saw the colours as they emerged, season by season.

I was also gaining knowledge about consumers. In addition to meeting the women whom we invited to sit on our testing panel, I moved around the country lecturing to women's groups in the Midlands, North and South-West. They asked me to talk on many different subjects. These were not serious lectures, but lighthearted topical presentations which caught people's imagination. I would share experiences with them and, of course, in the question and answer session which concluded each talk, I got to know the attitudes and ways of thinking of women from many different regions and levels. This was very important, because I was determined that we would not fall into the trap, while aiming to present Atkinsons cosmetics as elegant and up-to-date, of going so far up market as to lose touch with the far greater number of women who were the traditional Atkinsons clients.

The Atkinsons image did not have Rolls Royce exclusivity, although we did hold the Royal Warrant for supplying perfumes to the Royal Household. The Company was renowned across the world for the very high quality, superbly presented and traditionally stylish merchandise. It was necessary, therefore, that we pitched the new products in just the right way.

Deciding on the correct market level is one of the most significant aspects of any marketing strategy. It influences price, distribution and the ultimate success of the activity. The public, without always being conscious of why or how they make their decision to buy or not to buy, sense when a product is wholly credible. If the packaging doesn't promote the product in the right way, if its performance does not live up to the advertising claims, if it is not readily available in the shops where they expect to find it, sales will not result. There has to be a unity and consistency of presentation which calls for a great deal of care and thought as the product is coming into being. And with cosmetics, in particular, one is selling dreams and aspirations, not just functional practicalities, so the whole ambience has to be right.

A marketing team has, therefore to debate all these issues very thoroughly and there has to be unanimity of thought and action, from the top, so that the production team in the factory know precisely the standard they are aiming for, the advertising people catch the spirit as well as the essence of the merchandise and the salesmen, who have to persuade tough retailers to give them counter space and selling time, do so with enthusiasm and conviction. Only when this co-ordinated effort comes about does a product really have a chance of succeeding and even then there are unforeseen hazards.

This did not happen spontaneously at Atkinsons. There were conflicting ideas and disagreements at quite stormy meetings at which the quirks of people's personalities came out very strongly.

I came closer and closer to a comprehension of these factors and my own involvement steadily increased. This seemed to make it possible for me to transmit my enthusiasm effectively to other members of the team.

I had by this time been with the Company about two and a half years. One day I was called to a meeting at which Ambrose told me that as a result of my work, which was regarded as very innovative, I was to be raised to Senior Management status.

It was what I had hoped would one day happen, but I was very surprised that it came so quickly. I was sure that Alister as well as Ambrose had influenced this decision, which had to be endorsed by Unilever House.

It was at this point that I failed to follow through with further study. Figures were still my weak point and if I had improved my statistical and financial comprehension then, I would later have been in a much stronger position. As it was, I "picked up" the basics and achieved results much more slowly than I need to have done.

No-one counselled me on this, but whenever I give careers guidance today, I always strongly advise people to tackle these subjects as early in their careers as possible and never allow figures to become a negative phobia. Facility with quantification is an absolute essential in almost every career. Furthermore it gives confidence and a sureness of touch, which are major assets.

The packaging and advertising for the cosmetic range had been commissioned by the Advertising Director and the emblem of a little lady in a frilly skirt, a white cameo on a grey ground, formed the central theme on the powder boxes and jar labels and gave the range its name — "White Lady Cosmetics". The presentation was very attractive.

It always intrigues me when briefing creative people how carefully they need to be handled. Although often brash and seemingly self-assured, they have usually a great need for reassurance. If criticism or correction are called for, these have to be meted out in such a way as to leave confidence and self-esteem intact.

This is indeed true of all human relations and yet many Managers who are dealing with people all the time never learn this lesson, never learn to communicate, and so fail to bring out the best in others.

I came to learn from experience that the lack of awareness and sensitivity which produce the negative approach are the most common faults which make people into bad managers.

Changes in the Company

It was at this point that Ambrose Addis was transferred from Atkinsons to one of the Unilever companies in Canada and Alister Morison went back to what was called a 'Hard Soap' operation. These were splendid opportunities for both of them and sufficient work had been done on the cosmetics to make it possible for the handover to the new Chairman not to be too disruptive.

Such transfers which often happen quite suddenly in large companies can be both advantageous and the reverse. For the individual they can lead to the opening up of splendid new opportunities, but sometimes they break essential continuity, which is damaging.

Fortunately I was able to provide the continuity element. My task, therefore, at this juncture was, I felt, to create a purposeful relationship with the new Chairman. He had come with an excellent track record in the marketing field, but a somewhat colourful reputation.

I thought it was vital, therefore, that on the work front he knew exactly how ideas had evolved and been implemented. I was as open and honest as possible about the marketing plan.

I thought it was equally important that he knew where I was coming from as a person, so I spoke frankly about my personal tastes, work patterns and approaches. We were, after all, going to have to work very closely together and I felt that it would save time and make things much easier if any mistaken expectations were cleared out of the way immediately. It proved to be an effective tactic. We found we could work together very well. (Of course, I didn't actually say "No hanky-panky behind the filing cabinets, please", but the message registered!)

I think sometimes personal relationships between men and women get off track, because people are not open and confident enough to lay down the rules of the game and stick to them.

A deadline for the launch of the cosmetic range was set. During the next months work was very hectic.

Exploring Perfume in Italy

Apart from activities on the cosmetic front, there was an on-going pre-occupation with the perfume side of our business. One of the hazards in the fifties was the increasing price of essential oils. One of these, Bergamot, which is used in most high quality fragrances, became enormously expensive. Perfume Bergamot is not the old fashioned herb that is grown in many gardens, but a round citrus fruit which looks a little like a grapefruit. It is the product of a citrus tree, often old and gnarled like olives, and only grows to perfection in a tiny strip of land near Reggio di Calabria in Southern Italy. The essence is extracted from the skin of the fruit, which is pricked to release the gorgeous smelling oil, which has the property of stabilising and intensifying the quality of other ingredients with which it can be blended.

Atkinsons used a great deal of this oil and my Chairman thought, as it transpired mistakenly, that if he could meet and negotiate with the Head of the Consortium which produced the Bergamot oil, he could obtain a more advantageous price.

So it was decided that we would go to Italy, spend some time in the Atkinsons establishment in Milan, which was a very lucrative part of the business, and then go on to Reggio di Calabria, some 700/800 miles to the south.

I was very pleased to go on this trip. I had never been to Italy and I wanted to see the way the Milan business was organised and also the way that the essence market worked.

My Chairman had somewhat extravagant tastes, so we wined and dined sumptuously. I found Milan an extremely drab city and as we were travelling in December, we encountered the mists which frequently surround it. The dull exterior of the buildings, however, completely belied the interiors. They were luxurious, whether it was Atkinsons' Salon or the individual apartments which we visited. The hotels and restaurants too were stylish and elegant. The women we saw were intriguing. They either looked like little old cottage loaf shaped people always wearing black and bustling about the streets with their ubiquitous shopping baskets, or versions of Gina Lollobrigida or Sophia Loren!

Our meetings in Milan complete, we set off for Reggio — my Boss, the Manager of the Milan business (a Welshman who spoke excellent Italian) and myself. It was decided to go by train, partly because we could break our journey in Rome and visit the offices there of an advertising and publishing House from whom we purchased art work, and partly because the Milan mists could delay flights. As we went south, the weather improved and in Rome it was mild and quite sunny. Gilardi, the artist, took us to lunch at a famous fish restaurant. The men then settled down to some serious drinking, while I took myself off to see the Forum and other antiquities. A chance I felt not to be missed.

We met up at 6 o'clock at the huge Rome railway station, with its beautiful arched front, in time to catch the night train to the south. Inexplicably we had to change trains at Naples — with my two companions hardly in a state to march the length of Naples station, this proved a little difficult. However, consigning our luggage to a porter, I decided that a brisk trot was the best manoeuvre. So seizing them both by their arms, I propelled them up the platform. We made it!

Next morning, we arrived in Calabria and discovered that Reggio was a very small town with no taxis at the station, so we walked to the local hotel to tidy up before our meeting with the Head of the Consortium.

A quaint little establishment with no pretensions to grandeur, the hotel was able to give us breakfast and we set off in different directions for the cloakrooms. I discovered what I thought was the ladies. It looked rather like a decrepit Victorian conservatory. I dived into the inner sanctum, and coming out to wash my hands I discovered a gentleman, dressed in a pale grey suit with wide chalk stripes, the kind of garment my father would immediately have described as vulgar. He smiled ingratiatingly, and talking volubly advanced towards me; flinging his arms round my neck he tried to kiss me. I was astonished.

Unable to talk Italian, I somehow made it clear that I wished him to leave; shrugging nonchalantly, he did so and I followed. I then collided with my Welsh companion who asked what was going on. I told him; to my amazement he became tremendously dramatic and cavalier fashion, rushed off down the corridor seizing the grey suited gent roughly by the arm. In the exchange that followed, the bemused Italian said, "I only told the lady I thought she had beautiful eyes." I said to Gwyn, "Forget it. We're in Italy — you ought to know. After all there can't be many women who've been kissed in the lavatory at 8 o'clock in the morning. I ought to be able to dine out on that for years!"

We went to the Bergamot consortium HQ. I was astonished to see the enormous vats easily twelve feet high and huge in circumference, filled with the gorgeous, fragrant liquid. I felt I could not smell enough — it was piquant, never sickly and enormously stimulating.

I confirmed what I had known for a long time that certain types of perfume have a most beneficial effect on our senses: not only are they pleasant, they are therapeutic.

We were then taken round the countryside to see how the Bergamot fruit was grown and gathered. I had imagined orderly groves of well tended trees — not at all! Sometimes a single tree in the back garden of a tumble down cottage, clutching for dear life as it seemed, on to a rocky eminence; sometimes a few, up to a dozen or so trees, a little better tended but in no scientific way, were on the edge of farmsteads. It was incredible.

The peasants or the bigger farmers had to gather the fruit and take it mostly in little donkey carts to either small mountain stills or perhaps a village extraction point. The simplest of these were wooden vats from the inside of which protruded hundreds of sharp spikes. The Bergamot fruit was emptied into the vats which rotated on a central spindle. The fruit was then tossed around as the vat moved round, the sharp spikes penetrating the skin of the fruit from which the essence dripped down into a container underneath. The motive power which turned the spindle was inevitably a donkey, which harnessed to it marched round and round making the vat revolve.

It was all very primitive and casual — people looked grubby, but very happy and were delighted to show us all that went on. Some stills were being modernised and, where available, electric power and metal vats were being introduced. I am sure thirty-five years later the process is completely different, but it was most exciting to have seen the simple procedure and shared in the friendliness of this happy scattered community.

We returned to Reggio where the Signor back at the consortium was most courteous and showed great deference to us as important customers — but the price remained unchanged! He was speaking from the strength of a monopoly position. Bergamot needs a special kind of soil and warm sun, but the skin of the fruit is very delicate and, if subjected to too much heat from the sun turns brown and is ruined. The gentle breezes from the Straits of Messina temper this heat and bring the fruit to a high point of perfection.

Weather reports stated that the mists in Milan had cleared, so flying back there seemed the sensible thing to do. Enquiries revealed that there would not be a flight from Reggio for some thirty-six hours, but we were advised that if we crossed over to Catania, a port in Sicily, we could catch a plane the next morning which would go direct to Milan. Accordingly, as dusk fell, we climbed on to the overloaded ferry going to Messina. People, smelling strongly of garlic, all with enormous bundles, jostled about. At last, when it was almost dark, we somewhat bumpily moored up at the quay at Messina.

We then had to negotiate for a car, because Gwynn said it was no use staying in Messina, we would be much better off at Taormina on the coast half way to Catania. This would ensure that we did not miss the morning flight.

Feeling very tired by this time, we got into the rickety old car and climbed high up the hillside to Taormina. It was now absolutely dark and all I wanted was a bath. I turned on the tap in my bathroom and a miserable little trickle of muddy water came out and then stopped. I was a bit fed up, so I crept into bed.

Next morning I opened the shutters and there lay the glistening Mediterranean, the rocky coast line and the geraniums tumbling down in profusion from my balcony. It had been worth it.

We left the hotel and circled Mount Etna, sinister and black, and arrived at Catania airport, a relic of the war. The runway was just a strip of daisy strewn grass. A little apprehensively, we got into the plane and within twenty minutes we touched down — who would have guessed — at Reggio!

We Visit Grasse

Another perfume trip took me to Grasse in the south of France. Here the extraction was highly professional and the fields of roses, jasmine or violet plots were neat and orderly. Again, as an important customer, I was treated with great courtesy and warm hospitality. A memorable day was when having driven along the fabulous Gorges du Verdon. I arrived at the lavender fields on a high plateau in the Basses-Alpes — the fragrance was tremendous and the clear skies formed a perfect backdrop to the carpet of purple which extended to the sky line.

Whenever it was convenient, I touched Paris on these trips so that our liaison with Harriet Hubbard Ayer was really close. The Unilever personality that I greatly enjoyed being with in Paris and who by the example of his statesmanlike approach taught me a great deal, was Roger Francis. Happily married with a charming wife and two daughters, they were all great fun to be with. Later he returned to England and we met again in Unilever House.

There was also the Ransome's lavender and herb farm in East Anglia. This provided not only essential oils for the Atkinsons perfumes, but also flavourings, such as mint and sage, for the any number of Unilever toothpastes and toiletries. Richard and Hazel Ransome ran this unique farm beautifully and while their seemingly leisurely country life was most enjoyable, it was also very hard work.

All these trips and visits broadened my experience. Meeting an international community I learned to feel relaxed wherever I went and also how to put other people at their ease.

The Launch of White Lady Cosmetics

Perfume was, however, a secondary consideration for me. My major responsibility was the cosmetic range which was now ready to be launched. As was customary, the products were introduced in two phases. Initially, the Sales team sold the cosmetics to the trade, chemists, beauty shops and stores. They were readily accepted, because they made an immediate appeal and were backed by a substantial advertising campaign. Attractive show cards and counter display units had also been devised. These activities were the responsibility of the new Chairman and the Advertising Director, although I sat in and contributed to the decision making process.

The second phase was the introduction of the products to the Press, for which I was responsible. We held large parties and tied up substantial promotions, one with the Daily Telegraph, another with a chain of provincial newspapers. These had to be carefully worked out, our objective being to obtain wide acceptance for the products by a direct appeal to the consumer — but, of course, the papers had to see some real benefit to these schemes for them and their readers.

This called for extensive negotiation and planning, involving trips to the major cities throughout the country, where demonstrations were given. The success of such undertakings, which are never cheap to mount, are judged on the number of customer contacts that are made. Fortunately our figures were high and resulting sales were good — we met our initial targets.

One of the aspects which, of course, this kind of work entails is extensive entertaining, which inevitably includes a substantial amount of drinking. Without appearing to be a kill joy and because I, myself, enjoy socialising, I participated happily. I was fortunate enough, however, to have developed sufficient confidence not to be coerced into drinking more than I wanted. Others, staff members as well as our hosts and guests, sometimes fell rather heavily into the conviviality trap; like one of our elderly associates, rushing over to greet me, who fell flat on his face spilling his drink all over a beautiful white fur rug!

Unfortunately this type of indulgence can become a habit and I have seen so often people suffer from it very very disastrously, even ultimately wrecking their careers and their health. It is so easy to drift down the drinking path. The one thing which aroused my anger was senior people who led juniors, who felt they did not have the authority to refuse, into this kind of behaviour. It is difficult sometimes to stand firm. For myself, I felt there was some advantage here in being a woman, and usually the only woman. I could set my pattern in my way and I did not mind if I appeared to be out-of-step, but young men, who were trying to make their way, feared they would be regarded as not tough enough if they didn't drink.

The range met with great success and featured well on the product indexes. We obtained high ratings and gained a substantial market share against our competitors.

Looking for New Ideas

I felt we could not, however, rest on our laurels. I was always looking round for new ideas or products which would give us a real edge over our competitors. I did not know how such things would develop, but I just kept constantly on the alert.

Then in 1952 a very exciting thing happened. I was travelling to Birmingham to organise a promotion in one of the stores and I was not able to purchase my usual newspaper on the station. Instead I bought the Daily Express. In it was an article which described how a scientist at Sheffield University was working on substances that affect the skin. Healthy skin results from balanced skin mitosis — that is old skin cells flake off revealing new vibrant cells, which are growing up from underneath. Sometimes this process gets out of phase. The cells divide in an unbalanced way and multiply uncontrollably — sometimes causing cancer. The good healthy skin responds steadily in a balanced sequence. Certain ingredients encourage this healthy growth.

The scientist working on this was W.S. Bullough and he was, of course, using his research for medical purposes. But as I read the article, calling on my old 'probe technique', I said to myself that this research surely had cosmetic application.

A little hesitantly, I wrote and asked if I might call on Professor Bullough, as he was later to become, and discuss my ideas. I said that if he felt that commercialisation of his thinking was undesirable, I would understand.

Generously and openly he invited me to come to Sheffield and this was the start of a tremendously important business development, which had the added bonus of creating a friendship that has lasted nearly 40 years.

I found my meetings with Bill Bullough not only very constructive, but also very enjoyable. He agreed with me that the substance he was isolating in the course of his experiments was highly beneficial to skin health, and might well improve the appearance of the skin and, therefore, have significance in cosmetic development. We agreed that it would be well worth researching.

I went back to the office and explained to the Chairman the way my mind was working. His response was mixed. He was keen on the innovative approach, but he was hesitant about the acceptance of anything as novel and unproven to Unilever, who quite rightly were always very cautious about any product or substance which might have dangerous side effects.

Professor Bullough had reassured me that the substances he was working with were totally innocuous and could not be damaging in any way.

I was reluctant, therefore, to have the possibility of an exciting development turned down on the grounds of timidity or conventional thinking — before we had even worked it through.

Taking perhaps a risky initiative, I turned to my old friend, Jack White and explained that I wanted some samples of a cream made up which contained different proportions of the active ingredient being used Bill Bullough and would he collaborate with me "under the counter", so to speak. He was himself a scientist and could with absolute confidence endorse Professor Bullough's assessment of the safety of the ingredient.

He agreed to help — the samples were made. Professor Bullough put them under test in his laboratory and then we gave them extensive tests with the Bond Street Panel. Everyone who used the product loved it. It was soft, light, yet had a penetrating quality which on a purely subjective basis the panel members found delightful to use and claimed they recognised just the kind of benefits we were looking for. These tests took some months to complete and, although observations showed very promising results, that was not enough. We had to go for a much more scientific set of tests which would provide statistical results.

I now involved the Research Department at Isleworth where I gained great support from the Senior Research Scientist, Doreen Weddeburn. She encouraged me in every way possible, and we then decided to call on a Harley Street Specialist, who was prepared to make biopsy tests, which were nothing more than the removal of a tiny section of skin from the arm. A group of women readily agreed to permit this insignificant little operation.

The initial test was performed on women who had not used the cream and was then repeated at a 30 day interval, during which time they had used the cream daily. Under a powerful microscope close examination of the cells was taken on day 1 and again on day 30. The results were indisputable, the shape and number of the cells was universally improved. The product worked!

The feeling of elation which everyone concerned felt, was tremendous. These tests were repeated with a totally different panel of women — the results were equally as good.

We had a superb product, which, judged personally, women liked. We had an advertising story backed by scientific support which up to that time was unique. The whole plan, however, had to be sold to the senior people in Unilever House. The Head of the Toiletry Executive at that time was Paul Addis, the elder brother of my old Chairman. I had met him many times and had always found him a most sympathetic person, and although he did not suffer fools gladly, he invariably listened very attentively. He had a brilliant mind. A first class honours Classicist, his academic attainments were, unusually perhaps, combined with a keen appreciation of entrepreneurial matters.

I presented my proposition, showing him all our documentation, the scientific, the medical back up and the consumer reports which revealed such high acceptance. His pale blue eyes almost masked by near pebble lenses gave no indication as to whether he was accepting my case. I ploughed on to the end and then had to wait in a kind of agony while he pondered on the matter.

He said nothing for quite a while, turning over and looking carefully at the sheets of paper I had presented to him. Then he asked a number of penetrating questions which told me that he had absorbed in detail, as it seemed to me everything, I had said.

It was a joy to be with someone whose mental acuteness made possible such a quick, yet in depth, grasp of a new proposition. Challenged by him, my own thinking raced along and I found myself able to keep pace. It was exhilarating. He approved further work on the product, laying down the essential safeguards that were to be observed. We were away.

Now the lab samples had to be put into factory production and this proved no easy task. The active ingredient, which had never before been used in cosmetics, proved very difficult to incorporate in a cream base. In order to get the essential quality and consistency for the product, many tests and variants had to be worked through, which entailed long discussions at Isleworth. Then fresh user tests had to be set up to ensure that moving from virtually hand-tailored to bulk production in no way altered the efficiency, or the appeal of the cream.

There followed a whole series of meetings on the marketing side — Lintas, our Advertising Agents, were involved. The enthusiasm we all felt for the product was quickly transferred to the creative people and marketing and advertising strategies started to evolve. This was the work of many months. The cream was called *Skinfare*.

I become a Director

Partly, I think, for the creative work I had done over the last years and partly perhaps for continuity, I was made a Director of the Company. This was commented on most favourably by the Press, with whom I had very good relations. I also received many letters of congratulations from people throughout the organisation, men and women.

I did not delude myself that the title Director was as significant as it would have been in a different set up. Unilever was, and I think probably still is, a hierarchical organisation and the power does not wholly reside at subsidiary company level. Each Company, it is true, was regarded as a profit centre and the performance was judged on sales effectiveness and profit, but major capital and budgetary control was held at a much higher level in the organisation. Nevertheless, considerable authority and responsibility lay in the hands of so called Directors and had, therefore, to be properly utilised.

Coming on to the Board, I had to learn a whole new set of procedures. This was not easy, particularly as I was the only senior woman in the Toiletries and Cosmetic Group of Companies, but I did not allow this to concern me.

The actual work which I did, did not vary greatly, but of course I attended Board Meetings, studied the balance sheet, the profit and loss and cash flow documents and gradually took a wider view of Atkinsons and its relationship with the parent company.

While I was looking ahead and working on *Skinfare* so as to be ready for our next move, a drastic cut back on our advertising budget for *White Lady Cosmetics* was imposed by Unilever. It followed the annual financial and sales review, which it was the custom for the Chairman of individual subsidiary companies to present to Senior Executives at Unilever House. The reason for the cut back was because Unilever was involved with a number of big projects with other subsidiaries, where the overall profit would be larger than Atkinsons could produce, however successfully we traded. We were a small fish in a very big pool. I thought also that the lack of understanding of the luxury market caused doubts in the minds of the Senior Executives, which we never overcame.

We made very strong representations, trying to show that we had achieved excellent results in a competitive market in a very short space of time. This was acknowledged but the decision was final and so we had the unhappy experience of seeing sales of White Lady cosmetics remain static. Failure to support the initial success with sustained advertising meant that the potential of the range was never achieved. Everyone was very disappointed.

It was at this point that another change came about in the Company structure of Atkinsons' Board. After a mere three/four years, our Chairman left and was replaced by another one — very much one of the old school tie fraternity. He had been with Unilever for a long time, so he knew the pattern and working of the organisation very well. He had been concerned with the export of Atkinsons perfumery overseas, but knew nothing about cosmetics, nor the domestic market.

Further, he came of a social background where make up was considered outré. It was therefore something of an up-hill task to familiarise him with what we were doing, with such things as lipsticks, eye shadow, rouge, etc. We were on slightly firmer ground with *Skinfare*, because it was a skin care product and had a scientific basis. He felt more at home in this area. He decided to see through the advertising and presentation of the product personally.

This led to a great deal of discussion and not a little disagreement. Both the artwork and the copy platform were continually altered. The Advertising Agency became very despondent. Sometimes I was called into the meeting to give the history of the product's development and describe its unique properties.

After nearly a year of preparation and revision, we were ready for the launch. The Chairman, however, thought it was necessary to get final endorsement from Unilever House, although we had already had that in the early stages.

So a major meeting was called at which all the research, production and some sales people were represented. Our Chairman, who was extremely courteous with somewhat pedantic manners, avoided anything approaching confrontation, so when the senior Unilever man at this late stage showed some hostility to the whole scheme — the Chairman to appease him started to put forward a suggestion for further study and research.

My heart sank — I knew the product was right. I knew that further research would waste time and money, and prove nothing new. I feared that it would not be long before our competitors would be following down our route and that if we delayed, we might forever lose the initiative.

Screwing up my courage, I was determined to bring back the discussion to reality. I knew I was threatening authority, but I had to act because the whole team, sitting round the table, had worked so hard and I was sure that the fine edge of their enthusiasm would go if we dilly-dallied any longer.

I heard my voice, higher pitched than normal and very tense saying, "Gentlemen" — condensed, my comments were, "Do we wish to have this product or don't we? If not, let us stop wasting resources and admit to cutting out losses and foregoing the whole plan." I rapidly enumerated, yet again, the benefits of *Skinfare* and expressed the view that it would be a tragedy to lose it.

There was what is called in certain types of literature a "pregnant silence" and then the senior Unilever Executive turning his cold eyes and expressionless face to me, said "When could you launch?" Without waiting for our Chairman to speak, I gave the date. Once again we got the product on track.

Everyone round the table gave nervous little smiles and the Chairman took the Unilever chap to his car. My Boss never referred to the meeting, nor the way the product was endorsed. Perhaps secretly, like many indecisive people, he was happy for others to run the gauntlet of possible disapproval and have decisions made for him; also as I was the Director in charge of Development, there really wasn't much he could do about it anyway.

The launch of Skinfare

Both with the Trade and the Press, *Skinfare* proved a great success. It was so novel, the packaging which had an attractive design in gold and black was so outstanding, that the initial appeal was very strong. Added to these points, the dramatic story behind the cream, indicating the tremendous care we had taken in devising the product, put *Skinfare* in a category of its own. Initial sales were excellent and were sustained.

Among the people who came to the launch party was Raymond Haas from Harriet Hubbard Ayer in Paris. He was very interested in *Skinfare* and wanted to include it as an item in his range, though not of course under our brand name.

We at Atkinsons were anxious that this development did not happen until we had had a fair run with the cream in the UK. We did not wish to risk the product losing its identity and becoming confused with an item in another range. We were, of course, pleased that our work was finding favour outside our immediate circle, but we wanted to delay any action which might mean we lost the major initial benefit. Fortunately, this was agreed, although later *Skinfare* was manufactured in France and proved a great success there also.

Staff Management

In the twelve years that I was to work with Atkinsons, although the major emphasis was on marketing, product development and PR, there was quite a degree of staff management as well. To set up the original Test Salon I had recruited only two staff. As these activities increased, more staff was needed. April Hunt, who came as a Trainee, and Peverel Jeffree, a fully trained Beauty Consultant, were our next recruits. Jeff, as we called her, was not only a skilled operator, but a very hard working and loyal staff member.

I also always had a Secretary; the most efficient of these and my favourite because of her happy manner, was Joan French, who was a great support and excellent at all the contact work which formed a large part of our work. Her telephone manner, for example with the Press, who could sometimes be a little trying, was most professional and yet friendly. She also had a very good memory, which anyone working with me badly needs, because while I don't readily forget people and circumstances, I am hopeless at names, calling Smith — Robinson at the drop of a hat, or not even recollecting any name at all. It is an exasperating failing, which can land me and anyone who tries to help me into the most awful tangles.

I don't think in those early days I was a very good boss with secretaries. I behaved, as was the custom at that time and also too often today, in a way that did not involve them enough in the work. Later I came to develop a very different attitude with them, because I came to realise that they were indeed partners in any job which I undertook. Joan, however, seemed to understand me and fitted into my work style very well — one thing I can claim a little credit for, I think, I was a reasonably good communicator, sharing information as much as possible. We also laughed a great deal.

At different times, to meet promotional activities in the stores where we had Atkinsons counters, we had to engage demonstrators. Always at Christmas time, there were up to twenty of these girls, who had to be trained and whose performances had to be monitored. Mostly they were a very pleasant crowd. The best sales people, without any doubt, were the Australian girls who came to England to travel and needed short term jobs to pay their way.

One robust Aussie, Keiron, who was both good looking and a hard worker, invariably turned in results three or four times higher than all the other demonstrators. I think I intimidated her a bit, but I admired her very much — to come all the way from Australia on her own, find digs in London and then travel round the country staying in different towns for three to four weeks at a time, I thought was terrific.

Not that Keiron didn't have a bit of Aussie bluntness. For example, she was working for a while in a store in the Midlands, where the Manager of the ground floor was an insignificant, pompous little man, who liked to throw his weight about. Keiron's counter was always immaculate — she was a wonderful advertisement for us. One morning this stupid little man walked round the department and was foolish enough to run his finger along Keiron's spotless counter, as if expecting to find dust or grease. It was too much. Keiron rushed over to him and said, "If you've any criticism of my work, just tell me. That counter is spotless and if you ever do that again, I promise you I'll knock you through your bloody fixtures!"

It was retailed to me that the little man scuttled away without a word and, in as much as such wonderful sales girls as Keiron were not all that easy to find, he never reported her rudeness, nor did he ever cross swords with her again. Of course, the story was only told to me through the back door, so I never mentioned it to her.

The Bond Street Pageant

As part of my job was creating a public image for Atkinsons, I had continually to draw up different publicity exercises. An interesting one was the organising and presentation of the Bond Street Pageant which took place in April 1956.

For many years there had been an organisation called the Bond Street Association, which sought to promote the image of Bond Street as the foremost fashion shopping centre in London. From time to time, small items of news concerning Bond Street houses and shops would appear in the press. It was traditional that the Chairman of Atkinsons sat on the committee, whose members included such firms as Cartiers, Russell and Bromley, and many fashion shops. The function of the committee was to promote the style and elegance of the Bond Street establishment and so increase trade.

As a Director of Atkinsons, I was voted on to the committee when my Chairman decided to resign from it. It seemed to me that we needed to take some really dramatic action which would attract much greater attention than we had previously managed to obtain. I proposed that we should stage a pageant or festival actually in the street, in which we would seek to include as many of the establishments who traded in the street as possible.

To begin with the idea was received with some hesitation. Members said we would never get the police to agree, it would take too much time to organise — would the press really be interested? However, I won sufficient support to be able to forge ahead. The first major hurdle was getting the police to agree to close Bond Street for several hours on Sunday morning while the procession filed from Oxford Street to Piccadilly, round Albemarle Street and back up to Oxford Street. It would not, of course, be possible with today's volume of traffic — indeed the very idea is laughable — but I succeeded then in persuading the police to support the scheme.

Then I, and other members of the committee, approached every establishment in the street seeking their participation. We got the car firms to contribute their smartest vehicles. One was an enormous Ford Thunderbird, on which sat attractive models displaying fashions. Other models, both men and women, walked in the street wearing men's outfits or ladies' fashions. To represent the jewellers, because it would have been useless and too high a security risk to use actual expensive jewellery from Cartiers, for example, we got the famous Whitbreads shire horses to draw a float on which was arranged in a dazzling display replicas of the crown jewels. These had featured in London in a previous exhibition and we were permitted to borrow them. Programmes were produced and every firm participating was listed.

We all prayed for fine weather and mercifully it did not rain. A military band headed the procession and as the cavalcade passed slowly down the street, the spectators jammed the side walks and cheered with delight. There was film and radio coverage and I featured on the famous "In Town Tonight" programme.

It was enormous fun and drew the Bond Street traders together. It was certainly useful general image building publicity for us all and cost each organisation very little. Just how much increased sales resulted from the event, it was impossible to gauge.

Links with Hartnell and the World of Art

I tried each year to put on some event in the Bond Street Salon, which would encourage people to come to the shop and keep our name before the press and the public. One of these events was a fashion, cosmetic and perfume presentation, for which Normal Hartnell very generously allowed part of his current collection to be featured. It aroused a great deal of interest and enabled us not only to obtain press notices here in UK, but we were also able to send photographs to all the overseas centres where Atkinsons had a business, such as Milan, Buenos Aires, etc.

Another feature was an exhibition of portraits by Francis Marshall, an artist whose highly stylised paintings of women featured on the covers of most of the smart magazines of the time. I met him socially and learned that it was one of his aspirations to become a recognised portrait painter. He already had a small collection of pictures of well known women.

We decided that it would be necessary to increase the number of these portraits to about eighteen or twenty. Different celebrities were invited to sit for him, and working quickly but most effectively in delicate pastels, Francis, who was quiet and shy but very charming, completed eighteen canvases.

They included personalities such as Jill Bennett, Audrey Hepburn, Anna Massey, Annette Page — the ballerina, and Pat Smythe — the famous horsewoman. Each picture gave an interpretation of women through contemporary eyes, hence the title of the exhibition, "Beauty Today".

The result of this publicity was to increase the number of clients who came for beauty treatment to the Bond Street Salon.

Hospital Beauty Scheme

The longer I worked with cosmetics and saw the beneficial effects they had on most women, the more interested I became in the stimulating psychological results that beauty products and beauty treatments had. I had seen innumerable women come into the salon at Bond Street, perhaps after an attack of flu, feeling thoroughly depressed and looking tense, jaded and neglected — they were at a low ebb.

Then the beauty treatment would start. They would give themselves over to the luxury of being looked after, and for an hour or so they would sink back into attractive, soothing surroundings, totally relax and allow a series of care activities to take over. The delicious smell of the products started the process; then the sensitive, firm hands of Peverel Jeffree, our Chief Beauty Consultant, would gently cleanse and massage their faces and necks. With great skill, she would touch all the tension release points and finally, after careful discussion on personal colouring and fashion shades, a make-up would be selected, so that when they looked at themselves in the mirror, a fresh, radiant, wholly presentable person appeared. It was not possible to make plain women into beauties, but it was possible to refresh and bring out the personal sparkle and best qualities of each person. So a woman who had arrived tired and despondent, left stimulated and rested, looking better groomed and relaxed — she felt different, and therefore acted in a more positive way.

Whether it is beauty treatment or just listening while a person talks, care therapy relieves tension and builds confidence which is vital to everyone's sense of well-being.

I pondered on this a great deal, because about this time I happened to meet a number of people who were having serious nervous problems — suffering from stress, turning to alcohol or being completely mentally disturbed. The thought came to me that if we could help so dramatically the comparatively "well" women who came to Bond Street, could we not do something for the mentally sick ones? I contacted various psychiatrists and although they listened to my ideas, it was with a measure of tolerant rejection — interesting, of course, but .....?!

Nevertheless, in spite of this rejection, I was convinced that there was something in my thinking. So I sought out another approach. Through the introduction of his daughter, who was the physiotherapist at Unilever House, I met Dr. Somerville who was in charge of Goodmayes Mental Hospital in Essex.

Intuitive, enormously skilled in his field and very open-minded, he saw at once what I had in mind, which, simply expressed, was to try to link the interaction between health, well-being and appearance together.

We talked through detail and he invited me to go to the hospital to give a demonstration of how I felt the scheme could be introduced. It was, in effect, to give simplified beauty treatments to patients selected by him to see whether, complementing the other medical techniques which were being used on these patients, the beauty treatments would give an added lift and help forward the whole curative process.

Money had to be found — techniques worked out — and what Atkinsons' role in the whole venture was to be. A little beauty room was set up and the scheme started. It was decided that Peverel Jeffree, our Beauty Consultant who was as keen on the scheme as I was, would go once a week to work with the patients. Before many weeks had gone by the results started to reveal themselves.

The benefits were greater than Dr. Somerville expected. To start with, the nurses themselves, who played a significant part in the experiment, gained in confidence because we helped to raise their morale. Looking better, feeling smarter, the fatigue which so often beset them as a result of their very arduous duties, was somewhat relieved. Both I and Dr. Somerville had insisted that the tiny beauty room should be equipped as attractively as possible so a pretty colourful dimension was added to the drab old hospital building. This tiny development, consisting of a coat of paint, a few colourful curtains and a pretty mirror, cost very little. The only expensive item was the beauty chair, which I insisted had to be of the correct type.

Some of the women we encountered, who responded wonderfully to Miss Jeffree's skill, were really pathetic. One woman whose face had been badly damaged by a bomb in the war, was totally withdrawn, scarcely spoke and had not smiled for eleven years! Initially she refused to come to the beauty room. When eventually she was persuaded to do so, she was totally uninterested, didn't look at anyone and refused to speak. The treatment and the make-up, which almost completely masked the scars on the left side of her face, made her look really quite attractive. She sat up in the beauty chair, looked in the mirror, a smile wreathed her face and she said incredulously, "It's lovely".

Every time the beauty room was open she asked to come, and bit by bit learned to talk again. She learned to put the make-up on herself. Her whole condition improved markedly.

There were many other cases: depressives, schizophrenics, some long-term patients, and women suffering from breakdowns of many different types. It seemed they all benefited, some more than others, even if it was only to look tidier, which somehow made them more co-operative.

We never claimed that beauty treatments on their own could cure mental illness, but what we found, which Dr. Somerville was only too ready to endorse, was that attitudes improved, tension was lessened and because the women learned or re-learned to take care of themselves, their self-respect increased.

The scheme was established through the vision of Dr. Somerville at Goodmayes and made effective by the skill of Miss Jeffree, our Consultant. Once proved at Goodmayes, twenty-two other hospitals, one by one, followed suit. We set up the schemes in each hospital and trained the nurses to carry on with the work when we left, only returning at intervals to monitor progress.

When I gave a paper in January 1959 to the Society of Cosmetic Chemists, two years after the scheme had been established, it was acknowledged as a successful and valuable undertaking. The scheme was carried on by Atkinsons for quite a while and then was taken up by the Red Cross, who still offer a beauty therapy service in hospitals.

The benefits from Atkinsons' angle were not commercial, because resulting product sales were small, but they undoubtedly enhanced our reputation as skilled cosmetologists and a beauty house with a real concern for women. We also developed several products initially especially for the hospitals, which we sold on the general market, notably depilatory products and masking creams.

The public relations result was highly significant. Practically every women's magazine wrote up the story.

Domestic Problems

My mother was tremendously interested in all my activities, but unfortunately her health was deteriorating rapidly. Also my father's sight was very poor. My mother should, much earlier, have had what today I am sure is a comparatively simple operation. The doctors had refused to perform this when my mother was in her late seventies because of her age. Eventually the operation had to be undertaken when she was over 80. She was a wonderful patient, serene and tolerant, but the shock of the operation was too great. She returned home after the operation cheerful and determined to get well, but a few weeks later in November, she died.

Anyone who has a deep affection and love for a person, and has been really close to them and able to identify with them because of the empathy which has built up, will know the sadness and the feeling of emptiness which comes at the time of death. There are those who can say briskly, "Well, she/he has had a good innings", or "What a relief". While I think death is not a dreadful, fearsome thing and has to be faced stoically, to discuss it at the moment of parting with such banality, reveals an attitude which I find totally misses the genuine grief of separation.

It is true to say that my father, Ian and I were all shattered. But the wonderful flowers and letters we received were a great help. On the day of the funeral an almost impenetrable fog descended and I remember trying to deliver the flowers to sick and elderly people who might enjoy them, scarcely able to find my way in the fog bound roads. The distortion of sound and the feeling of isolation which heavy fog induces closed in on me. The weather seemed to re-enforce the unreality of my unhappy feelings.

Work, of course, is the great healer and this I found when back at Bond Street I moved into yet another project. There was at that time an organisation known as Political and Economic Planning. It was a research body which produced papers and reviews on all manner of topical subjects, some social, some political, some commercial.

I was asked if I would write a monograph on the Cosmetic Industry up to 1958. This was a prestige job, which did not even carry my name on the title page when it was published. It required a great deal of research, because it was a statistical and factual trade review, not a fashion account. I contacted people throughout the Company and the industry, also other Cosmetic Houses and Institutions, such as the Department of Trade. It was a fascinating study and I greatly enjoyed working on it.

PEP was at that time a very influential body and anyone who wanted information on almost any topic always approached them. Their booklets were regarded as very significant reference works. So I was very glad to have been asked to do this. Strangely this reputation faded and within a few years what had seemed such an important and prestigious institution lost all influence. PEP just ceased to exist. It was a great pity, because there is always room for an organisation which can produce informed and independent thought.

Personal Feelings and Philosophies

During these years at Atkinsons, which demanded a great deal of hard work and constant thought which I thoroughly enjoyed, I have mentioned the major undertakings in which I participated and I think it will have emerged how necessary it is to keep on trying, even if first attempts don't succeed. There were, of course, small irritations or pleasant day to day happenings which seemed so important at the time, raising one's spirits high or playing them down to the point where the horrid, latent sense of inadequacy, which I believe we all have, takes over.

One little happiness touch was the conclusion of the Under Buyer story from Selfridges — the lady for whom I had been able to find an alternative job when she wanted to throw everything away and resign out of hurt pride. It was after some trivial snub, which was for a moment making me feel a bit miserable and I don't now even remember what it was, that unexpectedly a little parcel arrived on my desk. I opened it and inside was a beautiful little cut glass violet vase with a card, which read, "I retire today — this is a tiny token of appreciation and thanks for what you did — you have given me three of the happiest years of my life!" I have to confess that tears came to my eyes — so perhaps sometimes one did do good things!

Contrary to some women's views, when negative or contentious happenings occurred, I did not feel it was because I was being got as *as a woman*. I saw men as people, who with high ambition and not always the talent and confidence to bring them the advancement they would have liked — often pushing aggressively, even deviously, to gain advantages. Not everyone was like this, but who ever stood in these men's paths got attacked. So if that's where I happened to be at that moment, I didn't expect any quarter. Their onslaughts were inevitably worded with barbs appropriate to hit me as a woman, but I tried not to personalise such ploys or digs. I saw them happening to men as well as to me. They would just be worded and carried through differently.

To illustrate, to a man who had never made Officer grade in the services, but who was going up the ladder, one sarcastic remark made by another man who had been an officer, I remember was, "Oh, so you're bringing 'other ranks' techniques into things are you?" The comment was unjustified and totally irrelevant, but none the less very hurtful to the man in question. To me the masculine irritation and macho desire to be proved right would be worded, "Don't think a pretty face and two penn'orth of charm is going to prove the point." To which I would flash back with a show of temper, but always with a final grin — "Well, I find that it helps, but I've got the statistics too, if you will spare time to look at them."

Perhaps I was lucky, but it is my experience that if you don't look for slights, you don't see them and so you don't have to bother — but you do have to believe in yourself and not mind much whether people like you or not. It's just a jolly good bonus if you feel they do!

I have always found enormous pleasure in women's company. For the most part I like them. I find their widely differing personalities, their capacity for loyalty and love fascinating. On the whole I don't think they are as selfish as men, although I do wish sometimes they believed in themselves a bit more.

Equally, I am attracted to some men, whose strength, gentleness, courtesy or brilliance of mind appeal to me. I am perhaps not tolerant enough with either braggarts or idlers, whom I dislike.

At one stage, I fell deeply in love with a marvellous man and enjoyed all the exhilaration and excitement and special elation, which being 'the only one' brings. Being able to give love and affection and share in a totally uninhibited way with someone you really admire, laughing together, even arguing furiously, only to return warm and comforted, all adds up to the special kaleidoscope of deep emotion, which happily came my way. It was a wonderful experience.

Perhaps inevitably because of the short comings of my personality, impatience and a desire to have things clearly outlined, and an overwhelming love of harmony, but also partly, I fear, because of the wild, ill-founded jealousy which crept in and which led to repeated disruptions, a long standing relationship ended sadly. In retrospect it was rewarding; at the time it was a destructive happening which left an empty feeling of isolation, which can only be compared with utter loneliness.

Gradually, however, rationality returns, the world in all its beauty goes on, and the truth, that we so often fall in love with what we want to see, as much as what is there, emerges. The deep and lasting affection which grows out of the initial euphoric stage, in my experience, only comes when constancy and forbearance and real commitment are established, which really has little to do with sexual attraction. But all this is uniquely different for every single individual. We, I think, need to evolve a personal philosophy if there is to be serenity and warmth. Stormy passionate turbulence may work for some, but not for everyone.

A recurring theme in this story is the occurrence of seeming coincidences, which have shaped the pattern of my activities.

People, for example, who have suddenly come into my orbit, such as the Selfridges connections — a little later the Unilever links, or again the apparent chance reading of a newspaper, which created an introduction into the scientific world and the creation of Skinfare — all these things which at the time had no perceived connection, put me in line to grasp new opportunities. I believe such happenings come from overall effort, which creates a framework — an ambience in which things can happen, rather than from aiming for narrowly defined targets.

I subscribe very strongly to the concept that there is a universal power, a hidden resource on which everyone can draw, providing we think of ourselves as a channel through which this creative strength can flow. Hard work, zest linked with patience and a certain disregard of self, clear the channel through which these forces can then flow, and work to our benefit.

Such philosophies or religious ideas mean nothing to some people. For me they are highly significant and enable me to regard my achievements, such as they are, not as personally attained, but resulting from my allowing the hidden strength to work through me. This simply does not permit of conceit of personal attainment, because it can never be entirely one's own. The blockages which inhibit access to that power are, of course, pride, obstinacy and insensitivity, which hinder perception. Sadly it is we ourselves who all to often erect them.

There is no other way that I can account for the many happenings which others would call "strokes of luck" which have come my way. I don't believe much in luck, but I do believe that the individual's search for attainment with harmony, brings significant influences to bear, *if the will to recognise and utilise them is there.*

Very much in this mode a seemingly unrelated event then occurred and made possible my next move within the Company. It was at a very mundane cocktail party. Among the guests was a number of senior Unilever Executives, including Edgar Graham, a Director of the largest single Unilever subsidiary, the United Africa Company, known as UAC. I had not met him before, but we talked at length.

I learned that he was responsible for several of UAC's different activities in West Africa, including a chain of departmental stores called Kingsway. He asked me how we had developed the cosmetic business at Atkinsons and I told him of some of the approaches we had adopted. He then asked whether I thought these techniques, which had resulted in particular products, could be used overseas.

It seemed a very interesting thought. I explained that I had no knowledge of West Africa, but that I presumed that if one studied the consumer and distribution pattern very thoroughly, as we had tried to do at Atkinsons, ideas adapted to suit local needs would emerge. Presumably also different products could be created and sold in an appropriate manner to meet the overseas market.

We chatted further. I found him very easy to talk to — not in the least intimidating, an attentive listener and with a kind of carefree, slightly amused, manner, but a very sharp intelligence. He was a stimulating personality, very different from some of the people I had recently been labouring with. He told me something about the rapid social and commercial developments which were taking place in West Africa; all of which I found fascinating.

I had not comprehended the close links which existed between Nigeria and Ghana, in particular, with Unilever — how the first Lord Leverhulme had gone to West Africa to develop the plantations, which were to produce palm oil, one of the major ingredients used in the manufacture of soap. It was Hesketh Lever's vision and far reaching plans in creating these plantations, which, back in 1909 and 1910, put him in a commanding position in the oils and fats market and added substantially to Unilever's profits. I was to learn a great deal more about this, but for the moment I was just pleased to have met such a delightful person.

I thought no more about this chance encounter, until some weeks later my Chairman asked to see me. I thought he was annoyed. He told me that the Chairman of UAC, Arthur Smith, had approached him and wanted me to join his Company. "Something about developments in West Africa", he said in his Oxbridge accent. "Of course you wouldn't want to go — not your kind of market at all." He also added, with quite a bite in his voice, "I don't really think in any case that I could release you."

I didn't know what to say as he had not told me what the proposal was. I judged, however, that it was unwise at that juncture to ask questions, so I made a few non-committal remarks and decided that I would wait and think about the conversation before I did anything.

I did not have long to wait. A call came from Roger Francis, my old friend of Paris visits, who was now in Unilever Personnel Department. He asked to see me.

At the interview, he outlined the job which was on offer. A person was required to build up the Company's trade with African women who were playing increasingly important roles in their countries and becoming more and more fashion conscious and interested in cosmetics, clothes and sophisticated things in general for themselves, their children and their homes. The scope of the job was partly market investigation, partly PR, with authority to recommend the creation of new products and marketing approaches.

It was a much wider remit than my present job. It would entail extensive travel to West Africa, although I would be based in London. I would not be a Director as such, but carry the title, Women's Adviser to the UAC, retaining my senior Management status with enlarged responsibilities and a considerable increase in salary.

It sounded very exciting. A little wryly I told Roger, who was a most sympathetic person and obviously wanted me to build up my career in the best way, that I feared my Chairman at Atkinsons was not at all keen on the idea. Roger laughed and said that if I wanted the job, my present Boss would not have the authority to prevent me taking a more important assignment. He made a point of saying that it was very much a part of

Unilever philosophy to make maximum use of valuable human resources in the best way — not to hold back people with potential for short term, possible smaller, overall gains. "Why don't you go and talk to Edgar Graham about it? He can really give you the gen on the job. You see if it comes off — you would report to him!" So that was the connection — I was even more pleased.

I saw Edgar and got a lot more information and then I had to wait. I knew the ball was not in my court. Back at Bond Street the Chairman never mentioned the matter to me, although his manner was slightly tart. I had no-one I could discuss this with except Ian at home — he knew some of the personalities and we chortled gleefully over the reactions I told him about. As regards work, I just carried on as before for several weeks. It was very curious.

Then one day the Chairman said, "They seem determined to have you at UAC — I'm very disappointed if you are interested; but you have to see Arthur Smith — I think you should be very careful how you decide."

I said I was sorry if he felt that I was letting him down, but as the development work on all that was planned to date both on products and PR was completed, perhaps I could be spared. He shrugged his shoulders. It seemed that whenever I made a move forward, it was accompanied by a tinge of regret. I was, of course, experiencing something which takes most of us a while to comprehend — we cannot progress without forfeiting something — none of us can do everything. We have to select — we must exercise choice, which is not always comfortable.

My real hesitation about the proposed job was my father. He was at 84, getting very frail and his sight had almost gone. Although I was not going to be based overseas, I was going to have to travel. Was it fair for me to leave him for months at a time?

Our housekeeper, dear Mrs. Morter, was marvellous with him, because like many older people, he did have trying moments of obstinacy. My brother was also around. But Daddy had always depended most on me; I seemed to be his focus point. He, himself, said I must accept the offer, but I felt very apprehensive about my journeys. I consulted our doctor and he said there was absolutely nothing wrong with my father, just a gradual lessening of strength. He told me he could go on for years like this and that I had no justification whatsoever not to go.

So following a very constructive and encouraging meeting with Arthur Smith and also with Sir Fred Pedler, a joint Managing Director of UAC, I accepted. I went to Africa about a month after joining the Company. Three days after I arrived in Accra, Ghana, the General Manager of Kingsway Stores Accra, broke the news to me that my father had died. A great sadness engulfed me — had I been right to take up the new job? Had I exhibited an unacceptable streak of selfish ruthlessness? I was deeply distressed. Ian was marvellous — he had encouraged me to make the change from the very beginning. He assumed all the responsibility before I left; now on the telephone he reassured me in his own specially supportive way and made me feel a little better. Yet another bond was forged between us!

The Atkinson shop in Old Bond Street after it had been re-decorated

Wearing a Hardy Amies creation, I test out a new perfume

I pose for a publicity photograph in the Ransome's lavender farm near St. Ives. The lavender is in full bloom

THE BEST-DRESSED SUNDAY MORNING IN BRITAIN

LOTS of people went for a stroll yesterday morning—but here's the best-dressed stroll of them all.

Women in elegant clothes—and equally smart men—walked in a procession through the West End.

It was part of a display put on by the Bond-street Association to represent every section of merchandise sold in one of London's most fashionable shopping centres.

Spectators were startled to see the Crown jewels go by on a brewer's dray, guarded by a single man.

They were reproductions of the real things done by one of London's leading jewellers and worth about £25,000. Other goods on show were valued at £30,000.

Eleanor Macdonald, who organised the show, said:

"It's about time we showed the world what Britain really can do. We make the finest goods in the world and produce the world's best fashions, our craftsmen are second to none and it's time we blew our trumpet a bit more."

The Bond Street Pageant, April 1956. Elegantly dressed women and men walked the length of Bond Street displaying the fashions and merchandise available in London's most famous street

To support the White Lady cosmetic range we mounted a fashion show in the Bond Street Shop. Norman Hartnell, shown discussing details with me and one of the models, kindly loaned a part of his collection.

The "White Lady" Fashion Show in progress

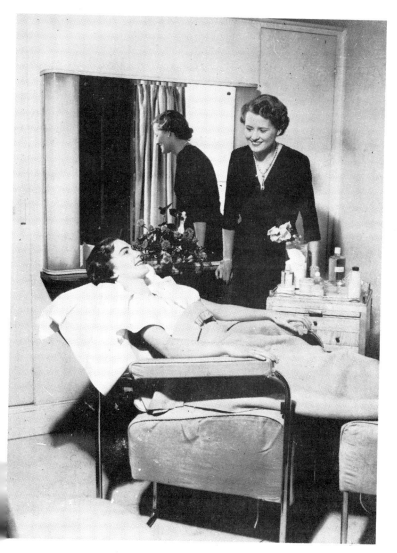

A client relaxes prior to a beauty treatment in the Atkinson salon

My portrait was included in the Francis Marshall "Beauty Today" exhibition

act as one of the judges in a Pin-up Girl competition at the Lyceum Theatre

Chapter Seven

The African Era

The announcement of my appointment as Women's Advisor to the UAC created a great deal of interest. Articles appeared in many different newspapers and journals. It intrigued the Press that a big company like UAC, which was known to be very male orientated, should make such a progressive step as to devote time and resources to African women, allocating a senior woman executive to the task.

Many of the articles were solid factual accounts as to what I was going to do — how I was to study the needs of the women in Nigeria, Ghana, Sierra Leone and the Gambia, particularly in relation to clothes, accessories and smart things for their babies and the home. Some inevitably carried fanciful headlines, such as, "Cosmetics for Black Beauties", and even got some of the data wrong suggesting, for example, that I was going to the Congo, which was not on my itinerary and which I never visited.

I could see that the job had great potential and would provide scope for social and community work, as well as interesting commercial development. I viewed the feminine merchandise with which I was to be involved, not as trivial, but as a great morale builder. To boost women's self-respect was, I felt, to make a considerable contribution to their confidence, which in turn would enlarge their status.

My London base was to be in Unilever House, so after a lovely farewell party at Atkinsons, I transported my belongings and moved into the Big House. Edgar Graham was splendid. He introduced me to the other Directors and the Heads of the different Divisions. The joint Heads of Kingsway Stores Division, Stanley Archer and Kenneth Weaver, with whom I was to work very closely, welcomed me most kindly. They had been with the Company for a long time and knew a great deal about the organisation, its background and the buying systems of the business.

My first task was to recruit a Secretary. I was very lucky as the best of the applicants, whom I selected, proved to be excellent. Rosalind Capper was a language graduate. I had to explain to her that it was unlikely that she would have any occasion to use her German. However, she came and set up my files, as I was preoccupied with reading and research about UAC as a whole and the Kingsway Stores Division, in particular. Her work was meticulous. She was tremendously interested in my assignment and made very useful suggestions, invaluable to me as I was trying to familiarise myself with the work. She was always smiling and helpful. I knew from the start I had picked a winner.

It was agreed that I should go to the Coast as soon as possible. I therefore had to set to work to purchase clothes suitable for the tropics. The woman in charge of Kingsway fashions kindly introduced me to her suppliers and I went round the various wholesale fashion houses and chose light coloured dresses and short sleeved jumper suits. I had been warned that there would be a good deal of evening entertaining, so I had to go well equipped with summer evening dresses. It was very exciting acquiring a whole new wardrobe. I had to project the fashion image of Kingsway. The Stores had grown rapidly in recent years and had become more modern in every respect, carrying an ever-increasing range of goods. The largest store was Kingsway, Lagos; the next in size was Kingsway, Accra, but there were smaller outlets in most of the major cities.

Another of the buyers in the Fashion Department was Terry Kennedy. She specialised in children's wear, undies and accessories. As she had been in West Africa quite often, she gave me a lot of useful advice about shoes and hats — so necessary to get right in a hot climate. I immediately took a great liking to Terry. She was open and laughing and very generous in all that she did. Her red hair and friendly manner I found most endearing; we struck up a great relationship. Although her skilful buying made a lot of money for the Company, her casual manner irritated some people and I felt that she never rose to the heights she deserved. The formal controls often limited her buying capacity. She sometimes ignored these, and as the merchandise she selected nearly always sold very quickly, she felt she was justified. This was not always the official view.

My First African Tour

Finally, equipped and ready, I took off on the long flight to Ghana in what I think is still my favourite aircraft, the dear old Britannia. It was a unique flight, and I remember seeing the moon shedding a soft blue light over the Saraha as we zoomed on our way. The next morning we touched down at Kano, Northern Nigeria, and were allowed to step on to the tarmac. As I gazed at the two large camels and their turbanned riders equipped with long trumpets, I realised I was in a totally new environment. The heat too even at 7.30 in the morning rose up and enveloped me. There was also the all pervading smell, not unpleasant, but impossible to describe, which I was to recognise always as the scent of Africa.

Back in the plane it took very little time to reach Accra, Ghana. I was met at the airport and driven through the orderly streets, white buildings on all sides and masses of flowering bushes — Hibiscus, Alamander and Bougainvillea — a riot of colour. There were all sorts of other sights to be observed; African boys teetering about erratically on bicycles, Ghanaian women in colourful National dress walking very gracefully and carrying on their heads enormous baskets or bundles up to 20 lbs in weight, and most comical, tiny objects, such as a single ink pot or a carefully balanced umbrella. It was exciting because it was all so different.

After unloading my baggage at the UAC Rest House, I took off for the Kingsway Stores. The Manager, Jimmie Bethell, who a few days later had the disagreeable task of telling me of my father's death, was supported by Tony Sweeney as his No 2. I went round the Store with them.

Almost immediately I started gathering my impressions of the Store, the customers, the merchandise. I talked with store staff, English and African. I noted everything as carefully as I could but avoided forming judgements until I had seen more. I was particularly anxious not to offend people whom I knew would have been working hard against considerable odds. I had no desire to come as a know-all from outer space — but rather to listen.

Nearly every evening there was a dinner engagement or a party. Many of the guests were the European Managers in charge of the different companies which were part of the UAC empire, so I had the opportunity to talk to them about their work. The Company incorporated, for example, a large textile division, which designed, manufactured and sold millions of yards of brightly coloured cottons, which form the very individual African dress.

The designs have special significance to Africans, who value fabrics in a very different way from Europeans. These cloths were sold to groups of influential "market mammies", as the women traders are called. They bought from UAC in bulk and sold the merchandise through smaller retailers in markets and tiny village stalls, so forming a national network. It was a thriving trade which had made some of these women, quite a number of whom could not write, immensely rich.

It was a crucial time in the history of the UAC which had originated as a trading organisation, that is, the Company had exported basic domestic, hardwear and food merchandise to Africa which was sold through a whole chain of village shops, which were run by Africans but capitalised by UAC. These were regarded as the main-stay of the simple economic life of African villages right up to the nineteen fifties.

The UAC Board, with considerable vision, then perceived that this era of trading was coming to an end, and that the Company should now be fulfilling a different role, that is to enter into the more sophisticated type of manufacturing business, which was for the most part technically based. These ventures required a great deal of capital and different types of expertise which at that time the Africans did not have. So the local stores ceased to exist and many Africans bitterly regretted their passing, but it was the right policy. It enabled the nationals to be in charge of all those things which they could do, such as straight forward buying and selling. By introducing such activities as motor assembly plants, textile and tobacco factories, initially run with expatriate management, which were gradually Africanised, we were enabling the Africans to acquire more developed skills. We were in fact implementing change.

As well as pursuing the policy of setting up factories, there were many Companies run by UAC, including the food, chemists and electrical divisions, which imported sophisticated merchandise which was not produced locally. These companies filled the role of wholesalers to independent African traders and shopkeepers. They also supplied hospitals, schools and research establishments. UAC had other huge interests, such as the ply wood production plants, which were based in the tropical rain forest belt in Kumasi in Ghana, and Sapele in Nigeria. These undertakings were concerned with export rather than supplying the domestic market. The capital investment was enormous and the expertise, both technical and marketing, which all these undertakings required, meant that there was at that time a large expatriate staff in all the countries I was to visit. As I have said, year by year the expatriates were replaced by African staff, who were trained to take up senior positions. Later it was to be one of my responsibilities to assist with this training and development.

Always present at the dinner parties and other social events were senior Africans, members of the Government or trading companies, also professionals, doctors, lawyers, etc, very impressive people, who usually wore their national dress; the men in flowing embroidered robes in bright coloured cottons with matching pantaloons. The ladies also wore the cloth, as it is called, draped in different ways according to their tribe or, in respect of the head-dress, styled to suit at least thirty different occasions such as weddings, funerals and parties. I think these garments are delightful. To see an African lady twist the two-yard square of cloth of silk, cotton or organza round her head in two minutes flat and emerge with a gorgeous head-dress, still amazes me!

In Ghana, there is a hand woven material made up of strips of shiny pure or artificial silk, in brilliant blues, golds and reds. The strips are then sewn together to make up the seven yards required to make a robe. This particular kind of cloth, called Kenti cloth, originated in Ashanti, Central Ghana, but became special occasion dress all over the country. These robes are very costly, but very lovely. I was privileged to be presented with some of this beautiful fabric.

Other cottons which are still much prized are the Dutch wax block prints. Through the Dutch Colonial connections in the Far East, these were introduced many years ago into West Africa via Holland. Designs were created to meet the African taste, but the manufacturing process was the same which had been used for centuries in the East Indies. It requires that each ten yard- length of fabric is processed several times. The pattern of the block is imprinted on to the fabric, colour by colour, wax having been applied to those areas where the colour is not required to adhere at that stage. It is a "resist dyeing" process, and when the material finally emerges the rich, vibrant dyes will have blended together into intricate and fascinating patterns. The wax gives the fabric a special feel.

Such prints have, of course, always been very expensive and much sought after. As machine techniques developed, manufacturers tried to imitate the wax prints, but shrewd "market mammies" usually knew instantly whether the cloth was genuine. If, however, they were unsure, they would put a corner of the material in their mouths. Immediately the taste or absence of the wax confirmed their opinion. A primitive, but very effective testing technique.

On my first evening I attended a very stylish dinner party and met a number of both the British and the African community. I did not, of course, know much about the different tribes which make up the Ghanaian population, but a short dynamic little man with flashing eyes came over to me and introduced himself. He gave me his name and then said, "I am from Ashanti — we are small, but full of fire!" It was delightful, because it absolutely described his electric personality.

My mind went back to accounts of the Ashanti wars in the latter years of the last century in which the British, with vastly superior weaponry, had considerable difficulty in defeating the brave Ashanti warriors!

I took much pleasure in all the West African countries at the flowery English, frequently derived from the Bible, which was used and was quite often very well spoken.

I Meet African Women

As soon as possible I met the leading Ghanaian ladies who were engaged in all kinds of activities, educational, social and community work throughout the country. The doyenne of Accra society was a marvellous older lady, who had been educated in England and had all the charm and the cultivated manners of the Edwardian era. She was Miss Ruby Quartey-Papafio, who did a great deal to encourage women's education and development. She was a Ghanaian in spite of her name. Many of the well-known Ghanaian families had, perhaps many generations back, a European forbear, hence the mixture of non-African names; some English, Portuguese, German etc, representing a catalogue of the different nationalities of the adventurers who had traded on the Gold Coast, as Ghana was previously called for centuries.

Ruby arranged for me to give talks to groups, predominantly Ghanaian, but sometimes including one or two English people who were working with YWCA, the Girl Guides, or similar societies. This was a two-way exchange. I learned about the African culture and aspirations, and shared information about the educational topics and women's career developments in the UK.

There were some really marvellous women in this group. I particularly liked Dr Armartefio, a tall handsome lady who had very constructive views on how to alleviate some of the terribly hard work, health problems and meagre rewards which many of the women had to put up with.

The men had many privileges and a much easier time than the women. So often the men were lazy and did practically nothing except gossip. As a matriarchal society, the women, and particularly the senior lady in the family, the matriarch herself, had a great deal of say in the "clan's" affairs. This did not stop the women having to work very hard. The men for the most part did not care for their wives in a really considerate way. Tenderness between husbands and wives was not a general feature of the culture.

It was important to have large families because of the need for extra pairs of hands, and the country women working in the fields, often with very primitive tools, perhaps fetching water and loads of shopping, kept going from morning till night. They never stopped. Some sadly were old at forty years of age.

Of course at different levels of the society, where there was more money and a chance of further education, the lifestyle was very different. I met many women doctors, teachers and social workers and one very enterprising young woman, Regina Addae, actually ran her own Advertising Agency. There were newspapers, magazine and radio by 1959, which made this possible.

The political situation increasingly over the ensuing years caused anxiety. Kwame Nkrumah had come to power in 1957 when Ghana became independent. The women had been a significant force in winning him the leadership, first in the position of Prime Minister and then President of the Republic. There was growing disapproval at some of the measures that he was taking. Democratic procedures were gradually eroded and were replaced by authoritarian methods. Ghanaians are by disposition happy, laughing people, at their most able, highly intelligent and very shrewd. Although there had been social and educational advantages to the British Colonial way of life, they were ecstatic to be an independent state. However, they were disappointed when it seemed that Nkrumah was not living up to expectations. In a mere ten years they came to distrust and dislike him.

To give an example, I was invited by some of my African friends to attend a meeting of the Accra Women's Association. I was the only European there, and so quietly I played very much the role of the spectator. The gathering, which numbered about 500 women, some well educated, some simple second or third wives of polygamous families with babies and little children trotting about, had come together to hear Judge Jiagge, Ghana's only woman judge, explain the meaning of the latest legislation concerning the status and rights of married women.

It was a complicated proposal which in the Judge's opinion would leave women impoverished and with less power and authority. There was considerable anger that such a statute had ever been proposed, considering the great debt which Nkrumah owed to the women, whose support, as I have said, had been largely instrumental in putting him in power. Flanked on the platform by a whole group of good looking, dignified and well qualified women, Judge Jiagge gave a wonderful address, which was translated on the spot into two local languages by interpreters, who were on hand. It was a stirring occasion which, I heard later, resulted in considerable modification to the legislation. The women did have a way of getting their voices heard.

It was strange that in spite of their problems and difficulties, the Ghanaian women thought that they had more authority and influence than British women at that time and told me so. In one way this was true, but for many women, the conditions in which they lived were pretty arduous.

Schools Lectures

I addressed a number of schools, talking of the need to gain qualifications and the careers which were opening up, even if gradually, in the UK. One such talk was given when I visited Achimota Girls' School a few miles outside Accra. It was to be an evening meeting and by the time my driver and I arrived at the school, the brief tropical twilight was over and it was quite dark. I was shown into the assembly room, to a group of about 300 eagerly waiting Ghanaian students aged ten to twenty, mostly boarders. I climbed on to the platform and started my talk, when suddenly all the lights fused. This was, I may say, not an infrequent occurrence.

There were titters and giggles and, speaking into the black pit of the hall in which I could see nothing, I said, "Shall we go on in the dark, or shall we wait for the lamps to come?" We agreed to carry on, although not unexpectedly concentration was momentarily somewhat lessened. There were whispers and more giggles, but I started again. Then the girls who had been sent for the oil lamps appeared at the back of the room and made their way up the hall, placing the lamps on the platform. Of course, I couldn't see my notes, so I just spoke without them. The dim glow of the two lamps showed up the first few rows of eager black faces and reflected uncomfortably into my eyes.

What I had not reckoned on was the invasion of myriads of insects of every size and description which attracted by the lights appeared, I am sure, from just everywhere north of the equator. They whirred round my feet, settled on my arms and my face and tangled into my hair, buzzing and biting with a kind of fury. I carried on, but it was one of the most unpleasant experiences I had had to date. However, before the end of the talk, the lights came back and the flying things again following the lights, rose up to the ceiling bulbs and left me in peace. This was typical of some of the hazards which besieged me as I went about my business.

Fortunately, the heat did not trouble me greatly. I always kept out of the sun and always wore hats. My drivers also were very clever at finding any available shade, while they waited for me to complete my engagements. Even then, getting back into the car after a meeting, I have sat on seats which had become so hot in the sun, that I had to sit on the edge until the breeze created by the car movement cooled the temperature down a little. Air conditioned cars were still something of a rarity.

Only on one occasion do I remember being laid low in public and that was when I went to Ho, a village some considerable distance into the country to the east of Accra. It lies in a dip in the surrounding hills and is, therefore, rather like a saucer trapping the sun and the heat. I had gone to view some community work, and a health and housing project. A large number of women had gathered in the open square, and the only shade which was provided was a tiny palm frond awning under which a few chairs had been placed. People were introduced with much ceremony; they showed me their handicrafts and their babies and chatted about their work.

The sun beat down and the temperature rose well above 100°. The spectacle started to swim before me. Reluctantly I had to ask to be excused. My guide, a very friendly community worker, took me into a little house where there was shade and a cold drink. I soon recovered and went back to finish my inspection. The show ended with a display of African dancing which was always exciting and I was presented with an enormous basket of fruit, which included the largest pineapple I have ever seen, easily 14" long.

I Travel to Sierra Leone

On the first tour, after Ghana, I went to Sierra Leone. This was a very different community — a much smaller country with not nearly so many resources as Ghana, which had rich exports and, when Nkrumah took over, a full treasury, although it did not remain like that. In Sierra Leone natural resources are much poorer, indeed gem stone diamonds are one of the most important exports. The colony was established in 1807. It had the oldest University, Fourah Bay, on the west coast which was founded in 1838, a source of great pride.

But Sierra Leone, I felt had a strange lifestyle. The descendants of the slaves who were released under the famous Cotton Tree in the centre of Freetown, and the prostitutes who were despatched from Bristol to keep them company, had over more than a century established a kind of élitist society, which I felt was not wholly black, not wholly African in outlook. These well educated Creoles, who lived in the area round Freetown, I found delightful.

I was interested to learn that at the end of the 19th and the beginning of the 20th century, as first Ghana and then Nigeria became more sophisticated, it was the Sierra Leonians who travelled down the West Coast and became their teachers. They helped to establish the education in both these countries, yet the Sierra Leonians who lived up country in the provinces out of Freetown, had a comparatively low standard of education even in 1959. This made for a divisive society. Also unhappily there was mismanagement and corruption. The attitude of superiority adopted by the Creoles to the disadvantage of the provincial people, was to alter somewhat when Dr Milton Margay, who himself came from up country, won independence for Sierra Leone and became the first Prime Minister; but progress was not rapid.

Many Sierra Leonians and other Africans too, seemed to lack the vigour and energy to work consistently. They appeared lethargic, lacked vigour and seemed unable to sustain effort. There is no doubt that poor health contributed largely to this, it was certainly not lack of intelligence and ability. This was brought home very forcibly to me when one very able community officer, Miss George, who, fresh from training in the UK, was put in charge of a nation-wide community service. She was very worried that she could not get her team to work really hard and push ahead as fast as she wanted them to do. Suspecting the reason, she instituted a confidential health check for about 100 of these men and women, and found that 92% had some health problems, many severe and unsuspected. High on the list was of course malaria, but intestinal problems from infected water or bad sanitation and the after effects of measles and malaria, such as bronchitis, poor sight and hearing, were all present. She said to me, "They are slow and appear lazy because they are not well." This group were all quite well placed; many others were far worse off. This research made me aware what enormous problems there were. I was deeply concerned by such discoveries, which made me feel very anxious to make as big a contribution as I could.

Lagos

I went on to Nigeria, arriving first in Lagos, a teeming city set round a series of Lagoons. It had originally been just islands of solid ground in amongst mangrove swamps. Since 1900, the city had grown larger and larger, land had been reclaimed, and harbours and roads constructed — the development still goes on. Even today the city has an unfinished appearance, modern office blocks stand cheek by jowl with tumble down dwellings and shops, many of which are very old and have touches of Portuguese type architecture.

Lagos and Accra are very different cities. There is also a marked difference in the appearance and the cultures of the various peoples on the West Coast, their ethnic origins giving very distinctive physical features and customs to each group. The Yorubas of Southern Nigeria, for example, are often round headed, plump people, while Northern Nigerians tend to be taller, leaner, more sinewy. Different again are the Ibos from the east of Nigeria, often shorter in stature with compact strong physiques. These are generalisations, of course, but I found that over the years as I came to know Africa better, I could often, but not always, distinguish the different tribes and nationalities. This was a great help as it enabled me to respond more sensitively to different people.

I was delighted that as time went on I made so many friends among the African women, a large number of whom I thought remarkable, outgoing, dedicated and very able. Mostly they showed great concern for those of their country women who were not well placed and were struggling with impossible odds; although some of the more commercially minded of them did not hesitate sometimes to take advantage of their weaker sisters. I came to realise that people are people everywhere — honest, dishonest — sympathetic or hard-hearted. One thing I found unacceptable was the patronising manner which some Europeans adopted towards Africans. The important factor was that they failed to take into account the fact that very well educated people were speaking a language other than their mother tongue. This often made the Europeans rude and impatient, but it was a profitless approach as the Africans invariably somehow got their own back.

The Lagos ladies were warmly hospital and extended assistance to me in as many ways as possible as they saw my activities as potentially very beneficial to the community. Many of them were the wives of officials, who in keeping with British Colonial practice, had before liberation been knighted for their services as senior administrators or members of the judiciary. So many of my mentors were *LADIES* — people like Lady Alakija of the YWCA, Lady Ademola, Lady Abayomi.

I travelled out of Lagos a great deal. In Port Harcourt, one of the important women traders was Mary Nzimiro, in Ibadan, it was Mrs Agbage Williams in charge of women's broadcasting. In the East Miriam Okagbue held a senior position in the TV set up in Enugu. In the North, there were some sophisticated women, but as it is a predominantly Moslem area, many of the wives live in purdah, only infrequently going outside their own homes and then only at night and veiled.

It is so easy to give a very wrong impression about West Coast society because the communities are so varied; it is very difficult to generalise. Many of the Africans belong to ancient tribes whose culture has developed over centuries. There is much wisdom in many of these early tribal patterns, which, because they are different from our culture, Western people in my view often too easily dismiss, although it has to be acknowledged that there are undesirable, even cruel, strands in the fabric of these societies. When, however, Western education and African philosophies are wisely blended, the best of both worlds emerge.

To quote an example, one of my trainees at one stage was Marion Asafu-Ajaye, the daughter of the Ghanaian High Commissioner in London, Sir Edward Asafu-Ajaye. Marion learned that I was going to Denmark on a merchandise investigation trip. At that moment she said nothing, but within half an hour Sir Edward rang me up and asked, since the time of my visit and a state one he was making coincided, if I would like to be included in some of the official engagements which were to be part o' his itinery.

Of course I agreed, saying that I felt privileged to accompany his family. So I dined at the Danish Foreign Ministry, eating off the famous Flor Danica porcelain which is absolutely exquisite, and heard Sir Edward repl in faultless English and with great humour to a toast which was propsed t him. Lady Asafu-Ajaye and Marion in the whole of that visit revealed th charm and impeccable good manners which are natural to West African which I did not always see exhibited by some of my compatriots. Styl dignity, courtesy are attributes which come very easily to the West Africa élite.

In Lagos I met a most brilliant and sympathetic English woman, wh became a firm friend. Margaret Gentle was Head Mistress of Queen

College, Lagos. She had a remarkable understanding of the Nigerian character. This did not mean that her disciplines, either in school or with her colleagues in the education world, were weak and floppy. She was firm, but fun, enormously hard working and a wonderful teacher. She had that mixture of laughter and authority which makes a good manager anywhere, but is essential in Africa. She gained the respect of everyone she worked with and had the satisfaction of getting the first Nigerian woman, Abimbola Okenla, to Cambridge University. Abimbola took an excellent degree in Economics and is now highly placed in the Ministry of Economic Affairs in Lagos.

I always gave talks and did workshops with the Queen's College girls, and in my later trips to Nigeria I stayed with Margaret instead of at the Rest House. This was marvellous, because we got a lot of support from each other. In the evenings we could compare notes on how her and my day had gone. Sometimes I was out on a dinner engagement; she too might have a meeting, but her house was very close to the Lagoon, and so in the late evening when we were back, we would walk along the sandy shore, the water lapping quietly in the darkness. Sputty, Margaret's little dog of indeterminate breed, would trot along with us or send the sand flying as he dug holes in the sand.

Across the Lagoon was an island where only Nigerians lived, and the twinkling lights of the flares outside their little cabins would be reflected in the water; the leaves of the palm trees would stir in the welcome breeze and the velvety tropical sky would sparkle with distant stars. Sometimes the moon rode high in the cloudless sky. They were lovely occasions, high spots for me in what were quite arduous tours on which I would travel up to 10,000 miles.

Margaret stayed at Queen's for several years and then was invited to join the Ministry of Education, as Advisor on Secondary Education. She was the last white face there. She was greatly respected and did much to help the Heads of schools play a balanced role, often in very difficult circumstances, such jobs were not made any easier by tribal differences between pupils and also between staff members.

Then happily Margaret married Peter Harwood, a classicist who came to Nigeria as Head of the Government College at Sokoto in the north. He too had this same "feel" for Africans, guiding them, helping them to attain their highest level, but never bullying, even the most dull and obstinate ones. Now they are back in England and I am a frequent visitor to their ever welcoming home in Suffolk.

Developing Ideas for the Store

The real nub of the work I was engaged in with Kingsway Stores, which spread over into community work, was to assess the service and presentation we were achieving in the Store. By getting to know the African women as closely as possible, I learned whether the merchandise we offered in the Store met their needs or failed to do so. Many of our shoppers were Europeans. We obviously did not wish to alienate their custom, but we wished to expand the goods which appealed to the Africans.

I would go round each department talking, particularly with the African assistants. I would then think through the improvements we could make. Two things which particularly interested the Africans were cosmetics — many of those which we sold were in the wrong shades, and fashion accessories, which were neither varied nor attractive enough. African women mostly have lovely skins and the many shades of their complexions can look most attractive. Paler skins are often favoured, but I think the deep almost plum coloured complexions, which glow with health, are marvellous. We had to devise a range of shades which toned with all of these colours.

As to the accessories, because so much national dress was worn and frequently clever dressmakers made up European style dresses for themselves, what the Nigerians and Ghanaians wanted were good dress patterns and sewing aids and lots of smart accessories — belts, clips, costume jewellery, lace blouses and smart shoes, to finish off their outfits.

I recommended, therefore, that the buying budgets for these items should be substantially increased in order to give variety and choice. I also felt that the whole tone of the women's departments would be vastly improved, if we had some permanent women managers in the bigger stores on the Coast. I knew that once the buying in London was improved, some feminine touches in the way the merchandise was displayed and sold would make all the difference.

Another category of merchandise which the African women continually raised with me wherever I went, was foundation garments. African women's figures are quite different from European women; many of them are much fatter than we are, they have larger behinds, and to design foundations which would suit these figures was not easy. What was required were girdles or a girdle and bra combined, which gave a slim waist line, controlled often ample hips and didn't ride up. This last was difficult, because of course very few people wore stockings. In the end, with the help of Terry Kennedy and a manufacturer in Germany, we succeeded.

Of course I got a lot of teasing about this from the men in the Company, but I didn't mind because I knew we were going to make profit out of these girdles, and that the African women would be pleased and impressed that their needs were being looked to. This led to their coming into the stores more frequently, so it was an important move.

I also saw that both in the areas of display and selling, if we were to be really up-to-date, there was need for improvement. The former required that more money be spent, and fixtures modernised. Concerning the latter, I didn't feel we would get it right until we could have someone in charge of training for both the selling and management staff — actually in Africa.

After each visit I made to the Coast, I wrote up my findings in detailed reports, which were given to the appropriate manager in HQ. I was particularly pleased that after my first trip, Edgard Graham congratulated me on what I had achieved in a mere two months and sanctioned work to be started at once on implementing my recommendations.

Unfortunately, soon after this, one of the many changes which I had experienced over the last twelve years in Unilever took place yet again, Edgar was moved out of UAC to the Food Co-ordination Group, an excellent opportunity for him, but very disappointing for me. There really wasn't anyone in the senior UAC management with his imagination and far seeing perception of the feminine side of the business to support my ideas. As a result, suggestions I put forward after he left, which Edgar would have seen through without hesitation, either hung fire or got lost. Skilful retailing requires imagination and the courage to take calculated risks.

"Live by Beauty"

However, back in the UK, I had an important personal task to complete, which filled my evenings. Before I left Atkinsons I had conceived the idea of writing a book on beauty, following on the many articles on the subject I had written for newspapers and magazines. I talked at length with Anita Christophersen about this and I was very pleased when she agreed to collaborate with me on it. I felt I could supply the technical aspects of the book and her skill in writing, I was sure, would enhance the style of the book. It was called "Live by Beauty". Secker & Warburg agreed to publish it and so we set to work to create a totally different kind of beauty book.

We worked out the format — Part I, which was subtitled "The Anatomy of Beauty", gave the practical advice on beauty care, covering every part of the body. Part II we called "The Spirit of Beauty". This dealt with the way women need to think about themselves if they were to find their best presentation and acquire that inner radiance, without which cosmetics are a mere superficial coating which achieves little. The last part was devoted to pictures and a short biography of women, whom I felt had that indefineable quality — style, as well as good looks. Eleven contemporary women were included in this section, which was called, "The Biographies of Beauty". They included one African, Marion Asafu-Ajaye.

I did not want the illustrations throughout the book to be the usual type of rather pedestrian sketches. I wanted really informative and attractive drawings. For this I called on the help of Elizabeth Suter, an outstanding fashion illustrator, herself a most sympathetic and attractive woman, who caught the exact spirit of what Anita and I wished to convey.

Finally, I persuaded Secker and Warburg to permit the book to be "designed". I thought that if there were just pages of script with a few drawings, however appealing, dotted about, a great opportunity to make the book come together as a unity would be missed. I visualised the drawings artistically placed on the relevant pages and with, at the end of each chapter, tiny old fashioned engravings or decorations forming a tailpiece. I envisaged that varied typefaces would add style throughout. In this way I hoped the book would have a character all of its own, and convey an artistic message appropriate to a beauty book. This was not a very usual technique at the time, but Secker and Warburg saw my point, that I wanted it to be a beautiful book as well as a book about beauty, and agreed that the layout was important.

The graphic artist who co-operated with us was Hermann Hecht, a gentle intuitive person, who having produced the most lovely layouts, would laugh a little apologetically as if he didn't expect us to like them. It was a wonderful team effort, exhilarating because everyone was contributing in their own special way and, although we frequently didn't initially see eye to eye, we always gave consideration to the others' views and, I believe, the concensus arrived at produced a satisfying whole. Such books are rarely, if ever, best sellers, but several thousand copies were sold, and it was serialised in a women's magazine.

Today, the first part, relating to the fashions current in 1960, has dated. But the other two parts, particularly The Spirit of Beauty, is I think as valid today as when I wrote it. It has also one merit, there is considerable consistency in my thinking between then and now, although I hope that my ideas have matured somewhat, moved on and developed since then. At least I have not been guilty of a complete *volte-face*.

The book was eventually launched in 1961 and received for the most part good notices, although one critic found it dull and conventional. You simply can't catch everyone's imagination! The publication of the book added to my reputation as an authority in the area of cosmetics and style, which was valuable for my job.

Creative Energy

It is perhaps worth noting that at each phase of my career, I had tried to pursue the main thrust of my development by exploring and engaging in support activities which I felt would build up the whole. This of course means quite hard work, because while I have talked for the most part of my ideas which came to maturity, there were others which didn't. I think one has to be prepared to see some endeavours fail without getting too upset about it. Creative energy has to be continually re-directed, not wasted on bemoaning what does not succeed. I don't mean by this that endeavours must not be worked at and carried through to a proper conclusion when possible – this is essential. But at a given point, ideas which are simply not winning and which perhaps one comes to see as not well conceived initially, or for which there is no hope of support, must be abandoned and others more soundly based, pursued. It is a matter of judgement.

As well as hard work, this requires energy. I believe that I am very fortunate in having been endowed with a very sturdy physique and plenty of zest, but I do believe that the drive, which is perhaps characteristic of me, is something that can be attained by anyone who is really motivated and has goals.

Energy generated by high drive thought, is in my opinion not expendable, but self-generating. The more one thinks about things with commitment and excitement, the more one is able to move forward to a conclusion, and the more one's interest provides the strength to go on to the end. The more people are preoccupied by thoughts of "fatigue", "needing rest", "I've done enough", etc, the more their energy trickles away – there is nothing so exhausting as lethargy. Whereas those who have a dynamic, élan vitale as one of my friends calls it – generate energy, and are exhilarated and able to go on. Essential to this concept is the capacity to relax between times and above all to avoid fretting. I think a very useful philosophy is to "turn anxiety into action", but if there is nothing to be done about a situation leave it and get on with something else. If not, I believe that frustration and misery can engulf one. I believe that this is as true of personal relationships as practical issues.

Furthering Management Training

At last my recommendation to have a resident trainer working in the Lagos store was agreed. I knew who I wanted. It was a woman who had been quite a junior in the Staff Department when I was at Selfridges. I knew that she made great progress, particularly in the area of training and had become an important support to my old friend Bill Fowles, who was now in charge of the Staff Department at Selfridges. Hesitantly, I went to Bill and told him what I had in mind — "Would he be prepared to spare Toni?" It so happened that while in one way he did not wish her to leave, he had realised that there was not likely to be promotion for her for some time in his Department at Selfridges. He could not expect a very able person like Toni to stay motivated with no new challenge. If she was interested in the job I had to offer he was prepared reluctantly to let her go.

So I was lucky. He fixed an appointment for me to see her. I discovered that she had, so to speak, grown up and developed into an assured and delightful person; lively, ambitious and, as always, full of fun. I told Toni that if she came to us, I saw her creating an entirely new post in the Lagos Kingsway, the largest of the stores. I explained that the job was to develop a whole training plan for all levels of staff from sales assistants to management. I had no idea whether she would welcome working in Africa and uprooting herself for an assignment, which would last probably only two years.

To my delight she accepted. I knew that her happy personality would appeal to the Africans, and I felt that she could make a really significant contribution to the improvement in store service which we were trying to make. Toni's appointment was a great success and produced just the kind of results I had hoped, largely due to the fact that she gave the Africans confidence as well as real expertise in what they were doing.

To round out the management training initiated by Toni on the Coast, it was decided to select certain very promising members for further development in England. Accordingly, therefore, they were sent over and it was partly my concern, co-operating with Staff Department, to lay down a course which would really build their management skills for store work. In a period of, say, 9-10 months, we would arrange for probably 3 months to be spent in London office learning the accounting and buying systems into which Coast activities had to fit — 3 months was taken up at a Technical College to have a course in basic management techniques and 3 months with a practical assignment.

Accordingly I sought store appointments for them. It is very much to the credit of John Lewis in Oxford Street that at this time, when black faces were neither so fimiliar nor so acceptable, I would always find a place there for my trainees. At the end of their visit they had to write a thesis on their findings.

They blossomed under the personal, if demanding, pressure to which they were subjected. But I came to realise the great strain imposed on them by leaving their own country and doing such different things in totally alien rhythm. Sometimes their assurance cracked and I had to talk, discuss, reassure and mend broken confidence.

For example, on one occasion an able African manager brought me a letter from her chief on the Coast which was intended as a friendly booster for her. She, however, had lost her nerve and saw it quite differently. Sh criticised every sentence in it, seeing a double, detrimental meaning. I had to talk for a long time before she came to feel happy again and believe that the Company did indeed wish her well. It was rather like seeing Cinderella pinch herself to make sure she was dressed for the ball.

As well as following through merchandise ideas, I built up activities on the PR front. I wrote articles for the local newspapers both in Accra and Lagos, indeed some of them became a weekly feature. I also did many radio and TV programmes. This meant that Kingsway's name was frequently before the public. The store displays too, improved tremendously. To give changing interest, on one occasion we organised an Italian promotion for which Terry Kennedy and I went on a buying trip to Italy. It was the most elaborate event the store had ever featured and it aroused a great deal of interest. The Nigerians were becoming more and more style conscious and the elegance of the Italian fashions made a great impact. At another time, a British design week was staged in conjunction with the London Design Centre.

I had been with Kingsway for several years now and, although there had been improvements, I felt that we were not moving very rapidly. There were disagreements in the Kingsway Department in London, and I found the dual-control which existed there, frustrating, reducing my scope and authority considerably.

External Activities

By contrast, outside the Company interesting things were happening. I had been asked by the Central Office of Information to act as Editor and contributor to a series of recorded magazine programmes, which were to be made available to broadcasting stations in under-developed countries throughout the world, with special emphasis on Africa.

Also I had been invited to sit on the Export Publicity Council of the Department of Trade and Industry, called then the Board of Trade. Here, representing UAC, I worked with very senior people, Managing Directors and Chief Executives from companies like Shell and Barclays Bank.

It seemed to me that I was being given far greater scope and authority in these non-company activities whereas inside the organisation I was not being used in a very positive way. I was hedged round with an inflexible system which was not producing rapid results. I thought about this for a long while and then irritated by the inaction and what seemed to me to be waste, I went to the Director in charge and explained how I felt. I pointed out that people outside the Company to whom I was only on loan, were gaining more from my work than UAC itself, who was after all paying my salary! I added that I was prepared to learn any necessary new techniques skills, if my work could in some way be enlarged and I could be given more responsibility. I was not sure that I was wise to do this, but I felt trapped and, therefore, decided that some action was essential if I was not to stagnate. Perhaps a degree of courage is a management requirement!

This Director was a cautious man whom I felt was never at ease with women. However, we talked constructively and he did not disagree with my assessment of the situation, but said he would need time to consider the matter.

A New Assignment

Fortunately what might be regarded as a risky approach, produced excellent results. Sir Fred Pedler, whom I found a very sympathetic and flexible person, as well as being enormously knowledgeable about Africa, called me to his office and told me that my remit was to be changed. I was to work with Dennis Buckle, who was in charge of the Public Relations Department. I was to retain my interest in Kingsway in an advisory capacity, but have much wider responsibilities for PR for the whole company, as a member of the PR Department.

I had had many contacts with Dennis already, as so much of what I had been doing really came into his orbit. We had had many discussions and I had frequently called on him for help and advice, which was always readily given. It was, therefore, a great pleasure for me to learn that I was to work with him. Dennis was open minded, had vision, was an excellent communicator and had zest for the work. I knew I would enjoy both the freedom and the support that he would provide. He also had great powers of persuasion. Tall and very good looking, I had seen him win over people, British and African, who under a different style of management would have become very aggressive.

One of the first tasks we agreed that I should undertake was to make a more comprehensive and co-ordinated study of African women. I already had a great deal of information, but it needed to be better co-ordinated if it was to be of real value.

I had at this time to recruit a new Secretary. Rosalind had an offer to go to the Foreign Office where she could make use of her German. I was very sorry to see her go, but it was entirely right that she should accept this opportunity. I recruited a new Secretary, a very shy young woman, who had excellent secretarial skills. She was the fastest most accurate typist I had ever worked with and her paperwork was excellent. She had not, however had much experience outside a typing pool. So when Eileen Bell joined me, I think she would agree that her concept of the secretary's role was to do what she was asked, without comment, whereas I wanted a different kind of contribution altogether. Eileen and I have become very close friends over the years and I have an enormous admiration for her and he achievements, which are great, so I do not think she will mind my telling this story, because I think it will help others who do not always see how to use their abilities, nor what is wanted of them.

Not long after Eileen came to me, I had dictated a draft, after which I said to her, "Now tell me, Eileen, what do you think of that?" She looked confused and said she didn't know. Rather testily, I am sure, I said, "Well you *must* know what you think of it — good — bad or indifferent!" She shook her head and said she really hadn't been taught to think like that. Rather cruelly I replied, "Oh, so you want to be a shorthand typist, not a secretary — okay, now we know!" I felt I had to jerk her out of her timidity.

Half an hour or so later, she came back and said, "About that draft — I think —"

"Hooray", I replied, "Now we're getting somewhere."

I *did* understand Eileen's problems which beset so many people — shyness, lack of confidence, limited experience, with rather bossy people which had left her feeling inadequate. We set to work together to change all that. It took a little while and sometimes I'm sure she found me very demanding. Today, having had the courage to abandon office work many years ago in order to pursue her violin studies which were her true interest, she has become a talented and highly respected violin teacher, with a growing school of pupils. Quite recently Eileen said to me, "How often have you said to me — you're in charge of you and don't let anyone forget it. I felt so much of my early life was spent sort of hiding in a cupboard — but that is all done with. I don't need now to ask anyone's permission to be me." I think we all have to say this to ourselves from time to time. Indeed, I think that is what I said to myself, when I went to the Director to try to change my role in UAC. Adverse circumstances come to all of us and we just have to master them.

I was now to enter into a very productive era in which, with Dennis Buckle's support, I evolved many different publicity schemes. Prominent among these was a series of teaching aids. The African schools were painfully short of books and teaching material and I frequently went into class rooms in village schools where the walls and shelves were bare.

To help with this situation we produced different types of teaching aids and educational material — wall charts, booklets on good grooming, cookery and various historical subjects. Usually they were very well received but occasionally the fact that they carried a Company logo offended some people's susceptibilities. They feared that schools were being subject to foreign commercialism. We had to be very careful.

The need for trade to build up in all the West African countries was a perennial preoccupation. How could industry be started, local materials used and employment created? A very well planned and managed pottery had been going for a number of years at Abuja in the centre of Nigeria. Michael Cardew, a well known British potter, had gone to Nigeria and re-organised and built up the local craft, producing some really beautiful work which was exported. His most famous pupil was a brilliant Nigerian woman potter, Ladi Kwali, whom I met and was charmed by her outstanding skill and serene personality. Her bowls, vases and jugs had a special elegance which won her an international reputation. It was a small but an effective undertaking.

I tried very hard with another scheme which was to use the raffia craft which had been developed in a small town in Eastern Nigeria, Ikotekpene. The tribe that lived there was quite a feudal society. At the most modest level, the completely illiterate villagers actually tore the raffia out of the trees, and separating it into strips, dyed it with different local plant dyes. These simple folk lived in little houses and always on rails at the back of them, one would see hanging these long strips in green, pink or yellow. The gatherers/dyers then sold their produce to the craftsmen on the other side of the village who were much more sophisticated people. Their leader was a really able Ibo, Chief Bassey. The normal output of finished goods from this village was baskets, mats and most attractive little toys, all made of raffia.

At this time I had become a member, in London, of the splendid Intermediate Technology Group which Dr Fritz Schumacher of "Small is Beautiful" fame had set up. I learned there that in the confusion which followed the withdrawal of the French from Algeria, the raffia trade, which had been developed there by the Algerians, had ceased to function. The raffia speciality which the Algerians had perfected was patterned strips of raffia which were called braids and which were bought, by amongst others the Luton Hat Manufacturers in England, to make into straw hats. The Luton hat businesses were therefore suffering from a serious lack of raw material, because of the failure of the North African supply.

I took the sample book of the raffia "braids" that were required to Ikotekpene and sat down with Chief Bassey and his "clansmen" to discover whether they could make these different kinds of straw braids. A great palaver took place and after several hours of discussion the raffia workers agreed they could produce these goods.

So here we were in a position where, in one spot, which meant no carriage charges, there was a supply of raw material, the skilled workers to convert it and firms back in England which wanted the resulting goods and were prepared to pay for them. Immediately I requested that samples be prepared and I obtained the help of one of the local UAC accountants to assist with the documentation. This last was very important because if the scheme was to become truly viable orders would need to be properly recorded and export regulations complied with.

It seemed like a perfect set up, whereas so often with such endeavours one or other element was missing — either the raw material had to come from miles away, maybe even be imported, or the local people who needed the jobs had to be trained, or the market for the end product was very small or non-existent. Here we had every element in place.

Chief Bassey was very excited and so was I. But it was not to be. Just as the samples arrived from Ikotekpene in Luton for examination, the Nigerian War broke out and the country, particularly in the east, was in ruins!

I deeply regretted the failure of this development because I felt it could have succeeded, with considerable benefits for all concerned.

Practical Aids

At about this time an article about some of the things I had been doing in Africa appeared in England in the magazine "She". The need that the African women had for all kinds of simple things which I described aroused the interest and enthusiasm of hundreds of women in Britain who just wanted to help. Here it seemed was an opportunity to run a very simple scheme, which we called "The Practical Aids Scheme". My many African friends collected together the names and addresses of the women in their groups who could read English and the "She" subscribers were given one of the names to whom they were to send knitting patterns, sewing and handicraft ideas, cookery recipes, baby care and household hints, cut out of magazines or newspapers. The only charge to the British women was the cost of postage.

The scheme was established very quickly. Many of the Ghanaians and Nigerians wrote back and thanked their British correspondents and so a friendship link was started — as well as the useful items which did give practical help.

Unfortunately, of course, some of the African replies turned into begging letters and some recipients never sent a word of thanks. This was very disappointing for the British women. Nevertheless the scheme did do quite a lot of good for a while but, as so often happens, the initial enthusiasm waned. It did illustrate the enormous fund of good will and generosity which exists in this country, which only needs to be tapped for it to flow out to help less fortunate people. On a really big scale the same sympathy point was touched when Bob Geldof, many years later, called for actual money for famine relief with such a miraculous response.

Results of the Nigerian War

The Nigerian War had many long lasting and damaging outcomes, not least the really severe blow to the already insecure economy. Today, 21 years afterwards, there are grave financial problems in Nigeria. Stringent import regulations and many types of belt tightening schemes have been introduced by successive governments, some civil some military, but they seem only partially to work. The society also, partly as a result of large numbers of people still having guns and weapons, has, like everywhere else, become more violent. Between 1959 and 1966 I travelled many thousands of miles over West Africa, frequently with only a trusted African driver, sometimes going into remote villages where there were few, if any, white people. No difficulties with people ever occurred and if by chance, as did happen on at least two occasions, the car broke down or got jammed in the mud after a tropical rainstorm, little villagers would pop up, as if from nowhere, to help.

I am very happy that I can look back on those years when people's true characters were displayed. I firmly believe in the basic goodness of human beings, but because we all have flaws in our characters, given the wrong kind of leadership or wanting quick returns, we set up chains of events whose damaging ends we do not always perceive — damaging not only for ourselves, but for others as well.

The outcome of the war difficulties was that there had to be cutbacks in expenditure by UAC and, from the security angle, it was not thought wise for me to return to Africa in the free and easy way that had been possible before.

It was a little sad. Nevertheless I *had* seen the curious thick walled mud houses in Kano and Sokoto, which were so cool inside; I *had* had an audience with the Emir of Zaria, whose feudal establishment included a master of horse and a juggler with a partially shaved head. When I asked this 6ft tall turbanned gentleman about his wives, he could scarcely suppress a yawn. However, when I mentioned his horses, he came alive and showed me a collection of the most beautiful tall, blue-eyed creatures to which I gave lumps of sugar.

There were also the Falls of Guara, a mere mud trickle most of the year, but after the rains a spectacular multi spray cascade. I had also spent an exciting day on the Igun River with hornbills, sunbirds and kingfishers flashing over the leafy swamps. I had loved also the gorgeous babies and children who, usually smiling and happy, survived often in the most appalling conditions.

One comical incident occured in Onitsha, the town which had the largest market in Nigeria. I was wandering round one day fascinted by the stalls with their intriguing merchandise, gossiping and laughing with the "market mammies" who were guarding their goods. I came to one stall where an enchanting little boy was sitting in his mother's arms. I went to speak to him, but he struggled away and howled with distress. A little disconcerted, I drew back and the Nigerians looked down, obviously embarrassed. Trying to remove the tension, I said, "I quite understand — he just doesn't want to chat". They shook their heads and then I learned that it was my white face which was the bother. "I'm afraid he thinks you're a ghost!" they added. We all roared with laughter. I thought it was very salutory that I had been reminded that white faces are not always the tops — some people prefer something different!

Because of these economic changes my work altered yet again. I was asked to become involved with the marketing of fabric, provided by our textile unit, in the UK. The Company plan was to put less emphasis on Africa, where returns were slow, and to diversify into the home market.

The Senior Executive in the Textile Division, Jack Kent, had the idea of selling dress lengths in packages. The material was already cut so that counter service was minimised, no-one had to measure out yardage and then cut it off, it was already done. The success of the scheme obviously depended on the display and marketing of the packs. A great deal of work went into this scheme. A small Company was formed and I again became a token Director.

To start with it was subjected to detailed Market Research, which Eileen Cole conducted for us. How did women in the UK buy their dress materials? What did they look for? The research provided some positive answers — it was worth going ahead. The distribution was organised, counter stands and displays were created and the washing instructions and labelling were carefully planned and designed and included in the pack.

As well as helping with these general marketing activities, I was in charge of a team of young salesmen who went round the country introducing the packs into departmental stores and fabric shops. It was a novel idea and with a shortage of trained counter staff it did have obvious advantages. We met with a certain amount of success, but to launch such a revolutionary idea required a great deal of advertising support, which unfortunately the Company did not at that time wish to run to.

We pressed on with determination, aiming for as much free editorial mention as possible. We encountered pockets of success, particularly after we had staged dress shows which we did all over the country, displaying attractive fashions made up from the packaged material in different stores.

I came, however, to realise that we would not get the major results which were wanted unless the advertising support was forthcoming. It was a chicken and egg situation. After 18 months I decided to call it a day. I no longer had the enthusiasm for a purely commercial activity. The blend of personnel, training and community development with the commercial element, had appealed to me very strongly when I was working with Kingsway and Dennis Buckle, but with this scheme a vital element from my point of view was missing.

I had become enormously interested in staff training and development. The success that I had encountered with the African managers, and with both supervisory and management courses, which I was doing as an extra mural activity to support Elizabeth Pepperell of the Industrial Society, led me closer and closer to the thought that I wanted to be concerned with staff development, particularly for women.

Although the Company was very training orientated, I had seen so many of its women staff fail to succeed because of their lack of confidence and self direction. I felt that I could meet a real need in this area. So, not entirely sure how I would tackle it, I decided to retire from the United Africa Company earlier than I needed to do, to set up my own consultancy and devote myself to the objective of Development Training.

Discussions with senior people in the organisation were friendly and supportive and I was praised for the work I had done. With a show of reluctance I was released. I remember one remark which Sir Fred Pedler made to me at this time which ran something like, "We never really made full use of your talents". I was obviously both pleased and sorry about this. But as I came to think back on the whole experience later, the climate for women's progress was not then positive enough to allow of their full development. It was too dependent on perceptive senior managers. I had happily had several of those, but also unimaginative ones who, without wishing me ill, did not know how to create a feminine scenario. I too must share some responsibility for this.

I have already said that my financial skills were not as sharp as they should have been and because I always enjoyed what I was doing, perhaps I did not push as hard as I might for the high spots. On the other hand, knowing what you want to do, like doing it and doing it well, I believe makes for a satisfying and happy life, which pressurising yourself beyond your limits will not do.

I had been with Unilever for 23 years. The time had slipped by almost without my being aware of it. There had been so much variety, so much change and interest, I had really enjoyed it all. I felt I had come a long way and I was very grateful to the Company, whose ethos I greatly admired.

I dare say that if I had stopped longer to consider, an alternative way of handling this arrest point would have been found. I had, for example, often been involved with the selection process for the Management Trainee schemes in Unilever House. Again, as far back as Atkinsons, I had done both supervisory and management training at the Unilever Training Centre at Four Acres. But my mind was made up — I somehow yearned for complete self direction and the freedom that goes with it. I was prepared to take the risk of breaking out on my own!

So an era came to an end.

My arrival in Africa in 1959

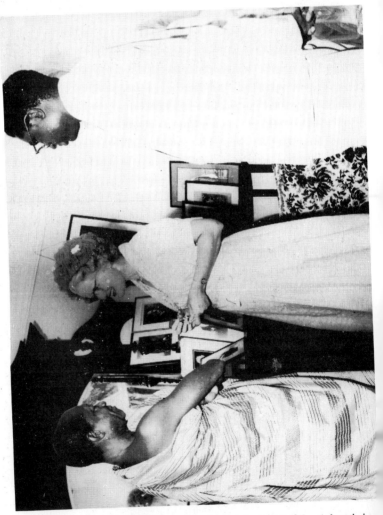

I have an audience with the Ashanti Hene, the head of the Ashantis in Kumasi, N. Ghana. He drive about in a very beautiful old Rolls Royce

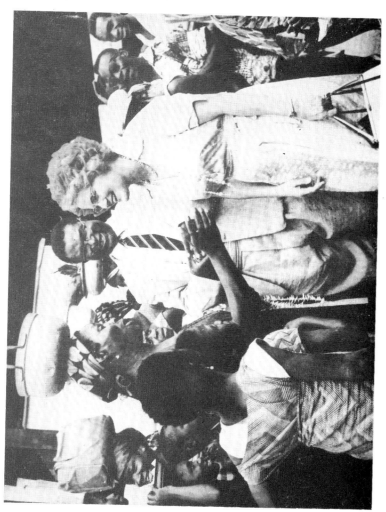

Here I am joking with market women in Accra and everyone else stopped to laugh. This picture won an award as the most natural, unposed photograph of the year

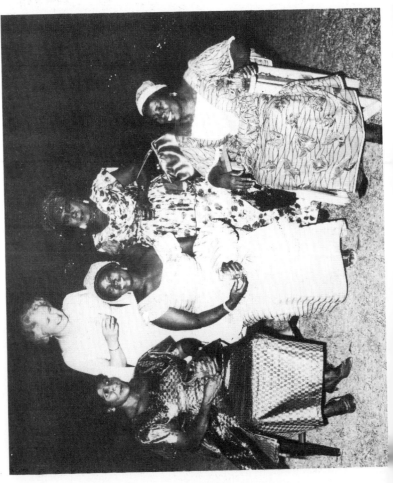

Attending an evening party with leading women in Accra

I am loaned a beautiful hand-woven dress of the Yoruba Tribe

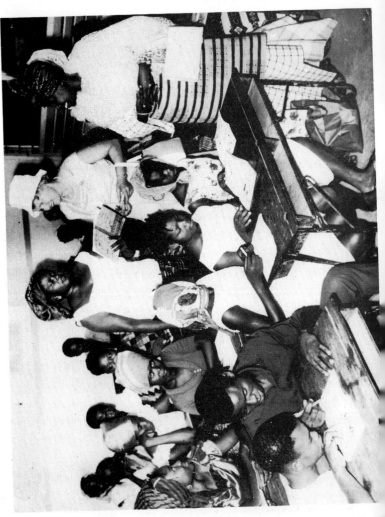

I visit a literacy class in Lagos where people who had missed out on school could learn to read

Examining enamel-ware in Dugbe market, Nigeria. I was received by influential leaders of both the market traders and the Women's Society

Ladi Kwali, Northern Nigeria's famous woman potter

African World

APRIL, 1964

Ladi Kwali, the famous potter from North Nigeria, who won many international awards

A group of distinguished women from North Nigeria in Kano. Yoruba, Hausa and Fulani ladies are present. Many were doctors, lawyers, Headmistresses

Chapter Eight

Launching my Own Business

As soon as my mind was made up to leave UAC, I started to think ahead — how could I tackle the future? I felt if I was to succeed in the area of Development and Training, I must go into the logistics of the proposition in real depth. The concept of people running individual consultancies was not so common then as it is now, so I did not at that juncture see how I could give practical shape to my ideas.

After some careful consideration, I thought the essential thing was to begin at the beginning. I had convictions based on observation, but I felt that a much sounder base than my opinions was needed.

My first step, therefore, was to collect facts and data which would support my conviction that many people did not make maximum use of their abilities and that, in particular, women neither evaluated themselves correctly, nor were they afforded adequate training and development. I regarded this as total waste.

At no stage did I feel anti men; I was just pro better utilisation of human resources, especially women's, who were so badly neglected. I perceived that a great deal of this situation arose from social patterns and stereotypes to which both men and women conformed. Indeed I saw men as much trapped by entrenched behaviour patterns as women.

Men for the most part could not perceive women doing other than conventional jobs, predominantly the wife and mother role. If they worked they were viewed as secretaries or assistants, perhaps occasionally rising to a supervisory role if no men happened to be available for the promotion, or the staff to be managed were women.

The marvellous war records of many women who had fulfilled highly responsible jobs were in many cases conveniently forgotten or put on one side. Managers found conventional rather than innovative thinking much easier to adhere to, and there were always snap arguments such as, "If we train and promote women to senior jobs, they'll only marry and leave, it's a waste", or "Our customers would be offended if we sent a woman representative", or again "Women make poor leaders. They get bossy and other people don't accept them", and "Anyway, many of them haven't the right qualifications". Some at least of these arguments were nothing but expressions of prejudice.

Women also all too often adhered to the stereotype. They did not, and in many cases still do not, have sufficient confidence to perceive themselves in senior or leadership roles. And it was true that their education and training had been in many cases inappropriate to the careers they wanted to follow. I am delighted that the educational pattern is changing rapidly. But women are still too heavily influenced and often confused by society's expectations of them — "Mother-in-law wants a grandson", or "I must not neglect my husband", or "I don't want to look bossy"; however, they do not always admit to these limitations.

Although there was some basis of fact in some of these prejudiced attitudes, not enough account was taken of the growing social and economic changes which were occurring. For example, two-income families were an increasing necessity because of, at one level, high school fees and mortgages and, at another level, the desire to meet the growing demands of the consumer society for washing machines, refrigerators etc.

The other significant, but frequently ignored, factor was women's own increasing desire for personal independence and recognition.

So I set to work to collect data — educational statistics — levels of women employed in companies and the Civil Service. I made this into a report in which I drew attention to such facts as the shortage of trained personnel at middle and senior management levels, and that 77% of women entering employment in 1967 went into clerical work or into positions offering less than two months' training.

Other statistics referred to were the insignificant numbers of young people, under 18 years of age, who were afforded Day Release by their employers. The figures were poor for boys, only 35% of them gaining this opportunity, but they were deplorable for girls, barely 9% of whom obtained places. Many other points were covered such as the employment of women graduates in jobs far below their capabilities, and the lack of any career progression opportunities for women in most companies. The conclusions pointed to ideas for actions which might be taken to redress this situation.

I circulated the report to 250 people whom I thought would be interested and would perhaps help me to formulate ideas as to how the pattern could be altered. The response to the report was most encouraging. People not on the original circulation list got to hear of it and asked for a copy. A few men and women expressed a wish to talk the report through with me. So I invited them to a meeting. Included in the group of about 10 were Joan Robins of The Gas Council, Sir George Pope of The Times, Francis Shearer of Cooper Sand Lybrand and Isobel Allen, an Economist who was working with Professor Fogarty on a series of studies on women and their careers. This eventually appeared as a book under the title, "Women in Top Jobs".

This group grew into an informal committee. There was unanimous agreement about the main thrust of the report. The debate turned on what we could do to draw further attention to the situation and how we could set to work to change it.

We also debated what we could call ourselves which we thought was important. It was Isobel Allen who came up with the very bright but simple title, "Women in Management".

This was in the summer of 1969. I could see that while it was a tremendous help to gain the support of this quite distinguished group, it seemed to me that I needed to influence employers and senior people in organisations, and also to get in touch with women themselves to learn first hand what their needs were, and work out ways in which they could be helped to build up their skills and confidence. I was already being invited to mount or make contributions to many different training courses, some run by Unilever, The Industrial Society and GKN, but also by other organisations. I noted that the more senior these seminars were, the fewer women were included. This led me in 1970 to put on a course of my own for women who had the potential to become Managers. I felt they needed to be encouraged.

First Women Managers' Course

It was the first course of its kind to be held in the country and took a great deal of organising and publicising. But I worked at it and succeeded, with the help of Pat Bowman of PA Management Consultants, who loaned me his Board Room, in getting the course launched. Leaflets were distributed and the programme devised. I succeeded in getting 17 delegates, most women who were working for promotion. Members of the WIM Group notably Eileen Cole, the Chairman of Research Bureau Ltd; Pat Down then Personnel Controller of British Home Stores, and Anne Mackie

Employee Relations, Personnel Division, Unilever, gave sessons on the course, which proved sufficiently successful for a second one to be put on in the autumn.

The Press were, of course, interested in this innovation, if in some instances for the wrong reasons. They were invited for a brief session on the first day to take photographs and learn what we were doing. There were a few sensible comments, but others were trivial in the extreme.

One press photographer, for example, when I was busy talking to someone else, got hold of the prettiest girl on the course poised her on a balustrade and took a low angle shot highlighting her elegant legs. This photograph was featured the next morning under the headline "Petticoats in the Boardroom". As the rest of the caption was quite informative, I took the view that perhaps there is no bad publicity!

One response which did worry me was an article which featured in a personnel magazine which attacked me for segregating men and women by running a woman only course. The comment ran something like, "If women want to be managers, they must face up to men managers and get on with it". I did not agree then and I do not agree wholly now, although the climate and women's attitudes have somewhat changed.

I believe that at the learning − the experimental − stage there is justification for women moving into management, who are so often hesitant and inexperienced, to gain their confidence without having to fear the derision or seeming superiority of men. Many women have endorsed this viewpoint.

Particularly in the early 70's, but also today, there is merit, I believe, in women "finding themselves" in a wholly supportive atmosphere with no masculine distractions. Once a feeling of self-belief and self-worth starts to grow, then working with men as colleagues is excellent and very necessary. Many women have a degree of sensitivity, however, before they discover their potential and believe in it, which responds excessively to men's height − powerful masculinity − deep voices − confident speech and positive declarations of their successes. They feel insignificant against this barrage and so give up before they've started.

I do not accept the argument that if these are women's reactions they are no managers anyway. The unconfident attitude, which is at the root of so much of negative thinking and projection, in men as well as women, so often arises from early belittling experiences. Father who says, "You're useless my boy − my girl"; mother who says, "Your brother is so much cleverer than you and in any case why didn't you do it yesterday?", or teacher who says, "Don't think you're bright enough to tackle that", and so on.

By the time these destructive comments have gone on for years, I believe that a negative mould is cast which it is very difficult to break. But it can be done, and then the true personality emerges.

It was to address this problem that led me to present all-women management courses and the results were very rewarding.

A Personal Loss

Developing these thoughts and planning the courses required a great deal of thought, reading and planning. Also it was essential to make contacts with schools — colleges, personnel and training departments in both the commercial and public sector. All this had made 1970 into a very busy year. By August I was very pleased that the time for the Scottish holiday, which Ian and I had planned, arrived.

Ian had long been established as the Maths teacher at Elmhurst School, the leading Prep School in Croydon. He had developed a highly individual teaching style and because he could identify closely with the 10–14 year old youngsters, who were his charges, he was successful. I think this success was also due to the fact that he had the ability to make figures come alive to boys who, without encouragement, would have paid little attention to, even developed a positive dislike for, Maths. By devising a blend of toughness with humour, he succeeded in making his lessons great fun, even to the least interested scallywag. He enjoyed his work enormously and inevitably so did the boys.

Sadly, a year before, Ian had developed cancer of the throat, which almost robbed him of his voice. He had never been a strong person. He had had recurring trouble with a duodenal ulcer and a heart condition which generated a great deal of fatique. To contend with these problems, he had developed considerable stoicism and with it a capacity to pace himself quietly without complaining.

When cancer had been diagnosed and he was told that he would have to have cobalt ray treatment for a month, he accepted the situation without complaint and with great fortitude. Each day he went from home to the London Branch of the Royal Marsden Hospital for the treatment, which lasted a mere 2–3 minutes. His neck getting increasingly burned and painful, he would then return home and read quietly, or work at his papers and problems preparing for his return to work. As a result of the stringent treatment the cancer was cured, his neck healed and his voice returned.

Unforgivably, in my view, having stopped smoking without any argument as soon as the cancer had been detected, he was given permission to resume this highly destructive habit once the treatment was finished! It was so wrong and I sharply resented the seemingly casual way permission was given to him to do this. I feel happy with the thought that the doctors would not do that today.

Ian returned to work and when the end of the summer term came, we went off on our Scottish holiday, which we greatly enjoyed. It was when we were in Poolewe, on the north-west coast that Ian had a monumental heart attack. Remote from anywhere, we eventually got an ambulance to take us to Inverness Hospital right on the other side of Scotland. The exquisite beauty of that sunlit drive across North Scotland and the ensuing weeks of watching him suffer are embedded in my memory for all time. My sole companion during these weeks was Sammy, my little grey poodle who stuck close to me wherever I went. Eventually, Ian was allowed to come south as I had had to do a little earlier. After making a tremendous effort to regain his strength and indeed making some improvement, he contracted pneumonia and died.

I think it is true to say that a little bit of me died with him. His sympathy and understanding of others linked with a gaity and sense of wit which made even dreary occasions funny, is something I have never experienced with any other man. In spite of undoubted ability he never, in my view, like so many people of his era, reached his full potential. In the last years of his life, however, which he greatly enjoyed, he had a significant influence with the youngsters who came into his orbit. Many of these young people when they were at their senior school, or even much later when they had taken up their careers, would come back and express their gratitude for the help he had given them.

The development of the quieter qualitites of inner courage and respect for others, linked with thoroughness and reliability at work, was the way which Ian and many others at all levels in British society lived their lives. I believe that this unspectacular but tremendously worthwhile way of life still persists, but I wonder whether the aggressive, vulgar, macho image, so heavily publicised and quite falsely made by the media to look so glamorous, has not in a measure taken over, lowering standards and making it very difficult for younger people to find a balanced way of life. Youngsters are all too often not aware of the insidious deterioration which can overtake them, and teachers and parents find it a great struggle to row against this tide. But if our values are to be preserved, I believe it is a task, however big, which must be tackled.

I am not talking about a prissy ineffectiveness, but a pattern of behaviour which rejects violence and cruelty, too often confused with strength and directness.

As I had found in the past, work was the great healer, but also crucial was the warm friendship which I received from my little inner circle, especially from Jane. She came, without being asked, as soon as Ian died and her matter-of-fact, practical and warm presence was a joy. Dear Mrs Morter also, our housekeeper, was a great stand by. Her crisp, detached voice talking about the shopping and the cooking, restored normality very quickly. Another great support was John Miller, the brilliant gynaecologist, who lived just up the road and seemed always on hand at a difficult moment. I was very lucky.

Like all deep emotional experiences, I found that, absorbed without self-pity, this whole sad episode had increased my capacity for compassion, built a greater sense of purpose and the strength to fulfil it. One thing I was quite sure about — that the "practice of misery" at such times, is damaging, unprofitable and a poor testimony to those we mourn.

Developing Further Courses

After the second Management Course, I discovered that there were all too few women who were being considered for development in their companies, and I had great difficulty in getting Training Managers to send delegates on the Management Course.

Re-thinking my strategy, I decided that since many women, however able, were for the most part in the secretarial grades, I had best go where they were and try to mount programmes which, although they were aimed at improving secretaries were also intended to raise women's expectations of themselves.

I reasoned that if I could get the secretaries to build their confidence and create a greater sense of self-worth, I was tackling the task I had set myself to do, but instead of furthering women with one foot already on the ladder, I was aiming to get them to that starting point.

So I set to work to devise programmes which were entitled Secretarial Development Course, or Development Courses for Senior Secretaries, etc. It was essential that I took the companies with me in promoting the seminars, and that the programmes included practical elements which improved current performance, as well as helping the delegates to widen their vision and aim higher.

Usually after the courses, the girls left with a very different attitude and often with the intention of doing further study at evening classes. But even if they had not arrived at that advancement point, the majority of them returned to their offices determined to tackle their work with more involvement and motivation.

It is very interesting to make a comparison between the delegates who came on those early secretarial courses and the secretaries who come on them today. The advancement is remarkable.

There are still very shy, intimidated people with poor qualifications — the most common defect being, inexcusably, poor English. For the most part, however, the secretaries today are much more positive and more purposeful — many of them thinking in terms of careers rather than short term jobs.

With the advent of the word processor and the computer, the whole approach to secretarial work has changed. Fifteen years ago it was for many girls a "do as I tell you" job which allowed little initiative to be used

The true PA/Assistant, even then, was a very worth while job, but too many bosses treated their secretaries, and perhaps still do, as shorthand typists. I always made the plea that girls should think about their work in depth, align themselves with their bosses' work and goals and think of themselves as contributing to results, that is, as a part of the management team.

Some secretaries just do not have the sense of self-worth and confidence to do this, and however resentfully they put up with dreary jobs and put downs such as, "She's only a secretary", they are unable to break out of the mould. As a result they are brushed aside and end up doing mundane tasks with no areas of decision making.

On many occasions I have had the great satisfaction of acting as a catalyst, which enabled women to review themselves more objectively, and, by changing passive attitudes, come to treat themselves as creative people.

One marvellous letter which I received from a girl after such a course, included the paragraph "Fear breeds uncertainty, but once fear is eliminated strength emerges. Once the catalyst reacts, the fire begins. With a changed awareness of my attitude, I was able to *do* something". Which is so true — fear is the real enemy of development and achievement. One needs to look closely and say, "What am I afraid of — what is the worst that could happen in this situation?" When one engages in this kind of self-analysis, one often discovers that the fears are not all that real and that if one takes hold of them with courage — one by one — they can be broken down and dispelled. But the drive to do this has to come from inside one's own being perhaps switched on by some sympathetic outside influence, or a snub which is so enraging that one drives oneself into positive action.

The Training Years

The Secretarial Courses have been a constant part of the training programmes I have offered because, as I have already said, there is so much unrealised potential in this area.

In addition, I have presented many seminars for Supervisors, junior and senior Managers for both men and women. I find the middle level training courses particularly interesting because they are attended by people who are just starting to mount the managerial ladder, who are sufficiently flexible in their outlook to be able to adapt to new ideas and techniques. They are, for the most part, very receptive and I feel that I am laying important foundations for their futures and perhaps helping them to avoid forming some of the worst management practices. Unfortunately some longer standing managers have already become too rigid and prejudiced to change.

Some of these junior managers come on the courses showing great promise and may have already developed impressive management skills.

Others have potential which has never been developed. They have been chucked in at the deep end, often with poor briefing about their responsibilities and totally inadequate job definitions. They know little about what is expected of them and do not know what the limits of their responsibilities are. This reveals that their bosses are very bad at communication, but staff also need to clarify their goals and job descriptions.

Delegation

One of the great problems, both at the senior and middle management level of staff, is delegation. Particularly when making the first upward move and having up till then been preoccupied with the "doing" areas of work, the first-time manager often finds it very difficult to let go the mini-tasks and concentrate on the broader issues of managing — planning and directing.

A typical young manager whom I met had no idea of the meaning of delegation. He interfered in the work that he had reluctantly given out, because he said that he couldn't trust his staff — adding sourly that they made mistakes and didn't produce results on time. So he took all the work back, and getting in early and staying late, he tried to do everything himself. Of course he couldn't manage it. He became exhausted and bad tempered and his staff were toally de-motivated.

When I talked to them, they said, "He is always in such a hurry — he never explains things fully so we don't know what we're about, and when we make mistakes from ignorance he gets angry and takes over. We've given up". Of course, primarily the manager was handling things badly, but the staff also were at fault because they should have talked to the manager and told him why things were going wrong. It is necessary sometimes for persons to have the courage to challenge senior people — to lead from behind.

The message has to be got over that a team of people responds far better when they are given specific tasks, or better still, areas of responsibility, when they are carefully briefed and trained and shown how they are expected to perform. Perhaps most important of all they must then be allowed to have the satisfaction of doing and achieving things on *their own*. Of course this means that the manager has to take some risk because if things go wrong he is still accountable. But if he has done the work properly, selecting the right people for jobs and helping them to gain the necessary knowledge and skills to do them, the risk should be minimised, but it has to be taken.

This is exactly what the young manager I describe did not do. So his staff lost all respect for him; they became bored, claiming that he did no listen to them nor accept any of their ideas, which made them feel inferior and frustrated. They lost interest and made no effort to support him.

An integral part of all management training must be to impress on managers the idea that, while the senior may be in control, the co-operation and the motivation which makes any work effective must come from the staff, who need the encouragement and the support of their leader.

Very often bad delegation and low motivation arise from supervisors or managers who do not have the confidence to trust their staff and release responsibility to them. The insecure manager all too often keeps information to him or herself, does not take time to explain and train, and so people are not identified with the job. The leader then feels let down and conflict situations develop. Frequently at this point the manager may blame people for poor performance and the staff begin to feel victimised and vengeful.

Considering People

Another problem that can arise is when the manager does not have the courage or the communication skills to tell the staff member where he/she has gone wrong and perhaps how the mistake can be put right. Trouble situations are not resolved by finding scapegoats, but by discovering the areas of the difficulty and the remedies. These need to be viewed objectively, not personally. In many cases the manager may have contributed to the difficulty and he must then be open enough to come clean. Putting things right has to take account of people's grievances, and while they must never be allowed to grump and moan for hours on end, being able to have their say will relieve tension and make it possible to make a fresh start with a new strategy.

On all our courses we spend a great deal of time putting over the concept of "people" management, because it is at the heart of the success of any undertaking. The need to develop positive human relations is paramount. It has been talked about for so many years, and may be accepted intellectually when people are on courses for example, but in many cases managers seem unable actually to put into practice techniques which take people into account.

Time pressures make ambitious managers, in particular, very short tempered. Being over enthusiastic to attain goals, leads them to harassing staff rather than persuading them. Blaming and condemning subordinates seems, in the heat of the moment, a much easier way to terminate arguments. Yet none of these perhaps understandable human short comings produces good results, particularly if there is inconsistency of attitude and performance — saccharine sweet today, because I was sorry for my rudeness of yesterday although I won't say so — bullying tomorrow. Staff get confused and do not know how to respond to this ambivalence. So they withdraw, because it is easier to say nothing if the open response only produces more criticism.

We always talk on all our seminars about the importance of self-analysis and awareness. How *do* I behave? What effect does my behaviour and attitudes have on others? What are *their* problems?

The people who are seeking to improve their work style must learn a measure of self-discipline and control. Yet it is also important to strike the right balance. I have seen people, managers and support staff, totally falsify their own personalities and become very insincere in an effort to conform to an alien standard.

To respond sensitively to the ethos of an organisation or adapt sympathetically to the needs of staff or the boss is wise, but totally to belie one's own character and allow either people or an organisation to rob one of personality and identity, is disaster. The young man, for example, who goes into an organisation open, sincere and straight-forward and over the years, because of the quest for power, becomes insincere, devious, even dishonest, is in danger of becoming a nothing. There are those also for whom success is a damaging factor. It goes to their heads, conceit begins to play a dominant part — and they lose humility. A sad example of this is a woman I have known for many years and for whom I had great respect who I feel has changed markedly. When I meet her now, instead of the attentive interested manner she used to have, she has acquired a certain superior detachment, her eyes look beyond me rather than at me, and she has a smooth shallow way of responding, a sort of cultivated charm, which spells egotism and lack of any real interest. Such behaviour makes me feel of little account and freezes communication — I find I have nothing to say to her. It isn't only film stars who succumb to the glitter.

Interpersonal relationships have to be thought about very carefully and with a considerable degree of self-criticism. I think it is quite likely that this great lady has no idea she is coming over as conceited and unsympathetic. She is trading on the good relations she made so readily earlier in her life. Now it would seem she lacks the humility to put herself under the microscope and perhaps there is no friend brave or perceptive enough to tell her what is happening.

Another problem which arises with human relations is when brash, goal orientated people do not consider that taking trouble with others, merits time and consideration. They expect things to happen and individual points of pride or doubts, which need to be considered, are ignored with disastrous results. It is a fact that very frequently more than half managers time is spent putting things right which have gone wrong from inconsiderate behaviour or bad communications. Almost invariably such disasters need never have happened.

Power Play

My mind goes back to a highly skilled scientist who depended heavily on a first class secretary to whom he was constantly rude. When one day he said to this able, long-suffering woman, "Don't think, type!", he was astonished that she resigned. Here was a man who either from arrogance or perhaps some inner insecurity, could only do his very taxing work by belittling others, particularly his subordinates, who could not get back at him. It was unforgivable that he denied respect to his secretary, refused to recognise her valuable contribution and by his selfishness and egotism, took away her "breathing" space.

At some stage this man needs to stop, think through his unfair behaviour and aggressive attitude and come to see that they will always produce antagonism, conflict and negative results. It is no use his saying, "This is "me" — I can't change". It is probably more accurate to say, "I don't want to change".

If he really stopped to examine his behaviour and saw how unprofitable it was, he could do something about it. Because his conduct is the result of deep seated attitudes about himself — his work — his secretary — perhaps women in general, it will not be easy for him to adjust. But with his most valuable supporter gone, he may have been forced to re-think his approach, particularly if the people he encounters, his new secretary perhaps, have no intention of being dominated by him.

All confrontations are in reality "power play" and the greater strength of one protagonist will seek to dominate the other. It is worth remembering, however, that no-one can exercise power over another except to the degree that they permit it. It is nevertheless difficult and requires very careful handling for someone in a subordinate position to exercise their strength, without appearing obstreperous or lacking in respect.

If our scientist wishes to alter, he will have to engage in some deep self-analysis and he will have to make repeated and conscious efforts to curb his disagreeable behaviour and, even more important, modify his underlying cynical attitude. Many people say that to change the behaviour of a life-time, because it is "natural", would make an individual totally insincere. This is not necessarily the truth, because taking up, in one's dealings with people some of their "space" assuming that everyone else's "territory" can be usurped with impunity, does not mean that the aggressor is acting "naturally", he has simply acquired the habit of using his power in a distorted way. To have indulged for many years in bad behaviour in an uncontrolled manner is not acting "naturally", it is acting without discipline, which becomes habitual because no-one has challenged it.

This man will have to make up his mind whether he wants to alter and how much effort he is prepared to put into the exercise. I have seen people over the years modify their behaviour quite dramatically. They may still retain at moments a flash of temper, or the capacity for a critical word, which is tolerated as being part of that person's character, but totally unkind disregard for others can be checked, if only because intelligence reveals that such conduct does not pay.

Finding the Balance

To attempt to exercise control and acquire a more disciplined approach is not the same thing as someone who continually dissembles, never comes out with an honest adverse comment, remains silent, giving no support at a moment of disagreement in order, at all costs, to avoid confrontation.

Such behaviour is no basis for a good relationship. It is perceived by everyone as insincere and hypocritical and generates distrust and lack of respect. People *must* know where they stand with others. So there are moments when the courage to be frank must be used, however tactfully the "frankness" is expressed.

The balance point between aggressive, tactful or weak behaviour is often fine, because there is a close relationship between negative and positive human qualities.

- Determination can quickly degenerate into cussedness
- Tolerance into weakness and indecision
- Courage into bravado
- Concentration into tunnel vision
- Leadership into bossyness
- To search for the mean and practise it with honesty is a lifelong task!
- It is getting the balance

I and my colleague, Ann Berwick, continue to train secretaries. Social and organisational skills and the vital need to work confidently with the new technology, are the important messages which we convey. It is good to be able to stress that it is far easier now for secretaries to expand their role, act as a true support to the boss or bosses, if they will seize the opportunities. They can become an information centre in a department, liaise with other staff on behalf of the boss and free him or her for the more complex tasks of management.

This all requires assurance, the capacity to speak and communicate, the good sense to project personality by clothes, style and a calm manner. Such attributes often need to be acquired — certainly polished. It is all part of the development process. They are incidentally just as important for those who are aspiring to management, as those who wish to maximise their secretarial role. The key factor is how we perceive ourselves, and the guiding phrase is, "If I can perceive it, I can do it."

Important Personalities

It was in 1970 that I had the good fortune to meet Peter Mulcahy- Morgan, the Training Manager at Guinness. His whole approach to staff was exemplary and he was particularly interested in, and sympathetic to, the idea of women's abilities being better used.

As well as joining the WIM Executive, Peter sent many delegates on my courses. We also often talked from time to time about our work, people's needs and aspirations, their responses and organisational attitudes to staff. I always found these discussions inspiring and stimulating. Peter was such a friendly and courteous person. He had been terribly badly wounded in the war and only just eluded capture by the Japs. Later, unfortunately, he developed diabetes, but he brushed off these trials and disabilities and gave himself whole-heartedly to everything he tackled. On the WIM Committee he was a tower of strength, wise and witty − quiet, when matters demanded careful thought, but fearlessly trenchant, although always polite, when waffle had to be dispelled!

I learned a great deal from him in these situations because, while I had had a lot of practice at running meetings in business, which is a skill, I had not chaired voluntary groups before. When members of a committee are employees and their jobs are important to them, a restraining factor is introduced and they behave very differently from those occasions when they are *giving* their time and expertise, perhaps from a base of strong conviction, even prejudice − and are *not* being paid. They will expand endlessly on favourite topics, wander off the point continually and even play hurt when their ideas are not taken up. I could get impatient and irritated with this kind of thing, but Peter kept his cool − this acted as a curb to me − I was lucky.

Chairing such gatherings calls for the exercise of considerable patience, but firmness. I came to rely on Peter. He had a great sense of personal responsibility and urgency which led him to tackle prodigious amounts of work. He had no conceits, he just felt that he owed it to all with whom he came in contact to make maximum endeavour, so that neither time nor personal potential remained unexplored or wasted. It is small wonder that people not only held him in high regard, but also had real affection for him.

I shared so many of Peter's views and I found that his interpretation of them deepened my convictions and also sharpened my endeavour. Such is the force of example.

Another early member of the WIM group whom I had known for many years as a Unilever personality, was Eileen Cole. I had always admired her and felt she would have a great deal to contribute. I was, therefore, delighted when she agreed to work with us. A Cambridge Economist, she had joined Unilever as a graduate trainee. A steady progression ensued as she acquired her skills as a highly professional manager. Then she leaped ahead and at 41 became the Chairman of Research Bureau Ltd. Later her authority was again greatly extended when she was made Chairman of Research International.

These two companies were the National and International Market Research organisations within Unilever. As one of the largest Marketing and Advertising multi-national companies, Unilever set great store by market research. Any major product required huge capital investment and subsequently vast advertising expenditure. Such resources could not be squandered on projects which had not been thoroughly examined in every aspect of market acceptance.

Eileen had a brilliant mind and a detached analytical approach, grasping logical argument and complicated statistical assessments with ease. Some people who perceived her as having a diamond hard brilliance found her a little off-putting. I didn't see her like that at all. Of course she had a quick pointed intelligence, but she was also most generous in sharing her skills and her time and she handled her staff with sympathy and insight. That she didn't always tolerate fools with equanimity, arose from the very high, perhaps even perfectionist, standards she worked to, and because I think to achieve to a high level requires a pace setter in a group, this is no bad thing.

In an area like Market Research where there is no room for guess work and error, I believe she was superbly well placed. Perhaps not apparent for all to see, there is a deeply understanding and compassionate aspect to Eileen's personality, from which on many occasions I personally have benefited.

As a role model for aspiring career women to look up to, particularly remembering that she rose to great heights in a multi-national company when women's progress was not all that easy, she is outstanding.

I also find it very interesting that since her retirement Eileen has taken on two very challenging positions, one as non-Executive Board member of the Post Office and the other fulfilling a similar role with London Regional Transport.

This new phase in her career has meant a complete change of direction. Eileen has had to adapt to two totally new organisations; different in nearly every respect from those with which she was familiar. They are public sector undertakings — not private industry — they have a Trade Union dimension which she happened never before to have encountered and, of course, in such organisations there is the requirement of working directly with Government and the Civil Service.

To establish credibility and acceptance in such changed circumstances required enormous flexibility and adaptability. This I believe is what attainment in the modern world is about.

WIM Activites

Gradually through publicising what we were aiming to do, more and more women became interested and wanted to be involved with WIM in some way. I felt that the most helpful thing at this stage would be to organise a series of Discussion Evenings, which would comprise the presentation of an important topic by a speaker, to be followed by questions and debate. We saw it would be unwise to get people to come on from work without refreshments, so we included these. I was determined from the start that they would not be of the "buns and butter" variety, reminiscent of a village hall jamboree. I said, "If we are, or are aspiring to be, managers we must behave like managers." So at a good hotel, wine and canapés were offered, and this has become the style of WIM functions.

The first Discussion Evening took place in June 1975 at the Basil Street Hotel. The theme was Career Progression. The event was well attended and very much appreciated. It was followed at regular intervals by other similar meetings.

These discussion Evenings are still a most popular and valuable part of the WIM events programme. Not only are members introduced to new thoughts and techniques relevant in some way to their development as managers, but they have the opportunity to meet other women over a glass of wine and a snack to discuss ideas, and problems, learn what others are doing and generally, in today's parlance, "network" supportively. It is all part of training to improve communication skills, so important in Management. Talking, questioning, discussing, discovering, even if when you pose your first question in public your heart thumps inside you, you can get over such nerves and learn how to face an audience. You are learning to play a participating management role.

The WIM group over the ensuing years took on many different tasks. One very important one was compiling a Women's Who's Who. This was a spendid idea contributed by Virginia Novarra, who had early on joined the WIM Executive. She is a lawyer, who has moved from banking to the Civil Service and now runs her own consultancy. Her clear logical approach to topics made it possible for her to perceive the need for this list.

The idea was to compile a register of women and so publicise their qualifications and experience. It included the names of about 100 women who were holding management jobs — some much more senior than others — with a view to encouraging the inclusion of women on to the committees of public bodies, or their participation in such activities as public enquiries. Also for companies who were "head hunting", here was a list of potential talent. We were only too aware that it was a very small effort and did not include nearly as many women as we would have liked. But the task of ferreting out names and particulars and putting it all together for publication was tremendous and, of course, was all done by voluntary help in the Committee members' so called spare time. At least it was a start. It aroused wide interest.

The great problem with WIM, like so many voluntary bodies, has been finance. My ploy for this in the early years was to syphon off from the courses that I ran under my own banner, sums of money to keep the organisation going. I argued that if I believed in women's development, I'd best put my money where my mouth was! Both the WIM Committee and I knew that we would have to earn our laurels and gain acceptance and credibility not as a cranky, bra- burning operation, but a group of clear thinking men and women whose aim was to improve the use of companies' most valuable asset — their people. We believed and, of course, still do that women's talents are just as important to the advancement of an organisation as men's! That is why I always sought to have men on the Executive as well as women, not only Peter Mulcahy-Morgan, but Norman Boakes — a most supportive marketing man — Roy Fielder of BP, Peter Wells of Shell and Nick Perry of IBM all concerned with Personnel Development. Each of them made valuable contributions to WIM's advancement. Their mere presence told the world that we were not a bunch of tiresome feminists, but a group of thoroughly professional people who had an important and valuable message to give.

Particularly in the early days companies, with a few marked exceptions, did not view what we were doing as very important and women themselves did not feel able to spend money on an organisation which, although carrying the promise of career development, could not at that stage show precise results. By which I mean no-one could say, "Because I belonged to WIM, I got a better job". The whole business of career development doesn't work like that and while WIM had to grow and gain its status, women also had to learn that career advancement is achieved by spreading their range of contacts, getting exposure and working with other professionals, outside as well as inside, their companies.

This has required a big change of approach for most women, psychologically as well as practically, because the whole feminine pattern up to the 1960's and 1970's was different. Women at home are often in a family enclave, women at work frequently as secretaries relate to one person, their boss — usually a man. Even heads of departments in hierarchical organisations are not always encouraged to cross fertilise with other departments, but have to report exclusively to their boss. So to open up contact with others on the basis of equality had been a male privilege and not a feminine practice. For decades men have realised the value of mingling with like minds. The great Political Clubs in Pall Mall in London, the Professional and Scientific Institutes, the Chambers of Commerce and Rotary Clubs, all over the country whatever their specific purposes, gave men the chance of mixing with others, learning from each other and acquiring status and confidence. The problem for women was that these bodies were exclusively male — understandably in the early days, because there were few, if any, women able to participate and, of course, habit knits into prejudice and assumes the garb of justified privilege.

As WIM's reputation grew and companies saw more clearly what we were about, they were happy to be identified with our aims and provided sponsorship both in the form of money and facilities for events. A most important contribution for which we are very grateful.

As time went on WIM became more formalised — subscriptions were charged and I was gradually released from the heavy burden which I had assumed in setting up the group, as steadily members of the Executive Committee took on more.

"Fact Sheets on Career Building"

A notable member of the Committee for 12 years was Julia Little, a Cambridge graduate; she had worked in Personnel Management in industry and then became a Careers Advisor for London University. Up to and after her marriage and birth of her two daughters, Julia and I worked together very closely. She not only presented many sessions on the different courses that I put on, but also gave unstintingly of her time to WIM. Perhaps her major contribution to the Group was the creation of a series of Fact Sheets, which set out a wide range of career opportunities, where and how the relevant training required to pursue those careers could be obtained, together with a mass of valuable reference information important for anyone wanting to enlarge their skills, change jobs or seek advancement.

It was a monumental task made possible only because of Julia's quick perceptive mind which produced results on paper while most people would still be thinking about them.

In her contacts with people, and particularly in a workshop situation, Julia has a splendid capacity for gaining and giving sympathy. A pocket sized lady, she projects a great deal of those essential management qualities, energy and vigour, and her laugh is unforgettable. She never makes her considerable expertise appear intimidating, so people are inspired to think more positively about themselves.

In addition to working together on courses, Julia and I wrote a book, *The Successful Secretary*, the theme of which was not technical, but personal skills. It stresses the organisational and thinking techniques required to develop fully the secretary's role, but even more important, it enlarges on the personal, communication, and social skills which are the elements which convert a shorthand typist into a true assistant — things which we both feel very strongly about.

Julia and I enjoy working together, and because she has moved to the country and her family are now her major pre-occupation, I greatly miss the lively exchanges we used to have, not always in total agreement, but always acting as a catalyst one with another.

Weekend Events

Two weekend Conferences which WIM organised opened up new dimensions for the Group. The first one called, "The Woman Manager — Towards the 21st Century", was held at Henley and planned by Lady Lindsay. Peggy Lindsay was a member of the Henley Management College staff and had been on the WIM Executive for a few years before 1978 when the Conference took place. 35 delegates participated, mostly men and women in senior positions responsible for personnel development in their organisations. The theme of the Conference was how to get more women into decision making roles. Education, employment policies in large and small organisations, Trade Union influence and the effect of social and family life, were all discussed. It generated many useful ideas and much enthusiasm.

The second major Conference was on "Microprocessors and their Impact". Peggy Lindsay was again responsible for the organisation of the programme, the event taking place in 1980 at Ashridge Management College. Eminent speakers in the field of modern technology contributed to the programme, which aimed at making the Microprocessor more understandable to the layman and encouraging people, particularly women, to acquire confidence in the area of the computer so becoming responsible participants, not hesitant observers.

These activities increased the reputation and credibility of WIM, which became an information resource about women's affairs for the Press and any other body seeking data on female managers and women' development.

WIM Newsletter

Every year I had compiled a report initially on the joint achievements of WIM and EM Courses, the title under which I ran my Training Consultancy. In 1979 there was a change, the formal link between the two bodies virtually ceased and after 1982 the Annual Report gave way to WIM Newsletter, which appeared three times a year. This publication appears regularly and not only tells about WIM's activities, but reports changes in the business and professional world which affect women — promotions — profiles of significant personalities — changes in legislation etc. It has a wide readership and forms a national and international link between WIM members.

Eventually in 1985, 16 years after its inception, I retired from the Chairmanship of WIM and became its President. This meant that the active organisation of the group was taken over by a new Chairman, and a changed Executive Committee.

We had come a long way in 16 years, but I felt the time had arrived for me to step down and hand over the planning *and* excitement to younger people. My feelings at this moment were a mixture of relief, regret and pride.

Valerie Boakes became the new Chairman. She had been a member of the Committee as early as 1971. In the intervening 14 years, Valerie with great enthusiasm and determination had worked at her own career, steadily climbing the ladder. In 1971 she was a Market Analyst, with a Corporate organisation dealing with agriculture. Moving through the position of Buyer to a multi- national food manufacturing firm, she is now a Director of one of the largest UK commodity merchants. Taking courses, learning new skills, winning a Churchill Fellowship and supporting her husband, Norman, particularly during the year he was Chairman of the Institute of Marketing. Valerie has never stopped reaching forward and like all the WIM Executive finds time to help others who are aiming for an upward career path.

I greatly enjoy both Valerie and Norman's company. They make a splendid partnership, supportive not only to each other, but far beyond that. For me their loyalty continues to be a cherished experience.

Although not now directly concerned with the running of WIM, I am still involved and enormously interested. I attend Executive Lunches, promote the Group and encourage others to join, because of the benefits I know they will gain. As I look back, I try to make an assessment of WIM's achievement. Of course, it is not as great as one would have hoped. Nevertheless, it has I feel sure acted as an agent of change, persuading companies to consider the women in their organisation more positively — and also encouraging women themselves to gain a greater sense of self-worth and be prepared to step a little more certainly and professionally into the remaining years of this century.

Although many of the splendid people who helped to build up WIM — gave time, ideas and used their influence to further the Group — have not been mentioned individually, the success of WIM is a testimony of their endeavour. It was, and indeed continues to be, a corporate effort.

As the first support group of its kind in the UK, there is no doubt that it has helped many women to view themselves more determinedly and gave them courage, perhaps at moments of difficulty, to press forwards when they might have given up. I believe also that it has contributed towards improving the general climate which is making possible women's further progress.

Home Affairs

Personal and domestic relationships changed continually in the early 70's. I have the delightful responsibility of being godmother to Caroline, the oldest daughter of April, my very dear friend from Atkinsons days. April has not been very fortunate in her married life, but her three children, all as handsome as April herself, are a great source of joy to her. The family lived in Devon, but it was difficult there to find the kind of training and experience which Caroline needed when she left school.

So we all decided that Caroline should come and live with me for a year and take a secretarial course at the local Technical College with the hope that it would launch her into her career. Caroline's basic education had not been of the best kind and so the start of her course was not easy. But Caroline was always a hard worker and gradually built up her speeds and skills.

It was a joy for me to have her. She has a sweet character and has a rare serenity and gentleness. Soon after she came, Mrs Morter, who had been with me for eighteen years, came to suffer very badly from arthritis. She felt she could not carry on. She was very sad to leave and for me to part with her, but I realised she could not keep going, so she left. The problem was then what to do about caring for the house? I was very busy with courses; Caroline was always ready to help, but that was obviously not a complete solution.

Fortunately, a little friend of Caroline's, Jess, who was going to train as a nurse, found she had to wait for several months before being admitted to her hospital. We agreed she should come and do her best with the housekeeping. Her best turned out to be very good, but it was a hilarious period. Jess, very small in stature but very vigorous, was a delightful chatterbox. She was a splendid companion for Caroline, but to see her trailing off to do the shopping in the gypsy skirts and print blouses of the time was comical. A sort of waif figure playing a grown-up housekeeper. But it worked. Diligently she would seek out the best bargains in the shops and triumphantly come home with her 3p-off coupons. At home she cooked and scrubbed with great zest and we managed splendidly. I loved the gorgeous alfresco kind of existence and entered into these young people's aspirations with great interest.

Of course, there were lots of phone calls and sorties with, to me, strange looking young men, some with bushy hair; others so lean and loose limbed that they looked and, I thought, spoke like "Goofy".

I remember one evening coming home and finding a whole gang of them sitting on the floor in the kitchen drinking coffee. They must have found me very staid, but they were always polite and no trouble whatsoever.

In between times Caroline would go off to her room to work at her desk. Unfortunately, she had acquired the habit of heavy smoking, and it was not until she left that I realised that as well as all the little silver stars she had scattered over the walls and ceilings of her room, above her desk was a thick layer of yellow tobacco smoke stain! I loved that nine months — I just hope it helped them and that they didn't find me too boring.

The Office

Meanwhile I had acquired support in the office — the increasing number of courses required thorough administrative back up. Pat Wellingham was early on the scene, a most supportive and happy person whose Irish streak enabled her to see the comical side of a lot that we were doing. She was an efficient and quick worker, tackling typing, filing and telephone work with a businesslike zest. Nothing was too much trouble and she entered into what I was doing with interest.

She soon needed further help — in Januuary 1971 Brenda Edwards arrived. Sixteen years later Brenda is still with me coping with apparent calmness with the worst excesses of my imagination. I am sure that there isn't anyone who has worked closely with me who has not groaned inwardly, at least, at the sound of the dreaded phrase, "I've got an idea!" Now they know me well enough to do it outwardly!

Brenda's early training in the Civil Service and her own meticulous approach to work has played a tremendously important part in the development of EM Courses. Orderly, perceptive and tenacious, Brenda sees jobs through to the very end, picking up error, but also by grasping very intuitively what I am trying to do, she gives ideas and words the shape which conveys their true meaning. The skill with which a report, for example, is laid out and presented, makes a substantial contribution to its ultimate readability and acceptance. Brenda's work in all these areas is superb.

Others joined the team, there were a few short term ladies, one or two of whom we labelled, "The impossibles", who had few skills and no motivation. These we sped on their way as soon as possible. The other members of the team, who have been with me anything from 8–12 years, Barbara, Hilary and Ann, not only do excellent jobs at their desks, but are known to all our contacts. They fulfil a very important PR role. They early developed special techniques, which fit together with a splendid team spirit. I am very grateful for the support I receive, framed in an atmosphere of a great deal of good humour and fun.

Of course there are tension points — irritating occurrences which give rise to differences of opinion and momentarily tempers may flash, but the overall objective of running the consultancy as professionally as possible, is never lost sight of. People arrive in the morning keen to get on with the day's tasks and, because it is such a small operation there has to be work swapping and sharing, which no-one gets up tight about.

I know I can go to Barbara and get an answer quickly about the finance angle and by using her prodigious memory, names and events will be recalled from years gone by. Hilary now in full charge of our WP will get out repeated drafts and manage endless alterations without a wry word. Ann, who flanks me, but also acts in her own right as a trainer on courses, has the outgoing personality and superb communication skills to which others respond so warmly.

We try to practise what we preach on the courses, real efficiency and supportive team work. It works. Over the years, although small in size, EM Courses is recognised as an influential training group with a very high reputation — we work for more than a hundred of the leading companies and organisations in the UK and overseas, advising on staff matters and career building as well as running courses.

As a training colleague from 1972–1978, I had the joy of working with Leonie Alexander, an Australian who was an excellent teacher, very creative and enormously loyal. We ran innumerable courses together and, like Ann, our different personalitites helped to draw out of the course members different responses. Leonie had a crisp down-to-earth efficiency which, by example, set standards for others to work to. Dark hair, dark eyes, a trim physique, always beautifully groomed, she had a great influence on delegates, whether senior men or hesitant junior women.

On one occasion, running a "handle your secretary better" workshop in the Midlands, which was attended by about 60 pretty tough engineers in a car factory, her no-nonsense but smiling approach checked any tendency to trivialise the occasion. Pointless, sexy cracks never occurred, because neither of us considered the possibility of them doing so. Unfortunately Leonie had to return to Australia to care for her elderly parents, but she is happily running a most successful Training Consultancy in Sydney and Melbourne — she tells me, much on the same lines as we established.

Leonie's avid interest in the threatre, in architecture and the culture of Europe, meant that when I went to the Cotswolds for a weekend she would have been to Moscow and back! Australia is an awfully long way on the other side of the world. Because we are great friends as well as ex business colleagues, we both feel this.

When Leonie left, her training role was taken over by Jean- Margaret Scrimshaw, with whom I had worked on one of the Training Boards. Jean-Margaret's great strengths were her knowledge of industrial legislation, which was at that time increasing rapidly and which we included in our programmes. Also using her long experience, Jean-Margaret was very adept at devising case studies drawn from real life, which gave the practical aspects of the courses great variety.

I was, however, moving into a less technical area of training and concentrating on the personal development and human aspects of people management which took me overseas. So Jean-Margaret returned to personnel work where her precision and logical thinking were well placed.

While many of the happenings in an office may appear common place, I have taken the trouble to record some of them, because they are nevertheless the essential ingredients in the structure of any venture.

The day-to-day events, the care and precision with which systems are observed and where necessary changed, the trivial comments which either irritate or spur people on, the kindly or annoying habits we cultivate, are the grains of sand which will eventually turn into the castle, if we know how to handle them.

Successful undertakings never depend exclusively on top level planning. In addition, they always require the efficient and enthusiastic carrying out of small, repetitive, often boring tasks which have to fit in to the whole. Once complacency or "corner cutting" takes place, there is always eventually disaster. Everyone in the team has to recognise this.

When thinking of these matters, I always remember Field Marshal Lord Slim's book, *Defeat into Victory*. It is full of good things for anyone, not just soldiers, who wishes to achieve. His foundations of morale, for example, are a masterpiece. But I like also the simple example which he quotes of the clock. Paraphrasing — he says — "The mainspring of the clock may be compared to the Top Boy — but there are dozens of other springs and wheels, large and small, which make up the whole. Remove one of the smallest wheels — and what happens?" Everyone *is* important.

Personal Back-Up

It is said that behind every successful man there is a supportive wife. Well, I cannot have a wife, but I have been fortunate enough to have one or two most valuable support people who have made it possible for me to develop my working life to the level it has attained, because of their care, interest and attention. Working as intensively as I tend to do, personal back-up is essential.

When little Jess tripped on her way, a new very important person joined me. Mrs Staples arrived in the autumn of 1972 and quickly adapted to the quite complex routine which confronted her. An office in a house adds a particular dimension to a domestic job, as there are always people coming and going. There is also a great deal of responsibility attached to running other people's homes. As anyone knows who has had even a tiny, little property, there is always something to attend to with the fabric of a house — a tile off the roof, a leaking pipe, etc, etc. Then, in my case, I was travelling all the time which meant that things had to be carefully monitored in my absence — yet another responsibility.

Over the years, Mrs Staples and I have become firm friends — an enormous trust and affection has grown up between us. She knows my needs and makes absolutely sure that they are met — she has, for example, taken on the charge of my clothes, so that with her careful packing I take off on trips, laundered and ready for any contingency. It isn't just a case of doing what I ask her, she anticipates, and that gives me a wonderfully secure feeling.

We have very similar tastes, so theatre visits and weekend breaks can be shared very happily. I am a solitary with no relations, though never, because of my wide circle of friends, alone. Mrs Staples has two sons and lovely grand children, but she makes sure they have independent lives, so we find we can share our leisure time with great satisfaction and pleasure.

To have someone backing you, who is completely loyal, is invaluable. Also because of the excellent business experience Mrs Staples had in the highly responsible administration jobs she did before she decided to turn her back on the city, she manages the service staff who come to the house, with great competence and courtesy. Paying household accounts, organising the domestic diary and reminding me of the thousand and one tasks which make up a busy life, from remembering a birthday to making a social appointment. All these things take loads off my shoulders and leave me free to do the wide range of work I have become involved with. As time has gone on, Mrs Staples' role has changed. She is less of a doer — more a supervisor; indeed I think of her as my domestic manager, so trust is high on my credit list, because the role calls for a special kind of confidentiality.

I have referred on more than one occasion to the heavy demands, which an energetic, quick thinking character such as I think I am, make on others. So I am mindful that uninterrupted tranquility will never be the pattern of our lives! This perhaps allows no boredom to creep in, but it can be tiring. Individually pacing ourselves to suit our personalities is one of the areas that needs to be watched with care. Just as some men are indebted and grateful to their wives, I feel the same with Mrs Staples. I hope I express those feelings adequately.

Preparation for the States

At the end of 1971 I was running a seminar when, through the office of the British Association of University Women, a woman from America asked to see me — and came and sat in at the course. At the end of it, to my great surprise and pleasure, Betty Ohrt asked me if I would be prepared to make a similar presentation in the East Washington State College in Spokane where she worked as Dean of Women. Of course I was tremendously interested, as I had long wanted to go to the States.

Betty was most enthusiastic and outlined the sort of thing she wanted me to do. I said I would be delighted to run some seminars for her, but I raised doubts as to whether my material would be suitable in America. I said that I knew my British audiences, but I felt that people might want very different things in the States and I added, "They might not like me and my English accent". Betty pooh-poohed all these doubts and convinced me that it would be fine. She returned to the States to get organised. I thought it was very courageous of her to take me so much on trust. By Christmas plans were taking shape — the topics and format of the proposed courses had been decided and I then submitted detailed programmes. I was very excited.

I present a course with a visual aid to a group of secretaries

*eter Mulcahy-Morgan attended a course we presented on the New Office
Technology in September 1980*

Sir Monty Finniston (centre) was the guest speaker at a Women in Management AGM. He is seen here with several Executive Committee members

The staff gather together to greet Leonie Alexander (right) visiting from Australia. Back row: Mrs. Staples, Brenda and Barbara , Hilary next to Leonie

Chapter Nine

Overseas Work with Travel and Ongoing UK Assignments

I go to America

I set off for the States in March 1972. I was really excited to be going. I had always felt that there was a freedom and openness in America which was a major factor in the innovative way that things are achieved there and I wanted to see for myself. Also the grandeur of the scenery I knew would delight me.

The programme that I had planned was quite concentrated. I flew to New York, where Ambrose Addis, my old Chairman from Atkinsons, with his gentle little wife, met me. They had been in North America, first in Canada and then in the States, for more than twelve years. They had not lost their English accents and ways, but they had adapted in a measure to American manners and both their daughters had married Americans.

Ambrose commuted daily to the Lever Office in New York from Darien, a luxury suburb in Connecticut. Summers were spent in a spacious, sunny house high on a peninsula at Cape Cod, which I visited a few years later. They entertained me charmingly, introducing me to a number of their friends. The weekend was a splendid start to my tour.

I had introductions to many people, among them a Marketing Chief at Nestle. The Company have an office not far from New York, so it happened that this was my first business appointment of the trip. A slightly self-satisfied person, this quite senior ex-Executive listened to what I had to say, but I perceived at once that he had little comprehension of what I was about. Women in Management? – he looked puzzled and unbelieving.

I learned that there was not a single woman at true Management level in the Company. I had to remember that it is a Swiss based organisation. He was very pleased to show me round the beautifully appointed offices. When it came to midday, he arranged for me to go to lunch with his PA and two other secretaries. I could see that he was not being, in his terms, rude, but just responding in his accustomed manner. He was not in the habit of entertaining senior women executives, so he just concluded that girls would want to lunch with girls – levels of interest did not enter into it. In spite of many women in the States having gone much further than a lot of women in England, I found nevertheless, that a strong streak of chauvinism existed, which I encountered from time to time.

For example there was the incident I learned about from a distinguished German woman scientist, who, when I met her the following week in Washington, was paying a repeat visit to the States. On her first visit, as an acknowledged authority in her field, she had been asked to address a prestigious Scientific Institute. She arrived at the marble portals and was told by the Commissionaire that this was not the ladies' entrance and that she should go to another door. Women were not normally permitted into the premises. She toiled round to the back of the building and after climbing over some garbage cans found her way through a narrow little door into the building. There was no apology, no explanation; she gave her talk and departed as she had come.

I am not a vindictive feminist, but my response to that behaviour would have been pretty savage and unless some really profound apology had been offered, I am quite sure I would not have delivered the lecture!

Perhaps things fifteen years later have altered. I was enormously impressed with some of the American women's achievements, and loved meeting and talking to them because they were so innovative and full of zest, but there was this strand running through the society which seemed to declare that the lady is not for promoting as a personality in her own right, but for pampering as a decorative and valuable extension of the Great Man.

There seemed several distinct streams in the society. The really strong minded successful business women who, either on her own or in a partnership with her equally successful husband, held top level jobs or ran her own business. Then there was the other type of woman who, sometimes with money of her own, had a lot of behind-scenes power or sometimes the devoted home figure with little external influence. These two last types, whatever their personal circumstances, were not individual personalities, they were in reality extensions of the Dominant Male. The DM, as I came to call him is, I believe, a direct descendent of the gun toting Wild West pioneer.

The low numbers of women in the Senate and the House of Representatives and, at that time the low number of female students at the Harvard Business School, were examples of the workings of the anti-female league. Of course the pattern exists here in the UK, but the Queen, Margaret Thatcher and some of our leading business women have undoubtedly changed the climate in recent years.

I am often asked, is it better or worse for women wishing to forge ahead in America or England? I do not think I can answer that question accurately. America is such a large country with widely differing cultures, so what goes in New York or Los Angeles can be totally different in Kentucky. There are, of course, enclaves in the UK also of atrocious backward anti-feminism. The worst, without doubt, is the University world, where the ranks of long established male academics are closed firmly against women — the City is changing a little — medicine also, but not I believe proportionately to the female talent which exists. How this compares with the States it is very difficult to judge.

I think there is so much which is forward looking and creative in the States, that perhaps the domineering anti-feminist characters whom I met took me by surprise. It was particularly apparent when some deeply prejudiced comment would come from a man who had shown meticulous courtesy.

Some of the "brawn is strength" brigade, who had not really moved forward in their attitude to women since the last century, I thought held the reins of power very firmly in their hands.

A close English friend of mine, Valerie Hammond, has also travelled in the States and met many American women in her capacity of Director in charge of Research at the Ashridge Management College. She notes that there is a higher proportion of women managers in the States, but there are very few women Chief Executives in top positions in major companies. She also thinks that American women pay a high price for success in terms of commitment, lack of family life, divorce, etc, but a similar price is also paid by men.

Travelling in the States

I loved Boston, the old buildings, the sea front and the traditional atmosphere were just what I had expected. In close-by Cambridge there is the renowned Harvard Business School where I was invited to speak to the 80 women students, two of whom were from England. The proportion of men to women students was 800 to 80. These purposeful women were very bright and very determined to make their mark. It was than that I met Ann Wohl who, when she left Harvard and went to the University of Colorado some two years later, asked me to do seminars for her.

From Boston I went to Northampton and visited Smith College, the prestigious women's college set in a lovely campus with many trees and a lake. I was armed with an introduction to the President of the College from Mrs. Boyd, my Scottish friend, an early alumnus. It is a delightful place, not only attractive to look at but beautifully organised and with a high academic record.

I stayed several days — I met many of the girls — I made a presentation about women's education and development in England, but the most fascinating part of the visit were the informal chats and talks I had with the girls over dinner or drinking coffee in the common room. I made several friends among these intelligent and entertaining young women, whose questioning attitude I was sure would open up their careers in a most positive way. I kept in touch with them and their successes in marketing, publishing and journalism proved this prediction correct.

Washington was the next point on my itinerary. I stayed in a little Quaker establishment which was very quiet and staid, but most comfortable in spite of the fact that no meals were served.

Washington is a very impressive city dominated by the White House on Capitol Hill. I went round the President's apartments, visited the museums where there are marvellous collections of Impressionist paintings. I also went to see Mount Vernon and the Tomb of the Unknown Warrior. The latter is approached by a long series of shallow steps. Unfortunately the weather had turned bitterly cold, snow had fallen over night and the ice was thick on the ground and on the trees. It looked beautiful, but as so often occurs at impressive and solemn moments, something ridiculous happens which stays in one's mind, perhaps more vividly than the thing one really came to see.

Such was the incident of the rotund lady who, having climbed to the top of the steps to see the Tomb, I encountered on her way down. Regrettably she slipped on the ice and because she was short and absolutely spherical, she could not find her footing on the ice and was unable to stand up. She rolled round and round and from side to side like one of those Russian dolls and to my shame I could not help laughing, though not openly. She struggled fruitlessly, looking more ridiculous at every turn. Then fortunately too very tall strong young men appeared and picked her up bodily and stood her down on her feet like a puppet. Comical events when recounted lose most of their savour — it requires a Chaplin to bring them to life — but I found this so very funny.

After Washington DC I headed for Spokane in Washington State some 4000 miles across country. I have flown back and forth across the States many times since, but these flights never lose their magic for me. Long interminable flat lands or the panoramic view of the Great Lakes — on other occasions crossing the Northern Ice Cap and coming across mile after mile of desolate snow covered wilderness, but most impressive of all are the mountain ranges. They are glorious — perpetually snow capped, with great ravines and crevasses, the mountains themselves are jagged and awe inspiring or cone shaped with crater tops, perhaps extinct, perhaps waiting to leap into life. It is always a wonderful experience.

Betty Ohrt met me in Spokane and I stayed with her. There were to be three different presentations. I participated with other speakers on two courses and presented one of my own — under the title "Career Women and Managing". Until I had completed these different exercises, I felt I could not be sure of Betty Ohrt's conviction that I would "go down" with Americans. I need not have worried — my technique worked. On the shared course I was voted the best speaker and on my solo effort there was a really great response. There were questions and comments and an enormous amount of enthusiasm. Before the 2- day seminar was finished, people were talking about my returning to make further presentations. It was highly satisfactory.

I was tremendously grateful to Betty for having backed her judgement of me. She had, I learned later, staked a good deal with the College Management by inviting me to come.

I was concerned whether my idiom, my method of presentation and the case studies I had chosen to get delegates to work through would be appropriate. There was also for me another major difficulty. In England I never had more than 15/16 people attend the courses and here I was addressing sometimes 25, sometimes 50 people. Apprehensive to begin with at this added hazard, I found that the delegates were so enthusiastic, so full of drive and wanting to learn and ask questions, they took no notice of the numbers. If they couldn't see me easily from one position, they got up and moved their chairs to get a better view from a different spot. It was delightful. American audiences are so much less inhibited and want to share ideas. Also, they enter so readily into what is being presented that the fear of looking silly, which so often worries British people, does not concern them at all. The questions and comments come tumbling out and everyone benefits.

The suggestion that I should return to the States was taken up very strongly and I returned to do an ever increasing number of workshops and courses all over the country annually until 1981. I always went back to Spokane, not always under the banner of East Washington State College. Through the skill and perception of a most charming and positive woman, Gladys Cottle, who is a Federal Government Officer, I did several courses for Federal Government employees in Spokane and also in Washington and Minneapolis.

I also went to many colleges and commercial companies. Frequently events were organised by different people who, having attended one of my courses, recommended me to do another one for another group. So I worked at New York University, William and Mary College, Williamsburg, University of Colorado, University of California, Los Angeles, University of Washington, Seattle, and innumerable one and two-day workshops for companies such as IBM and Lockheed. It was very stimulating and I found myself, with the help of such able women as Gladys and Ann Wohl, evolving new titles for the seminars and adding different modules to meet the demands of local audiences.

One very popular course was called "Climbing the Management Ladder – a People Approach"; another was "Executive Women's Workshop". These courses would be attended by some men and many women, perhaps running, for example, their own real estate or publicity businesses or employees of companies such as Samsonite Luggage, Bell Telephones or Public Service employees from Electricity and Water Authorities, or the Department for Indian Affairs. From the last organisation came a most interesting man, a Navaho Indian, small and compact with a degree in Music, who had come to vet the course to see whether a similar exercise could be set up exclusively for the Indian community. He had very considerable powers of concentration and a shrewd penetrating stare, which allowed little to go unobserved.

The delegates varied tremendously; many degree people with clear sharp minds, others with less formal education, but widely experienced, who absorbed the Management courses with great perception. As I went back year after year I saw many delegates from previous sessions, some just to meet socially, others to attend another, perhaps a more advanced course. For example, from being on "The Secretary Update" workshop, say in 1974, they would return having been promoted to Administrative Assistant or Office Manager to join the "Climbing the Management Ladder" seminar in 1977. The appreciation these people, who really were developing, showed was most rewarding.

The style of many of the women was outstanding: some were well groomed wearing simple elegant clothes which had a Katherine Hepburn look. Others were almost frumpy little characters with laughing puckish personalities, who were enormous fun to be with and who were often very skilled at their work – another type was the very sophisticated be-jewelled ladies invariably with long beautifully manicured red nails. They were a little frightening. The majority, however, were solid hard working, well motivated women who had set themselves goals which they were determined to meet.

A particular woman who came on one of the management seminars was one of the elegant types but instead of having the usual outgoing friendly personality, she was cold and detached. She made some very superior put-down comments to several of the other delegates and was quite plainly not a popular group member. One of the exercises called for some over-night preparation for about six of the delegates. The next morning the presentation started. This lady elected to go last. Everyone else participating had taken a great deal of trouble to put their contributions together very professionally and made a first class impression. The group members applauded very positively.

The superior lady had obviously made no effort at all to prepare carefully, because she thought she could do the exercise, which was not as simple as it looked, off the top of her head. Her presentation was awful and the reception it got, though kindly expressed, was very negative. Fair, very critical comments were made, and of course she was devastated, but more than that she was furious and returned to her place with pink spots on her cheeks and tears of rage in her eyes. At the end of the afternoon I went up to her as gently as I could and asked if she would like to talk anything through with me. She refused bluntly to the point of discourtesy, adding, "If I make mistakes, I must learn to live with them", and swung out of the room.

I learned later that this undoubtedly intelligent and able woman had some six or nine months before been promoted, but had made such a mess of the people management side of the job that the company had had to change her duties — they did not take her rank away from her, but no longer was she given staff control. Her supervisor had sent her on the course with hope that she could pick up a little on Human Relations techniques — she obviously hadn't got the message.

It was a clear example of the principle, "If I can perceive it, I can do it". Her enormous arrogance made it impossible for her to see herself as she came over to others. She was totally blocking her own progress.

American Friends

Some of the social contacts which I made right across the country sometimes started through people being course members, others through introductions. I have come to regard one or two of them as some of my closest friends who are enormously significant to me, although we see each other so infrequently.

Very special people for me are Gladys Laston from California and Betty Jay from Spokane. They are so hospitable, warm hearted and generous and always interested in everything I do. More than that, each in their own style has wide interests and a cultivated way of thinking which makes them refreshing and inspiring people to be with. Despite the thousands of miles which divide us, their friendship and support somehow annihilates the distance, and even if I do not write as often as I intend to do, I know the friendship and the warmth is there and it is a great joy to me. This is what I believe friendship is about.

Gladys has taken me about and introduced me to so many of the wonderful places along or near the Californian coast. Yosemite National Park with its five waterfalls is truly inspiring, as is the giant Redwood Forest. The old Mission Stations down the Coast Road, Highway 101, between San Francisco and Los Angeles are fascinating examples of early Spanish/American architecture and represent a most intriguing slice of American history, as does Sutter Creek where the Gold Rush started. These are just a few of the interesting and beautiful places I have visited with Gladys, so knowledgeable about the history of her country and a superb driver!

I have also seen much of Washington State, Idaho and Montana with Betty Jay, and have been welcomed into her family so that I feel like a near relative. I shall always remember the care and concern which Betty extended to me when, on one occasion, I arrived almost voiceless with a roaring temperature. Within minutes I was between cool sheets, and warm drinks and antibiotics were summoned as from nowhere. It was heaven.

Another member of the self-appointed "Teach Eleanor about America" syndicate was my delightful friend Ann Wohl. After Harvard, she had become the Head of the Continuing Education Department of Colorado University. It is quite common for American Universities to fulfill the function, which would be undertaken by Polytechnics and evening Institutes in the UK, of presenting short courses on a variety of topics, some of which can gain credits for any degree course which is being followed.

Ann has two lovely sons, Charles and Richard, whom I had seen grow up during my visits to the States from little boys, to six feet two or three splendid young men. From the bottom of Ann's garden we could see the foothills of the Rockies, but we went much further than Ann's backyard — to use the American term. We took day or weekend trips to the towering peaks of the Rockies in such areas as Estes Park and the ski-runs of Vale. Or we would investigate old mining villages, such as Leadville or Center City, which looked like ancient filmsets with wooden side walks and slatted swing doors leading into the saloons, all of which have been carefully preserved.

But undoubtedly one of my greatest thrills was out visit to the Grand Canyon, the one mile deep — ten mile wide gorge, cut deep by the mighty Colorado River. It is breathtaking in its grandeur. We arrived after dark in a mini-blizzard, snow hurtling down and the temperature well below zero. Ice had formed on the roads and we actually slithered into our parking space and were very glad to have a warm dinner and a night's rest in the lodge. I had a horrid fear that the snow would continue and that we would see nothing of the wonderful spectacle I had so long wanted to witness.

My fears were groundless — the next morning radiant, golden- pink sunshine filled the clear blue sky and made every snow- tipped gnarled tree and ledge of rock, glitter. I was entranced and I feel I must quote a sentence from a well-known description of the Canyon.

"Once you are exposed to its stunning beauty and mysterious power, you will never be quite the same again — to your advantage." This is absolutely true.

Also very exciting in our Arizona trip was seeing the ancient cliff dwellings in the Canyon de Chelly. It is not so big nor as spectacular as the Grand Canyon, but it is still tremendously impressive. 1200 years ago tribes of early people lived in little dwellings tunnelled out of the ochre coloured sandstone hundreds of feet below the upper edge of the gorge. The shape of their dwellings and some evidence of their way of life have been discovered and one has the feeling of going back in time in a rather mysterious way.

Two other dear friends, Margaret Nicholls and Andy Harlan, live in a dear little mobile home on the very edge of Trout Creek in the heart of Montana. I've stayed there and been surrounded by the mountains, which rise fold on fold to the horizon — Montana is indeed 'wide sky country'. Andy makes dozens of bird houses to assist in the preservation of the glorious mountain bluebirds. He also helps to teach illiterate children round about. To be with them both, is to enter a tiny, safe world where things are good. This warm hospitality has come to me from so many Americans, for example, Bob Clifford and his family in Williamsburg, who loves his jokes about 'getting rid of the British'!

So from Coast to Coast there is always a welcome. Of course one will never see half the beauties of the fabulous North American Continent, but I hope I may return to re-visit some favourite places and investigate some new ones. There is no doubt that the size and grandeur of natural things give one a better perspective of one's own insignificance. It is so difficult for us to grasp the paradox that human beings are all-important, and yet of little importance. It is vital that everything I do is done to the very best of my ability, but if I disappeared tonight? — such thoughts are a salutary cure for pride and conceit.

It is an all too frequent custom for Europeans to take on a slightly superior attitude towards Americans. I resent this very strongly. Americans are enthusiastic collectively, perhaps to the point of being a bit overwhelming at times — they do chase after, sometimes without due consideration, new ideas whether they are slightly cranky religions or health cult, but they are warm, hospitable and generous and have vigour and energy.

I personally have learned a great deal in the States and every time I go am invigorated by the willingness to discuss, investigate and experiment. To aim high and to possess good things are considered worthwhile goal across the Atlantic. This raises people's hopes and, most important, the expectations of themselves. Sometimes, unfortunately, this turns int sordid money grubbing, but that goes on in Europe too, perhaps without the zest which somehow gives others a stimulus.

Ireland

Two years after I started visiting the States, I went to Ireland for the first time and started a trend of two or three visits a year, which has continued until today. My Irish visits have been most happy and satisfying experiences. The earliest courses I presented there were for the Guinness Company, but I have not only worked with Guinness, but also with the Irish Management Institute and a number of other companies.

The reputation of Guinness, established in 1759, is tremendous. It is not, I think, fully appreciated in Britain the dominant position that this fine old company has filled in the economic and community life of Ireland and its influence has spread far beyond Dublin — to Britain — Nigeria, and elsewhere. These exports are of great significance and represent an important trade factor in each country, more influential perhaps than the actual size in financial terms of the company itself. I think this is due to the fact that a tremendous tradition has been built round the organisation, partly because they make a unique product to the highest possible standards, but also because of the deep respect and involvement which the Iveagh, the Guinness family, *and* the company have always shown to the community wherever they have traded.

Financing the Opera at the Wexford Festival — organising study grants and mathematical scholarships in the UK, as well as Ireland are just a few of the splendid community activities which owe their existence to the family and the company.

It is this most honourable and sharing reputation which makes the recent cloud which hangs over the Company all the more unacceptable. Whatever the outcome, wherever the blame for this situation, to talk about cheating and thieving in the same breath as the activities which have been the Company's lifestyle ever since it was founded, it intolerable. Integrity and fair trading has been its hallmark.

In an age where high endeavour and razor sharp efficiency are essential for survival, there is no room for complacency or resting on past successes — so change had to come to the Company, but it is to be deeply regretted that it took the form that it did.

Perhaps revulsion against disreputable practices, which are all too common today, may be so strong as to result in the re-establishment of better standards everywhere, so it is hoped that good will emerge from this unpleasant affair.

I did many different courses at Guinness for secretaries, office supervisors and managers. The outstanding aspect for me was the quality of the women staff. Highly efficient with a most loyal and supportive attitude to the Company, they are in addition, probably the most attractive and stylish group of women that I address anywhere in the world. They have for the most part a quiet smiling manner, linked with a sharp wit which is an enchanting combination. I find myself instantly drawn to them. I fear, however, their gentle, courteous approach, derived from the convent education most of them receive, has a negative side. It results in their being too often trapped by the stereotyped conduct which society has created for them. Compliant rather than independent, prepared to defer rather than to challenge — they are only now beginning to perceive their real worth and act courageously, sometimes in conflict with long tradition. They are starting to participate fully at the levels they are more than capable of achieving.

This is not easy, because there are quite a lot of DMs around, some of whom simply do not measure up intellectually or in terms of personality with the sheer quality of the women. I have to say that Guinness and most of the other Irish companies do not use this resource very well.

Happily, however, things are changing, even if slowly, and on many of the workshops which I hold at the Irish Management Institute I now encounter really able, well qualified women, managers in Banks, Insurance and Public Companies, as well as determined, creative women running their own businesses.

The very uncertain state of the economy in Ireland does not make Irish women's growing desire for progress any easier. The notion that every Manager's job held by a woman deprives a man of a chance, is still very commonly held, and in a small country of four million people where more than one million are jammed into Dublin, it is difficult to avoid this thinking.

As wherever else I have travelled, Irish people have generously offered me their hospitality and friendship. Noirin Slattery of IMI, one of the shrewdest politically clever people I know, is great fun to be with, whether at an Art Exhibition, the Gate Theatre or a celebration James Joyce evening.

I have made a number of women friends whom I see whenever I am in Dublin. I have also toured different parts of Ireland with several of them. A glorious country just as beautiful as legend and song describes, it has a fragile, ever changing beauty which is most alluring. The Ring of Kerry — the Wicklow Mountains — the cliffs of Moher, giant black granite walls rising 700 feet above the sea crashing at their feet — the curious Burren country, land of limestone slabs which give a moon-like look to the landscape, but made most exciting with tiny orchids and ferns hidden in the crevasses. All these form a wonderful miniature kaleidoscope of soft-edged beauty.

I love the hospitality too — warm and open — high on the list of wonderful hosts are the Turpins, Phyll and Jim and brother Fred, whom love to be with, but there are many others who have attended workshops and who loyally keep in touch.

There is also Mary Parnes who has worked with me as a most effective co-tutor on many courses. She is Scottish, but has lived in Ireland for many years. Her home is always open to me, which is a great pleasure and privilege.

I like the Celtic style — the humour and the escape from too much black and white logic — the gentle responsive 'floating' attitude which settles over things when leisure time has come is rather like the soft beauty of the landscape, nothing harsh and craggy.

All right, not everyone keeps time, and maybe saying harsh things is too often avoided, but as long as behaviour does not descend into mannered insincere charm, there is a pleasant easy-going atmosphere which is very relaxing. I think sometimes that too many hob nail booted 'I'm being frank' statements can make life very dreary.

United Nations Assignments

From 1978 a European dimension to my training activities opened up and I started to present courses to the World Health Organisation in Geneva. Initially they were for secretaries, but gradually they expanded and covered the whole range of staff up to Senior Specialists and Directors.

These seminars were organised by the Staff Development and Training Unit, which for several years was under the able and sympathetic direction of Dr. Bill Barton, aided by his very able Assistant, Bernadette Rivett, then when she went to Manila, Judith Munzinger took over her role.

WHO is a part of the United Nations family, although it has a very separate remit. I was later to work with the United Nations Training Division itself, which co-ordinates training for many United Nations Agencies based in Geneva, such as the International Trade Centre, the International Telecommunications Union and the Committee for Refugees. I also worked with the separate Division which handles training for the International Labour Office.

As is to be expected, these are highly bureaucratic institutions which function on a strictly hierarchical basis. This is necessary to safeguard the vast sums of money which are allocated to the UN by the member states, and to organise the complex tasks that are covered by the various Agencies. The pattern of working is further complicated in that while the separate Agencies report their activities to the United Nations HQ in New York, individually they are directly responsible to the member states, particularly Third World countries, who seek the co-operation of the Agencies to solve their problems. So whether assistance is required to handle a flood of refugees, improve a water supply or establish an injection programme for measles, whatever the technical implications, the appropriate UN Agency has to work in harmony with the wishes of the member state.

This means that progress and achievements are slow in coming, because they have to pass through so many levels. Marvellous projects, therefore, which could bring relief to millions are sometimes on political grounds, delayed endlessly and the frustrations of the HQ's staff mount.

I had to acclimatise myself to this totally different rhythm of working and also to adjust to the multi-national, multi-cultural groups which I encountered. Specialists are recruited from all over the world and the organisations try to ensure that the widest geographical representation is accorded, so that they are truly international. This meant that in a group of twenty delegates I might have twelve nationalities − Korean, French, Italian, Russian, Brazilian. The specialists would all be highly educated, doctors, engineers, economists, agrarians, nutritionists, etc. The support staff, administrators and secretaries would all have two, if not three languages and be skilled at administration. English is obligatory for everyone, so I conducted my courses in English, occasionally pausing to enlarge on a point in French. But I had to be very sure that the meaning I was trying to convey was the one that was being taken. I tried to achieve this by careful and sympathetic feedback and by encouraging and posing questions.

The cultural differences also had to be noted and very genuinely respected. Points of pride or deep seated national prejudices would from time to time emerge. Mostly I got my responses right, because I am genuinely concerned with people, but not always. For example, I would make a brisk, what I hoped was a time saving comment, only to discover that I had deeply offended someone. It was not always east to strike a balance between what I felt needed to be said and what a delegate could take. When I was aware of having made what was felt to be a clumsy remark, I would always make a point of apologising either in front of the group or afterwards one to one. Sometimes I was not conscious of it and this, very rarely, might result in what was to me a totally unexpected and inexplicable outbreak of argument.

In the many years I have organised courses both in the UK and overseas, I can only recall such a happening occurring three or four times. But I always take these events very seriously and examine how my own conduct and attitude might have contributed to the negative outcome. I try to begin at the point that it was I who was responsible − could I have gone a little slower? − consulted a little more? − allowed the group to *do* more and me to talk less? − this is the kind of probing which every conscientious teacher must engage in. But at the end of the day, we have to face the fact that not everyone is going to like us; not everyone will approve our aims and philosophy and one cannot allow a few adverse happenings to destroy one's confidence.

A significant factor which must be taken into account — every trainer has an 'off moment' or day. One of the major factors which produces the 'off' day is fatigue. Whether one is aware of tiredness, mental or physical or not, if it is present it will rob one of the energy and the inner strength, which induces people to listen to what one has to say if it is backed by conviction and power. If not, the delegates lose confidence in the teacher and the critical, even rebellious, attitudes present all the time below the surface will rise up and produce conflict. A mere one or two members only need to adopt this behaviour, and a major disruption can soon follow. The other members of the group perhaps unconsciously respond to the negative vibes which have been released and go where the power is being shown.

This kind of happening is the result of the group dynamics which take place whenever a collection of people gather together. Positive interaction equally can produce splendid results, but if the leader, even momentarily, loses his/her power, negative happenings can be released. It is very important that people who engage in negotiation or the presentation of ideas to others are aware of these often hidden possibilities. Of course adrenalin can come to the rescue if the trend is spotted in time and the trainer then steps up the level of the presentation and the flow is renewed.

Team Building and Personal Effectiveness

The Geneva courses, which in my view had the most significance, were the Team Building and the Personal Effectiveness seminars. The former were aimed at building a greater awareness, both by the senior and the support staff, of the work of their partners. On the one hand there were often brilliant specialists, probably world famous in their fields; on the other administrative staff, who had to understand and adhere to the UN systems and protocol and produce vast quantities of reports, letters and memos often with impossible deadlines.

There was undoubtedly the tendency for some specialists to develop a superior attitude and disregard the vital role which their secretaries and administrative assistants played. This probably derived from the exaggerated sense of self-esteem resulting from their medical or professional training. This attitude was very hurtful and destructive of motivation. On the other hand, support staff all too often denigrated themselves, did not challenge or state their case positively. In other words, they found it difficult, if not impossible, to say, 'No', giving the reasons quietly and cogently. Both types of staff needed to learn a great deal about communication and human relations.

I have witnessed really able women assistants lose their confidence and drive and become cynical and lethargic. The option which is open to everyone to leave a job if it does not in the end suit then, was not open to many of these women, because British girls for example who had married say an Italian or a Swiss, and could not return home because of children, were not allowed by Swiss law to take jobs outside the UN posts. Positions in Switzerland were reserved for the Swiss. So if these women left their UN jobs, they would be unemployed and perhaps were not able to do without their salaries.

The real purpose of the joint courses was, therefore, to give the women more confidence and enable them to speak up frankly, but politely, and to make both sides of this great divide, harshly categorised as professional and general staff, realise that in reality everyone was working for the same objectives, which could only be attained by team work. The specialists so often took up the attitude that the 'real' part of the job was the technical achievements which they were concerned with. So they often became impatient and rude and got into the habit, probably because they were bad time managers, of keeping staff late night after night, or forgetting to pass on information or ever view tasks from their secretaries' point of view.

This same wasteful disregard goes on in most offices, but seem to have particularly disagreeable overtones in non-profit making organisations. Waste of money and resources, particularly human resources, is not quite so common in the commercial field as in the public sector, because the bottom line is important.

The workshops incorporated sessions for the specialists (usually men) on their own and similarly for support staff (usually women). When at the end they came together, it was very encouraging to see how much more open and positive their attitudes were. Both managers and support staff were almost invariably able to compare and talk through a joint work plan.

The Personal Effectiveness courses which I had been developing steadily over the years had a special message for the UN and WHO staff. Because the opportunities for promotion are very infrequent, often non existent, morale was sometimes low. Most people came into the Agencies with high hopes of the importance of the work they were committed to. If, however, over the years they found that they were not given support, and often never heard where their contribution fitted into the overall objective, perhaps never knew whether the plan had even succeeded, they lost hope. Their initial high commitment would be whittled away and despondency often took over, particularly when world opinion was couched in sneering terms.

The popularity of the Personal Effectiveness courses arose because they renewed people's sense of purpose and emphasised the fact that everyone's work is significant, even if little recognised. Also the course gave them much needed training in the techniques of communication self-projection and interpersonal skills. The enthusiasm for the seminar was tremendous. Unfortunately, shortage of funds meant that it was neve possible to offer enough of this type of training.

As time went on Dr. Barton, because he saw the courses were so useful, suggested to the Copenhagen, Alexandria and Manila offices of WHO that they should run similar training exercises.

In each of these places the work style and the level of staff was very different. In Manila there was a large number of local Phillipino staff; smiling, happy people who very much welcomed the courses, because they felt so far away from the centre of things.

In Alexandria there was a wide variety of Middle East nationalities in the offices; many of the older Egyptians having been extremely well educated in the French tradition.

In Copenhagen there were Nordic/Scandinavian people, well educated, direct in thought and speech, a little serious perhaps. The specialists in all these offices were the usual multi-national mix — of German, Czechoslovakian, Russian, French, etc.

Although the content of the workshops was very similar because the objectives were the same — greater efficiency and effectiveness — the method of presentation had to vary to suit not only the people but also, in Manila and Alexandria especially, the climate. Manila is tropical and very enervating — Alexandria can be hot and clammy, but also at times very cold. The pace of the training had therefore to be adjusted to meet this.

I loved getting to know these very different countries and in Geneva and Copenhagen I made a great many friends.

Geneva, surrounded by mountains, sits low down on the Lake edge. It is a most attractive city with a long historical tradition. The streets are clean and orderly, the gardens and the beautiful lakeside estates are truly luxurious. There is neither litter, nor poverty, and the exquisite jewellery shops are more numerous than in any other city I know. Because of the dozens of international organisations, not only United Nations, which have their headquarters in Geneva, there are innumerable apartment blocks — there are also properties held by old Swiss families, but there is not all that amount of mixing between the foreign invaders and the indigenous population. The Swiss are a little withdrawn and I think I understand this. I believe I would act similarly if I were in their situation.

The mountains and the countryside round about, particularly when the spring flowers are out, are delightful. Nearly everyone skis and there is much boating on the Lake.

Important Colleagues

I loved working with Bill. He was a tremendously hard worker and dedicated to training. He was always deeply concerned that people should develop to their maximum potential. I have seen him by a mixture of encouragement and discipline lead people to go further and further, often far beyond their own expectations.

His generosity to me was something for which I was very grateful. We would talk about management skills and, expounding his very creative ideas, we would discuss how they could be achieved. I found it inspirational to see him stand against any form of disloyalty and procrastination, when many people, aiming for a quiet life, would not have bothered to make a stand — but that was not Bill's lifestyle.

His beautiful wife Libo (short for Elizabeth) with her serenity and cool judgement was always a great support to Bill.

They had both spent much of their youth in Kenya which they loved very much. They were kind enough to introduce me to that marvellous country. The two to three weeks I spent touring with them "On Safari" were some of the most thrilling I have ever spent. Whether riding across the plains in an open Land Rover or exploring the Great Rift Valley or looking at the hundreds of birds on Lake Naivasha or the coral reef at Malindi with the multi-coloured fish which tamely come and nibble your toes, it was all most exciting — an experience not to be missed, which they shared with me so generously.

They both also have a wonderful fun streak which enables Bill to imitate anybody and so we laugh a lot when we are together.

Other close friends in Geneva are Judith and her family. She has two youngsters, two dogs and a gentle solid husband, John. They live outside Geneva and Judith commutes daily, driving six or seven miles along the Lake side, braving the most awful traffic. She is highly intelligent, an excellent linguist and very well informed. She always looks smart, businesslike and is right on top of her job, which she handles with great skill and adroitness. The high respect in which she is held in her senior training role in WHO and her acceptance and credibility in it, come I believe from a combination of all the attributes I have mentioned.

She is an example to those women who wish to continue their careers yet not neglect their family and home. Of course there are problems and it is hard work, but the key to the situation is — *Judith knows how to organise* her private life and her professional life.

We share many interests, particularly lovely jewellery, not I think so much because of its value, but because of the workmanship and the beauty of the stones. John laughingly calls us — "Magpies Incorporated".

Copenhagen is another city of great charm — one is never far from water, either the sea itself or an inlet, a lake or a river. The curious wedding cake spires and the onion shaped tops to the buildings in the old city are very distinctive. But my interest in the City is the many friends I have there, members of WHO or the American Women's Club, where they gather to socialise and where I have sometimes addressed the group. All these people, of course, have widely differing personalities — some of them very generously say that my confidence building workshops have given a new meaning to their lives. I myself do see a vast improvement in their powers of self-projection and the serenity they seem to have at their command.

In Copenhagen the courses were organised by Ivan Tolstoy, a descendant of the great Tolstoy. It was fascinating to hear him talk of his early life which, when the family escaped from Russia, was very difficult.

His quiet, stoic response to these unhappy experiences, always filled me with admiration. He is without doubt a truly brave man — his mild manner completely misleads some people, but he takes no notice and quietly goes on his own way usually attaining his objectives without fuss or protest. There is quiet dignity about him which I find most impressive. Now having retired, he is devoting himself to painting and already he is making a great success of it. I learned a great deal from this unusual, highly intellectual man.

A highly significant factor in the success of the courses in Copenhagen was the support of the Regional Director, Dr. J.E. Asvall. He, himself, attended the Team Building seminar for his Division. It is this kind of commitment by Senior Management which makes all the difference.

The widely varying responses on these overseas courses were most intriguing and revealed a good deal about the character of the different people.

On one occasion a huge Russian was a delegate. He had a somewhat shaggy appearance rather like a lovable sheep dog. He paid meticulous attention to all I had to say, watching me intently. At one of the breaks he lumbered over to me and smiling, said how much he had enjoyed the morning. He then asked if I had "my methodology", as he called it, written down.

I told him that I did not, but that input, blended with discussion and debate, and case studies which delegates had to resolve, was not a training system unique to me, but was a style frequently adopted in the UK and the States too.

He said he found it very interesting and very different from practices used in Moscow. I asked him how the approaches differed and he replied quite simply, "In Moscow the lecturer talks!!". I was indeed sorry, I did not have precise documentation to give him!

Other very revealing situations arose when secretaries and clerical assistants attended courses with their administrative assistants, who were of course senior to them. All these staff were usually women. Some administrative assistants obviously had splendid relationships with their group and came to the course to share and learn together. Others were basically nervous, insecure women who found it very difficult to play a positive role, either on the course or, I suspected, in their offices. Some just could not make a contribution in public and I felt sometimes worked on the assumption that if they did not open their mouths in front of others, they couldn't be proved wrong. I did not, of course, allow this to continue, but drew them gradually into the discussion.

But I could see that these administrative assistants were neither liked nor respected by their team, whose members often told me, off the record, that they did not consult their AA except when absolutely obliged to do so. I had the message confirmed yet again that where any job calls for leadership, there has to be trust and support between people both upwards and downwards. There were many excellent AAs.

The courses in Alexandria were the very first that had been planned for the Unit and their gratitude was touching. Many different cultures and religions were represented in the office and this meant that there were problems, but for the purposes of the courses there was a common approach and the courtesy and involvement were outstanding.

While there I was able to make use of my weekends to go to Cairo and up the Nile to Luxor. I did all the usual tourist trips and, of course, was enchanted with what I saw — the Pyramids, the Valley of the Kings, the wonderful museums. It was all enthralling. As I had experienced before, seeing really ancient things and going back in time has a very curious effect. In Egypt there is another dimension, the foundations of so much from which we benefit today derives from this ancient civilisation, one cannot but be filled with admiration, even wonder, at what they achieved. I find the long march of history is not intimidating but inspirational, and gives one a sense of purpose and a niche, however minute, in the pattern of things. We all owe so much to what our predecessors have contributed.

The Philippines leave a very different impression. The uncomplaining acceptance of terrible conditions by many of the simple country people is very sad to see. Their low expectations of life and their struggle to survive in very damaging climatic conditions, demonstrates how tenacious life is, but the sickly little children dragging out an existence in terrible little shacks is grievous to see and is made all the more disturbing by the contrast with the luxurious life style of the wealthy plantation owners.

Bernadette was in charge of training at the WHO office, Manila, and looked after me most beautifully during my visit. The courses followed similar pattern to the Geneva seminars and were presented to most of the staff. It was wonderful to come back to Bernadette's house, set in a very pleasant tree-lined compound, after a really stretching day, relax, and get little cool under the whirring fans. We compared notes, and what a joy it to be able to share ideas and thoughts with someone whose approach to things is very similar to one's own — yet sufficiently different to give stimulus and point to discussion.

The whole idea of talking through problems and happenings is, I believe, one that is not practised enough in management. I it important to go over events in one's mind or with someone else. In this way the trigger points of successes and failures are recalled and mentally recorded for future action. Mistakes so often are repeated because when they occurred previously, how they came about was never fully comprehended. This is all part of the necessary "Think" process for which time must be allowed. It is said today that 5 minutes of preparation time only is required for activities which take 25 minutes to complete; whereas the formula should be reversed, 25 minutes preparation – 5 minutes of action. "Think" time is always being squeezed out by people who believe they haven't got the time for it.

I left Manila at the weekend and went up country through some quite wild places to visit my friend, Janet Miller, an American woman who had been Art Librarian at Spokane Library. When she retired from this, she took on the job of Librarian to the large College which her church was building in a very remote area 50 miles from Manila. She was devoted to this work and was very prepared to give up two years of her life to it in pretty stark conditions. She did not have air conditioning, nor a car and her bungalow was adequate, but by no means luxurious. Janet faced all this with equanimity and cheerfulness and so made a great impact with the staff. She realised that both the administrative and the teaching staff at the College were in need of personal training and counselling and, as I was on the spot, I was very happy to help.

I knew that Janet was doing her best to build up the skills of a very new team, so that when she went they would have some valuable personal resources to call on. There was very little money available for training and I did not have much time, so I had to limit myself to presenting two brief workshops, one on Sunday morning, the other on Sunday afternoon. As we were about to start the afternoon session, a monumental thunder storm broke. The Conference Hall, where about 100 people had gathered, was a very new circular building with a deep overhanging roof which covered the walkway which surrounded the hall. The thunder rattled and cracked and after a few minutes down came the rain. The noise was deafening – the thunder and the noise of the spots of rain crashing on to the roof made an incredible din – we just could not hear, so I had to wait.

But the sudden outburst soon stopped and I was able to go on again. A mere few hours was so little to cover the topics which needed to be addressed and I was very aware of the inadequacy of my effort, but I was thrilled when questions came in large numbers at the end. It was a marvellous responses and I felt very pleased that I had helped Janet a little her enormous task.

Driving back to Manila we saw in the distance the blackened landscape which surrounds Tagaytay, the ancient smoking volcano curiously located within the craters of even older eruptions. I greatly regretted not having time to do more than glimpse this and one of the orchid farms which are fabulous.

Putting Ideas on Paper and Other Workshops

After each overseas trip I would return to England and as well as carrying on with training and counselling, I did writing.

A book — "The Successful Secretary" — innumerable articles on Personal Development — and a year or two ago I compiled a Tape entitled, "Building Confidence". I knew that I could give new perspectives and renew determination in a very positive way in the few days that a seminar lasted; indeed men and women continually write to me expressing their gratitude, which I have to say makes me feel very humble.

But when back in the work place old familiar influences take over again. It is then very easy for even really determined delegates to lose their vigour and enthusiasm. I thought, therefore, that if the positive messages one needs to build on could be recorded, so that people could play the tape over and over — in a car, when peeling the potatoes, or whatever, the stimulus could be re-generated. This again seems to have worked for many people. But no single teaching/learning technique is right for everyone — what helps one person is no use for someone else, so it is a matter for both individuals and the trainer to experiment and try out new communication ideas, only some of which will succeed.

There are two courses which I present which offer a major challenge and are, therefore, very exciting. One is for the junior to middle management staff, men and women, who belong to commercial TV Companies. The courses came into being some years ago when the ITV Companies decided that there were not enough women in senior management roles in television. So I was asked to put on a course which would improve women's effectiveness and build their feelings of self-confidence.

The delegates vary widely — some in production, some in administrative posts. Many are doing creative jobs, others are engaged in budgeting and legal work. They are sent by any one of the 15 Commercial TV Companies which operates in the UK. These organisations are very different from ordinary commercial companies. The jobs are highly sought after and relatively highly paid and there is an excitement about the whole industry, which means that there is little boredom, but the atmosphere is often very artificial, and the tactics adopted to gain advancement can be devious.

It is true to say that although there has been some improvement, skilled and knowledgeable women are only gradually being considered for promotion. Yet, I have been told that there are more secretaries than managers with degrees.

The courses are directed towards helping the delegates to have a sharpened appreciation of their strengths and weaknesses and also to learn how to handle conflict and stress. So often when not achieving and moving forward, women, particularly in sophisticated environments like TV, can feel belittled.

Reacting negatively serves no good purpose. To convince people of their worth — hurts have to be examined for any lessons that can be learned from them and then forgotten. In spite of its initial raison d'être, men now come on some of these courses. When this happens the atmosphere is different and reveals attitudes and behaviour which occur between men and women, which are then opened up for valuable discussion. Both types of courses have their value.

Many of the delegates who have been on these courses have been promoted to more senior jobs and readily admit to more positive, relaxed and effective approaches at work. The courses are most thoroughly and imaginatively organised by Sue Davis of the Independent Television Association.

Another exciting course is the one I have run many times for IBM. This was designed to re-inforce the Company's Equal Opportunity policy and, although presented in England included delegates from all over Europe, many of whom were highly qualified. One of the most able of the Administrators that I worked with on this course was Edwige Drouhin-Atlan, who gave tremendous support and dynamism to the workshop.

IBM sets high standards and looks for commitment, but their practices are very fair and there are many opportunities for advancement. But even in a well structured and managed organisation, it is important for women, in particular, to recognise the need for tactics. The attack direct does not always succeed — it may be necessary to pause — take an alternative route — re-phrase arguments to succeed.

Everyone must set goals, long and short term, and monitor their progress with realism. Up-to-date techniques such as appraisal help with this and are now practised in big organisations such as the IBM, Shell, and Unilever, but not everyone has the vision or the determination to make the adjustments, particularly personality modifications, they are advised are necessary.

Damaging Management Styles

Some men's management style presents women with a special kind of difficulty, which I think is more evident today, than say fifty years ago. I am referring to the increase in crudity and drinking. It is a fact that vulgar language and sexist remarks which some men indulge in, actually result in robbing them of the respect without which they cannot function effectively as managers. The whole tone of an organisation can be let down and reduced to lavatorial school-boy levels, because no- one has the courage to call a halt to such activities. They are even thought clever.

I also find it deplorable that senior management in some companies choose to ignore the insidious increase in drinking which is happening and even quite unnecessarily extend the opening hours of the company's bars. Many dozens of staff members on courses, not just one or two, tell me that it is useless to approach their bosses after lunch, because they are incapable of making decisions — the waste of company time and the detriment to health is appalling.

It is not only that this is disagreeable to some staff members, it is a damaging disease which has disastrous results on the effectiveness of many organisations. It is a situation which needs to be addressed on a corporate not just an individual level.

The problem can also take the shape for staff who, while they may like a drink, are not "drinkers" and who discover that they miss out on information which is disseminated only in the "office extension", ie, the bar or the pub. These people can lose on the promotion stakes and may feel ostracised and tend to be regarded as "spoil sports", "dull", etc.

No-one would wish to act like a prig and a good tactic is totally to ignore such stupidities, but I believe that other people's bad behaviour, even though they may be very senior, cannot be allowed to intrude beyond a certain point into one's own work pattern or offend one's own standards. It is a matter of balance. One thing is certain, women cannot adopt a "holier than thou" approach.

Learning from Others

Two outstanding women, who have inevitably encountered all these aggravating peripheral stupidities, which can dissipate energy and achieve nothing, have much to share. Because they are shrewd, wise and have a quiet disciplined manner which automatically acts as a curb to bad behaviour — they have learned to handle such situations very professionally.

I refer to Pauline Graham and Valerie Hammond, whom I have already mentioned. Pauline is an older women with a long career of high achievement behind her. So it might be thought that only seniority is the safeguard in the situations just described. That is not the case. Valerie Hammond is much younger and while she already has a formidable track record, she is only on the way to high seniority.

Both these women are brilliant in their field and have been closely associated with WIM. Pauline is a splendid example of someone who has surmounted enormous difficulties and risen to very senior positions.

Sometimes I invite her to take part in my workshops. I persuade her to tell her own story which she does with great wit and vigour, because I feel it is a learning exercise for everyone. Her laughing voice, lustrous dark eyes and colourful clothes make her an inspirational speaker.

Pauline is Spanish by birth, but was educated in Egypt in French. She came to England with her husband and was soon left a widow with two little girls and very little money. She mastered this terrifying situation by early on doing translations, then learning accountancy and budgeting; finally her love of fashion brought these skills together and she went into Retail Store Management. This resulted in her eventually becoming Merchandise Director of a national fashion chain store with a multi-million pound turnover.

Her life philosophy is fascinating — she speaks of the paramount need for goals, backed by personal integrity, self-determination and self-management. She sees the problems of women aiming to achieve very clearly, because she has experienced so many of them. The aphorisms that she has collected along the way, and which she delivers with humour and zest, are delightful and full of meaning. In some cases they are other people's words and ideas but they represent a distillation of her own thinking over many years — "He who stops being better, stops being good" — "It is the poverty of our aspirations which is our downfall" — and, most inspirational of all, "One must always wear the victorious attitude!"

After her distinguished commercial career Pauline has turned to study, lecturing and writing. Her current work is a book, shortly to be published, on *Dynamic Management,* based on the ideas of Mary Parker Follett. This little known American lady was one of the earliest writers on management. She has the most challenging views on power and how it can only be effectively used when based on a real sense of personal and joint responsibility.

I have learned so much from Pauline who has a deep appreciation of the tremendously important fact that we live our lives on different levels. Many of us do not perceive this, nor do we grasp that we are not a single entity but many-facetted creatures who respond wholly differently in different circumstances. Yet, paradoxically, because our behaviour is the inter-connecting factor, we create our own environment. So in Pauline's view, with which I agree, we must regard life as unfinished business.

In Pauline's presence I find that life takes on a new meaning — joyous and full of subtleties. Sparked by her originality I find new and exciting possibilities opening up. For good or ill, it was she who gave me the idea for this book and encouraged me to write it. I feel very grateful to her for leading me to this.

Valerie's story is very different, but equally inspiring and worth examining phase by phase, because she sees so clearly where the trigger points of her advancement lie. Initially highly qualified in the secretarial field, winning several prizes:

- Her first approach for a job was to the BBC — no vacancies existed and she was told to re-apply in six months — she didn't.

  "Learning Point — The world and I, move on — I seldom go back."

- "Next, when with an international firm of lawyers I resolved a management/staff issue, concerning serious inconsistency and injustice in salaries paid to some of the girls. Although very new, I negotiated for the situation to be put right. The girls got a rise and I was offered promotion."

  "Learning Point — Acting on a moral principle — one person *can* make a difference."

- Filled a technical liaison role with an advertising film company. "It was fun but a bit shallow, women treated as objects — the only place I have ever been chased round a desk!" The devious way in which her ineffective Boss was fired by the Management, she found very distasteful and so resigned.

  "Learning Point — Organisational politics can be really disagreeable."

- Joined a subsidiary of an American Office Equipment manufacturers. "I learned about the new technology and also international finance, insurance and property management."

  "Learning Point — I discovered I had enormous energy and even more persistence."

- Became self-employed in the area of office systems.

  "Learning Point — Left to myself I work too intensely. I really need to care for, and be cared for, by others."

- "Joined Mobil having decided I was really a large company person. Worked in their Data Computer Centre. Was promoted, picked a post where I knew I could shine and using my past knowledge helped Mobil automate. I produced what became an industry standard and then a training programme. Mobil encouraged training and I started my degree at the Open University preparing for the future."

  "Learning Point — Learned how I should think about how to combine my skills. What I alone could do to make a difference, because this is what the company is buying."

- "Joined the Petroleum ITB as Training Adviser, as the only woman professional, and given additional responsibility for work on Sex Discrimination Legislation, so a wider range of issues opened up."

  "Learning Point — There are advantages to being a 'novelty only woman' employee. I used it to develop my understanding and contact and to include other women."

- Stimulated the oil industry involvement in an EEC project.

  "Learning Point — I learned how to make one piece of work relevant to more than one direction, eg, develop conceptual skills through awareness.

- Joined Ashridge Management College as Research Associate, having to handle difficult internal circumstances, came to be regarded as the Manager of the Project..

  "Learning Point — Diplomacy brings its own reward."

- Pursued active involvement in external organisation and took every opportunity to represent the College overseas where we wanted to be better known. Job continued to expand.

  "Learning Point — It is possible to progress with little power; but preparation and care with personal contacts, essential."

Valerie believes in taking specific points from different role models. She also thinks that mentors are important. Her earliest was her grandmother. Several senior men have been a great help and she respects them, perhaps more important than liking them. She also believes that women have a vital role to play in business, bringing different skills and abilities to the work place.

Where women, and men too, express themselves and fulfil their potential, she believes everyone gains greater freedom and the organisation is more effective. This has to be for the greater good of society, but women must never become pseudo-men. This would result in a stereotyped kind of glue, people stuck in roles for ever, never questioning, never asking. In seeking development it is essential that the culture within which women are inextricably bound, must be taken into account. Custom, history, values and beliefs are all important. If we don't take account of them, we may introduce change, but it will be transitory; as soon as the situation alters, we will revert, eg, women in the war did splendid jobs and then went back to minimal roles.

She has a vital and stimulating philosophy with which I find myself closely in accord.

Introducing a course at the Lokheed factory in Los Angeles, California

My great friend Betty Jay in front of her house in Spokane, Washington State

Ann Whol from Boulder and her two sons Charles and Richard

Visiting the Grand Canyon in 1980. It was very cold!

With Ann Wohl on our way to the Grand Canyon

I visit the Arizona Desert where the great cactus thrive

Dr. Bill Barton and his wife Libo attending a dinner party

he delegates of the first IBM Equal Opportunities Workshop which I ran in 1983 at Henley Management College

Pauline Graham, who blends great taste and fashion appreciation with keen entrepreneurial skills

Chapter Ten

Building a Life Philosophy

The theme of this book, as I indicated in the Introduction, is about making the most of human abilities. I have used words such as achievement – success – attainment, to convey the concept of personal growth, development and progress. I would now like to put this into context.

To think of advancement in purely material terms is to narrow down the scope of life to a very mundane level. Development for me is the reaching forward by every individual to a fuller interpretation of character, personality and spirituality, which may have little to do with commercial success. The two are not incompatible, they are equally not mutually exclusive.

It could be said that Mother Theresa of Calcutta has soared to heights of spirituality which few of us will attain, but the thousands of absolutely unknown people who are moving forward year by year in their simple sphere to a more perceptive understanding, and are using that increased sensitivity and their abilities to achieve a more worthwhile purpose, can be said to be achieving.

A petty criminal just out of prison who has evisaged and is striving towards a more honest use of perhaps minimal talents is a growing person.

If we are indeed to reach forward to a more complete life in which the various parts of our entity weld together with harmony, I think we need to create some kind of life philosophy which can gather up and make a pattern of our creativity and reasoning, our physical and emotional elements.

Trite perhaps to state this — much more difficult to achieve.

Winston Churchill expounded a concept which, I think, sets out wonderfully clearly how ideas can be transposed into an achieving philosophy, and can help everyone to come closer to themselves. Without some guidance or exposure to the thoughts of greater personalities however, we can fail to assess our inner reality and, therefore, never understand our own true potential.

The concept, though not expressed in Churchill's words, has three aspects. It requires that we have:

- a consciousness of the past, without regrets
- an awareness of the present, honest and fearless
- a vision of the future, with realism.

Here is a framework which can help us to treat ourselves as an action centre, whatever the level of our attainment or our circumstance. So much of our thought is non analytical, incomplete and wanders about in a fragmented way, leading to nothing which we can grasp. We all need signposts to guide us. So we need to remind ourselves that we all have a past — personal — family — national, which includes the culture of our country.

It is these which have conditioned us and given us our attitudes, which we frequently are not aware of. It is often difficult to detach ourselves from, but make proper use of early cultural, religious or family influences. But at least to develop a consciousness of them gives us a clearer perspective of where we are coming from.

We all have a *today*, which, if we will but sharpen our awareness about it, can give clarity of perception and a depth of feeling which can vitalise our imagination and our efforts, making them truly productive.

There is also the future which can give us an exciting image of what could be, with as yet unexplored dimensions. It is this kind of forward looking which releases our abilities in hitherto unimagined ways and brings benefits for years to come.

The ultimate extension of a single creative thought is fantastic. For example, not long ago a little girl, eighteen months old, was trapped down a well in Texas in the US. She kept herself happy and was able to sustain the ordeal by repeating "Winnie the Pooh" rhymes. It would have been utterly impossible for A A Milne, when he told Christopher Robin his bed-time stories, to have envisaged the enormous influence as well as the commercial success his books were to gain; nor that 60 years on he would be instrumental in saving a little girl's life.

So how can we produce results form that inner creativity which lies within each of us? To follow the Churchill formula, I believe that we must start from the known — the today — inspired by the vision of tomorrow — the future — but given the realism of the actual, by a full comprehension of what has gone before — the past.

As I spur my thinking and my imagination towards my chosen objective, whatever that may be, I believe it is essential to verbalise. Unless the vagrant, wandering notions which so often we choose to call thought are given depth, and shape in words, they will not work for us or anyone else.

As soon as I have defined or delineated my ideas, I have to give them substance by putting into words. As a little girl once said, "I have now drawn a line round my 'think', so I can tell you about it." Unless I do this I cannot use my hopes and visions. My sad experience is that if my thoughts are not crystallised they fade and drift off and are never re-captured.

This turning of visions into reality is the hard grind, but to achieve it is something we all have to do. Many of us dodge this taxing and exhausting task and follow safe familiar tracks, doing today what we did yesterday automatically without reflection, thereby denying ourselves the exhilaration of creativity.

One of the difficulties which face us when we try to dig deeper into ourselves and reflect on our failures and successes, is time. There is always some mundane task waiting to be done — "I must get a loaf of bread" — "I must pay the gas bill" — "I must mend a broken fuse". All these are necessary chores if we are to live in an orderly way. Nothing is more enfuriating than living with people who do not get on with such jobs, but it is important also that we give time quietly to take stock and review past events, how *we feel and what we want to do.*

It takes a shock sometimes to reveal to ourselves exactly where we are. On a course some time ago, a very successful woman suddenly became aware of the fact that she had no time whatsoever for herself. Her job was very demanding and filled many hours of the day. Her second husband, whom she loved, was a very dominant character, and her son by her first marriage was a typical teenager at loggerheads with his step-father. They lived in some style in an attractive home.

Reviewing the situation, this woman suddenly discovered that she had no time at all for herself. A wonderful employee, a loving wife, a mediating mother, a delightful hostess — she was nothing to herself. She resolved there and then to alter the pattern of her life and to take time out regularly to review her own needs and to ponder and reflect about what *she* wanted from life. At first she was deeply upset and could not restrain her tears and then as we talked she became very calm. When I said I was sorry she had been so distressed, "Oh no", she said, "It took this shock realisation to make me comprehend how I had been ignoring myself. I am very grateful, because I was very unhappy. I now see what I have to do".

Risk Taking

Two essential facets of high achievement are taking risks and making choices. Usually neither of these things is easy and often many of us are too fearful to attempt them. Yet if we do not dare to risk, we will not win. Usually, little is achieved by staying safe and holding to the familiar. Nothing has changed since the poet Spenser wrote that, "Faint heart ne'er won fair lady".

Once an idea has been turned into an action plan, that it has not been tried before or someone disapproves of it, must not intimidate us and divert us from our course if we believe we are right. To think and plan ahead and consider all possible points of failure and, if necessary, reject a whole scheme if it does not bear second investigation, is the careful preparation to which every strategy should be subjected. At the end of the day, however, we must believe in ourselves and our judgement and act courageously. More good ideas have been lost, more careers forfeited on the joint prongs of timidity and indecision, than almost anything else.

We need to examine our doubts and fears and the emotions which make us poor risk takers. On what our fears based, how do they arise, why do we feel apprehension and uncertainty? So often our hesitation come from a dislike of looking foolish, of being shown up as wrong or just different and a very powerful deterrent is the fear of being laughed at. These are in reality small things, but if they touch our pride, we may well lose our courage and our determination. Again many of us have a great fear of being rejected, which has to be chanced.

So, however our minds, thinking logically push us forward, seeing or imagining other people's disapproval, we draw back and may well miss a wonderful opportunity.

At the simplest level, how often have we been at a meeting, heard a debate when into our minds has come an excellent idea, a solution perhaps to the problem being discussed? But we did not advance it because we thought others knew better, or we feared it might sound silly. While we sat tight and anxious in a tizzy of indecision, saying nothing, someone else stepped in and said exactly what we had in mind. Everyone was delighted and full of praise for the brilliant thought that had been put forward. Yet again, we have lost a trick just from timidity.

This uncertainty not only arises from fear, but because we over estimate the significance of a single mistake. All right, let us assume we did make an error and come down on the wrong side. Is it so disastrous? We must not over emphasise the importance of one wrong decision. There are not all that number of faults that cannot be rectified. Much more damaging is continually holding back so that we acquire the habit of hesitancy, of seeing so many sides to a problem that we cannot come down positively on anything. We acquire the awful habit of procrastination. This holds back progress and earns us no brownie points in the leadership stakes.

It has been said that unless people risk being rejected, they never find a love they can trust. Put another way, until people take a chance and test their powers, they will never be sure of their strength. Playing safe is stagnation. To quote Helen Keller, the marvellous blind and deaf lady who rose to such incredible heights : "Security is mostly a superstition. It does not exist in nature, nor do the children of men as a whole experience it. Avoiding danger is no safer in the long run than outright exposure. Life is either a daring adventure or nothing."

There is, in addition, another very important outcome of never taking risks, of continually drawing back and assuming a negative attitude, we encourage others to dominate us and our opinions. As soon as we demonstrate that we are weak and uncertain, people may well accept our valuation of ourselves. We come to be thought of as lacking determination and leadership qualities and so any hope of winning respect as a full team member and certainly of gaining promotion, disappears. People will tolerate a bold mistake, skilfully at a later stage put right — they will not tolerate hesitant waffle.

There is another dimension here. As a manager, by my receptivity and willingness to listen and accept others' ideas, I can help people to be bolder and take risks. Indeed as a manager, while I must emphasise the need for careful evaluation, I must positively encourage risk taking. It is at the heart of development.

Exercising Choice

The exercise of choice is closely linked with risk taking. It depends on our perception of opportunities, which do not always lie on the surface. We need to probe and look at situations from different points of view.

So often we do not see events as a whole, we stick to a tiny narrow view of our job and the people in our immediate circle and do not focus our mind on broader issues. So we do not see what lies beyond, nor the causes of many things which would give us a view of the options. We are, so to speak, ploughing our own furrow, which becomes so deep that we cannot see over the edge. We have no perspective on what is happening beyond the furrow. My job does not end at the edge of my desk. While I must exercise thoroughness and persistence in dealing with my responsibilities, I must not allow them to seal me off from broader issues. We need to look around and question ourselves on wider things as well.

In a company, for example, where does the power reside? — by no means always with the person at the top. What are the really significant happenings both inside and outside our organisation? If we do not ask such questions and so develop a broader understanding of what is going on beyond our immediate patch, we will confine ourselves to narrow detail — not even perceiving the opportunities which are there.

On one occasion, a young woman manager of a multi-national company working in Germany, was invited by the Chief Executive of the whole organisation to attend a one-day meeting with a very select group of woman managers in London. It was the first meeting of its kind and a great breakthrough for women in the company. Her immediate manager did not want her to accept, because the following week they were launching a new product. From a feeling of loyalty and conscientiousness to her immediate job, the young manager did not attend the London meeting. The Chief Executive was annoyed and formed a very negative view of this young woman's judgement.

We have to ask ourselves what should she have done? What would we have done? It was a difficult choice. It is my view that by working late, perhaps delegating some tasks, she should have attended the London meeting. She needed to think more broadly, to evaluate the long, as well as the short term benefit of this meeting, not only to her, but to the company, although this might have meant encountering the censure of her immediate boss. I don't believe she did this and I suspect it took her a long time to regain her status with HQ.

At the back of every choice is not only the acceptance of one course of action, but also the rejection of the alternative or alternatives. We cannot do or be everything, so we have to select and set priorities. Perhaps this alternative is right for now, the other one may have to be deferred or even abandoned. We have to perceive, rather like a game of chess, where this move will lead us tomorrow, next week, next month. Often some seemingly attractive, even flattering, short term opportunities are in reality long term traps. We need to think very carefully, as did Valerie Hammond and I, myself, at the break points in our progression.

A Self-Discovery Course

It is discussing such topics as these and trying to find solutions to personal problems which is the purpose of the Building Personal Effectiveness Course, which I began to evolve about 10 years ago. I ask every person present to think through carefully who they are, what they are, what they really want from life and what they are going to do.

The vitally important skills of communication and sensitivity for others are discussed at length, because this is not a course so much about practical techniques, but about self-development and personal growth.

An atmosphere of trust and confidence is established and people discover that by being more open and not having as before to defer themselves, because in that situation there are no enemies, they can come out from their protective "cupboards" and share with others. They can speak and find they have something to say, they can share because they are beginning to value their own actions, their thoughts, their experiences, which are worthy of sharing.

The starting down this route may be slow, but even within the space of the week of the course, people who have practised "silence" for many years begin to talk — people whose manner and somewhat selfish philosophy have crushed or inhibited others, quite often their staff, begin to take up a different attitude.

To witness these changes is rather like seeing the release of a bird from a cage; people begin to realise and discover how they can reach to a fuller life and project a confident, more harmonious image which not only makes them feel better, but also releases the potential of others with whom they are dealing.

One particular approach which I enlarge on is the technique of "imaging". I encourage people to visualise themselves in their mind's eye actually doing what they want to do and *succeeding*. This self-visualisation can be made into a habit and by giving shapes to our thoughts and inner reflections, we can point our endeavours in a sharpened way to our goals and so release the energy which will turn then into reality.

This positive thinking becomes an energy source, it helps us to eliminate the negative lumber which perhaps for years we have been accumulating in our sub-conscious, by continually saying such things as, "I can't", "Others are better", "I know I will fail". We begin instead to programme our thoughts for success, achievement and co-operation, and so we begin to take charge of ourselves, cultivating thoughts and reactions from others. We set change in motion, because we can perceive that we can do it. We give up worry and anxiety in favour of laughter and action; but the technique has to be practised with conviction.

The best exposition of it that I know occurs in the book by Maxwell Maltz, an American Psychologist. "The Magic Power of Self-Image Psychology".

This is not fanciful imagination which has no basis in reality — it works. I think this is one of the reasons why this course has proved so successful.

The Role of Leisure and Pleasure

We also discuss the leisure and pleasure aspects of our lives on the course, because they have such a marked effect on our careers, our lives, our family, our own personality, giving balance and a sense of mental, physical and emotional harmony.

One of the factors that should be taken into account when important decisions are being made is not only the effect they will have on our careers, but also on our lives, our family, our own personality.

I believe that to spend all one's life glued to one's job without breaks or relaxation is both unwise and limiting. There are times when most of us have to work very hard. When I decided, for example, to take my degree, I knew that I would have to work all day at my job and study and read every evening, with perhaps only an hour or two weekly for play time, for several years. But I *wanted* to do that — it became a pleasure in itself and I could see the long term benefits I would gain.

Once, however, a special effort like that is finished, we need to relax and develop other interests, because these, apart from the sheer pleasure they afford us, will have important contributions to make to our work life, indeed our life as a whole. We become more rounded people, hopefully not in terms of avoirdupois even if our interest is food! — but mentally and psychologically.

Everyone's taste and activities are different. For me the world of natural history is all absorbing — particularly birds and flowers. I have been fortunate enough in the course of my work to go to places where there is wonderful wildlife to see. I feel I must share the joy and excitement that some of the experiences have given me, although I wouldn't wish to turn this into an ornithological check list, because it would be boring. When talking of our special loves that is something which is all too easy.

The first time I saw the beautiful, but somewhat elusive, mountain bluebird of America, he sat for me for at least 15 minutes on a garbage can at the back of a ski slope — not very glamorous surroundings, but he was exquisite; similarly the day that Janet Miller took me to the St. Jacques river in the Western United States and from a launch we saw at least 20 nesting pairs of osprey sitting on, or building their nests, or swooping down catching fish — my mind then went back to the times I have waited patiently for hours in Scotland, where with luck I have spotted the quick flight of just one osprey.

On an even larger scale were the hundreds of birds at Lake Naivasha in Kenya, flamingos, pelicans, waders of every kind, but that great spectacle does not obliterate the day I saw the tiny Dartford Warbler, flitting secretively in bushes on heathland in Dorset, nor watching the wonderful gliding flight of the Marsh Harrier over an estuary in Suffolk with my dear friends Mary and Howard Elliot Lacey. Incidentally, these two make a wonderful team — she paints with exquisite finesse and he researches, writes and photographs.

I cannot resist mentioning the Bharatpur Bird Reserve in India where with delight, I saw the stately Sarus cranes, dazzling sunbirds, the bizarre snakebird and about a hundred other species.

I love the motto of this park — no shooting except with a camera — wonderful reversal to the huge stone edifice one comes across in one of the clearings where hundreds of names, many of famous people, are listed with their "bag", 400 – 200 – 600 birds recorded alongside! Thank heaven that today many people at least feel ashamed if they wantonly kill or in any way destroy our wildlife heritage.

I have said elsewhere that sentimentalisating over the landscape and the animal kingdom is not either sensible or helpful, but we need to listen to and act on the wise and balanced words of people like David Attenborough, Peter Scott, Philip Drabble and Gerald Durrell and others like them. Money is needed to save the forests and the wild things and find solutions to difficult local problems of agriculture and the provision of fire wood. But wanton cruelty must be exposed and dealt with, with the utmost severity.

In this respect, I want to record a special word of appreciation to BBC Bristol for its amazingly beautiful nature programmes and for the writings of Ian Niall. He is one of the main reasons why I take "Country Life" every week. His and Phillip Drabble's impassioned condemnation of badger baiting and slaughter is very important and a confirmation of Francis Bacon's phrase "The nobler a soul is, the more objects of compassion it hath."

I could go on about birds, which anyone who knows me has learned to their cost, but I will turn instead to flowers. Perhaps just one phrase will suffice – my garden is my joy. I have one marvellous mentor in this area, Mr. Moore, who was the Head of one of the Parks Divisions in the Borough of Croydon. A countryman, with an encyclopaedic knowledge of plants and flowers, he has shared his expertise with me and while I am still imping far behind him, I am improving. To see his powerful, but so gentle hands take up a tiny cutting or with quick precision prune a rose bush at exactly the right point, is in itself an education.

I have already talked about Music and Art, which are of growing importance to me. I should, I think, add a word about my interest in antiques. The value is not the really significant factor, although that is why many people indulge in the hobby today. For me the exquisite workmanship of a cross banded table, the perfection of an 18th century repeater bracket clock, or the delicate brass inlay on a Regency cabinet, is the lure. As one studies these, yes – works of art – it seems that the old craftsmen designed objects in such a complicated way as to set themselves almost impossible tasks. The pursuit of excellence was certainly their motto.

I love just walking in the countryside, although there is never enough time to do as much of that as I would wish – although I do accept the fact that to a large extent time – is a matter of motivation – we do what we want to do.

One of my great pleasures has been my two Godchildren, Caroline and Deirdre Maclure. I have watched Deirdre with her generous, sensitive, loving, character develop into a charming young woman. I am delighted that her career in Television is growing apace. It is a harsh, at times an artificial world, but Deirdre has the common sense as well as the creative imagination to do her job superbly well *and* keep her feet on the ground. The latter is both important and difficult.

Her sister Philippa is also a close friend and was the guide when I toured Rajasthan in India. Tremendously knowledgeable, she has an understanding of Indian culture from which I joyously learned a great deal. Both these young people are the daughters of my war-time friend Mary — it is marvellous for me without a family to have these friends.

Faith and Belief

The thread which runs through all my activities and has, in considerable measure, illumined every thing I do is my religious belief. I am not perhaps the constant churchgoer which I should be although I go very frequently to the quiet early service in my little local church, St Andrew's in Old Croydon. I have been a communicant there for about 50 years, indeed since the days of a splendid vicar, Will Evans, a Welshman, who had all the celtic fire and fervour of his country. I found this infectious. He also had great courage — he fought the local council furiously in order to preserve St Andrew's Church Schools — and won, and somehow he made religion a happy experience. He visited me once when I had a brief spell in hospital and told me deliciously funny experiences which happened when he was a young curate. His blue eyes twinkled and we laughed uproarioulsy — I felt much better after that.

Canon Roy White is another Churchman who has taught me a great deal, not at least a little how to pray, not that his teaching is 'little', but rather my capacity to learn.

Roy has a serious, thoughtful way of talking, yet somehow makes me feel he is learning with me, which gives me hope and some how confirms that we are all on a journey — although some of us have a good deal further to go than others. There is an emanation of sheer goodness about Roy which I find most inspiring. The same feeling comes from Michael Mann, the Dean of Windsor, whom I see occasionally. I first met him many years ago in Port Harcourt in Nigeria. The respect that he commanded in that community was tremendous as he moved about, inspiring trust and hope among the poorest, most squalid parts of his Parish. The circumstances in his present job are obviously not the same, but I am sure that he has the same effect.

Faith is a very personal thing, but one conviction I have is that tolerance is an essential part of Christian teaching, yet it is sadly so often lacking and dogma appears to be more important to some people than reverence and faith.

This results in making people hesitant to declare any beliefs for fear of provoking argument or appearing to be out of step by professing an unfashionable conviction. Yet the Christian ethic which is at the basis of our society, is weakened by this silence. Individual faith also is not helped, because weaker characters wait for a lead from others and when that is not forthcoming, their own belief, can wane. Yet there is no doubt that the absence of any consciously held standard for living is highly damaging. Perhaps this is one of the contributory causes for the deterioration in morals, which we are currently witnessing. Too few people are prepared to stand up and be counted. They will blame institutions, but it is in reality personal behaviour which without any preaching at street corners changes attitudes.

For myself I know that I owe a great deal to my very modest version of Christianity, although I feel sometimes I do not do enough to justify my calling myself a Christian, I do not believe, however, that religion and reverence for God and his creation has essentially to come from hassocks, so perhaps — some of my work can rate as service — I hope so. One thought is central to my philosophy, I have no desire to bargain with God for a place in Heaven. Indeed, that is an aspect of the Christian faith, as it sometimes comes over, which I cannot accept. Whatever rubbishy little proposal or gift I might make, I am sure will earn me nothing in the ultimate. I must do what I do out of conviction and love and be prepared to admit and pay for my errors and my inadequacies and leave it at that — I quote a prayer I wrote many years ago.

"Oh Lord, set my life in a pattern so that the accumulation of my days of labour may bring joy to those around me and be a testimony, however humble, to the Glory of God."

My labour, as I have written continuously throughout, is to give training and counselling to people who wish to grow. I am delighted that sometimes at least I seem to succeed in this, though obviously not always. If, however, one can give a fresh perspective, stir interest and build in the individual a greater sense of self-worth, the growth process will have started, or as one delegate wrote back six months after our encounter — "You sowed the seeds; they are developing".

I Re-Visit Nigeria

Just after Christmas 1987, I had the exciting opportunity of returning to Nigeria to give a course for Nigerian Management Women. Arranging this was not easy. Currency restrictions, problems of travel and Nigeria's economic difficulties which result in a desperate shortage of sterling, required that a great deal of negotiation was needed to get things organised. I was, however, so intrigued to return to Nigeria after nearly 20 years, that I was prepared to forfeit some of the normal financial rewards just for the purpose of seeing old friends and old haunts. I also felt that I could perhaps be of some help and give a boost to Nigerian women, whom I knew were making tremendous efforts to rise to better levels in their jobs and were meeting with some success in spite of typical opposition.

The visit proved to be as pleasurable as I had anticipated. I met many old friends and worked very co-operatively with a new educational body, the Business Education Examinations Council, which is seeking to spread technical education and qualifications. 28 women attended the course — they all had a degree or some technical qualification, and were employed in middle to senior level positions in Banking, Insurance, Commercial firms and the Public Sector organisations. There was a high degree of concentration and the debate and questioning were very perceptive. Many of the difficulties that British women have experienced in seeking promotion, were encountered by these women.

The personal problems were, however, I felt, more complex as the marriage convention is not as stable as it is in the UK. Many of the delegates were considering divorce or struggling to maintain jobs and families on their own. But they are powerful women who do not give up easily. They undoubtedly appreciated the course and are considering forming a network group to carry on the mutual support they developed during the week.

Other events were a brief unprepared half an hour with the top managers of the National Oil Company, where unexpectedly I was asked to address their senior men on a management theme. Off the top of my head I chose to talk on the vital importance of self- responsibility and self-motivation, which I feel very keenly about. The message was about maintaining high standards *all* the time, of not cutting corners and not leaning on other people's energy and creativity, but showing your own initiative. It was well taken. The theme is, of course, universal and requires to be re-inforced all the time.

I stayed in Lagos. It was marvellous to see so many old friends again — a group of them gave me a delightful tea party, where there was a good deal of reminiscing. There was also a splendid bonus, in that I was taken bird watching on the creeks just outside Lagos and saw brilliant yellow weavers, flashing ultramarine rollers and one of the tiniest species of kingfishers, blue and black with a little crest. This, plus making many new friends, made the trip memorable, although I was sad to see the economy of the country in a pretty desperate state.

Feminism

Perhaps it is worth commenting on a slightly perverse reaction which I have at times. This perversity is, I believe, typical of most people — a sort of momentary revulsion against what most interests us. Although I have for so many years of my life been dedicated to the improvement of women's development, in which I passionately believe, there are times when the mere mention of the word feminism — infuriates me. I am utterly convinced of the justice of equal opportunity, and the absurd waste which results from not developing people, men and women, to their highest attainment — a subject which I have commented on many times in this book — yet I have to say that women, who go on and on about their difficulties and their rights and the shortcomings of the male sex, can be utterly tiresome. I think it is the emphasis which gets distorted.

There are good and bad examples in both sexes and for either side to elaborate to excess on the shortcomings of the other is to me a fruitless pursuit. There is no doubt that we are going through a social revolution, and one of the areas which is most markedly affected is the status of the sexes. Touch button automation has removed much of the need for brawn. The culture of our society has long been based on belief in male superiority, derived in the first instance from physical strength. Women with less physical strength have, as a result, been relegated to the inferior role of a mere supporter of the male. Since the basic premise that physical strength accords the senior role can no longer be regarded as valid, many social conventions which derive from this thinking have been overturned. The intellect, the mind has become of much greater significance.

I believe that, as yet, neither men nor women have wholly adjusted to this enormous change. Centuries old behaviour, attitudes and the legal patterns have just not caught up. In many situations, both men and women find it difficult to know how they should behave. The old safeguards and social patterns have gone, but few new ones have been set up in their place. It is absolutely right that both men and women should have a just pride in their masculinity or femininity respectively, but this gives neither sex the right to dominate the other.

Unfortunately, following the social norm, a man's pride is too often based on his superiority over women, affording him apparently the right to disregard them as equals, and permitting him to patronise them as inferior. But if there is no longer any validity for this behaviour, it follows that in many cases men's pride is at risk. Equally, women who have been taught not to challenge male domination, may well behave in a way which re-enforces the man's so called superiority and her own inferiority. If suddenly this attitude has no significance, she is left not knowing exactly what is expected of her.

Dear Agatha Christie, whom one can admire so much in so many ways, felt that women had forfeited a great deal by seeking equality. The life of a pampered lady, she believed was far more rewarding. A strange attitude for one whose mental ingenuity and earnings had put her in a class where such considerations were really without meaning. But she was a daughter of her era, which makes my mother's independent attitude all the more remarkable.

The power behind the throne, the manipulating second-fiddle woman, lacks the openness and honest which I am very pleased to see is gradually developing.

I do, however, perceive that in many circumstances neither sex know what attitudes and manners they should adopt to the other. We are in effect re-writing the social code and at the moment not always very effectively. Many fair minded men, for example, who will accept and support the principles of Equal Opportunity legislation, find it difficult to reject the stupid rigidity of some promotional patterns within their own organisation. In such instances, they fail to be impartial and regard change as a personal attack or deprivation.

Women also are guilty of the same kind of inconsistency. They will demand equality at work, but will not invite a single woman to a dinner party, because it breaks convention by making the sex representation round the table unequal. Expectations determine our attitudes and sometime when breaking away from old established patterns, which may still have merit in themselves we are in danger of throwing the baby out with the bath water. Courtesy is a plus quality which implies respect, and has nothing to do with inferiority or superiority. Remove it, in order for women to prove to themselves they are free, or for men to retaliate against a false sense of lost importance, and a gracious helpful element is removed from existence.

But the man who is overtaken by his wife in the promotion race, being graded lower in salary and position than she, will have to learn how to handle his pride which he may well feel has been assaulted. The wife who, at the break up of a marriage, expects to be treated "extra generously" by her ex-husband can quite wrongly feel deprived if she only gets a *fair* settlement. She has to ask herself are her norms right?

There are all kinds of sensitivities which come from long established custom, which while newer freer conventions are being worked out, it is well to respect. The wife who continually belittles her husband in a demanding way in front of others, is not proving anything and may well pay with a great loss of respect and affection.

As I see it, the way ahead is for a much greater sense of partnership to be developed, based on a recognition of the different qualities and abilities which men and women have, not as stereotypes, but as individuals.

The 300-Group and Working Woman

It is this approach which prompted Lesley Abdela some four years ago to set up The 300-Group, the aim of which is to encourage more women to enter Parliament. In the present House there are a record 41 women (6.3%), but compared to the total number of 650 members the proportion is very low. The population in the country is roughly half men, half women, so to have an equal representation in Parliament, the number of women MPs should be approximately 300, hence the title of the Group.

Lesley explored the need for women to become more interested and involved in politics, and train in order to get their voices heard in the national debate. She set a splendid activity going. Any group which attempts to implement change runs the risk of being regarded as cranky and way-out, but in the end, women who are prepared to blaze a trail, provided they act from logic and reason, not exclusively emotion, will effect progress. Having observed developments over many years, I quite honestly see so many changes for the better which would not have happened when I first started my work.

One splendid initiative which occurred two years ago was the Publication of "Working Woman" magazine, which as its name implies, was for women who were developing their careers. Audrey Slaughter, who was instrumental in launching this journal was unfortunately not able to make it into a lasting success. There were several reasons for this, among them finance, but also the failure of the Advertising Agents to recognise the publication as a really important venture and sell it hard enough to their clients to gain revenue for the magazine.

Oddly enough, there is still a considerable amount of sexist advertising, which seems to please short sighted advertising people in agencies and in companies more than it pleases women who so often are the purchasers they are aiming for. Audrey, a most courageous women and a brilliant journalist, in spite of putting a great deal of her own money as well as her expertise, into the magazine, couldn't win this particular battle. But both she and this type of magazine have a future, because they meet a growing need.

Two Outstanding Women

No review of women's progress over the last 20 years would be complete without mention of two outstanding women, Baroness Seear and Elizabeth Pepperell. Nancy Seear, a member of the Upper House, an erstwhile reader in Social Studies at the London School of Economics, has for many years supported women's progress in a most balanced and steadfast way. She adds her reasoned voice to debate on many subjects and to none more cogently than to women's affairs. There is never the slightest hint of feminism in what she advocates, she simply states in a most logical and matter-of-fact manner that as half the brains in the country reside in women's heads, no government, organisation or company can afford to disregard them. Talent is never so plentiful, she says, that it can be ignored and so her advice to employers has always been to take advantage of the abilities that lie on their doorsteps. Still conventional in their thinking and often unable to break away from the stereotype, these recommendations are all too rarely followed by companies.

Elizabeth Pepperell was a woman I was enormously proud to know. Her story is almost legendary — she came from a simple East End family. Her father was a drayman, who drove his delivery van with two horses about the crowded streets of the City of London, while Mrs Pepperell acted not only as mother to her own family, but to many of the girls who got into difficulties in the area. Whatever their problems, there was always help, a kindly word, often a bed in the Pepperell household for these unfortunates. This same warm generosity was the outstanding quality which Elizabeth herself always displayed. One could not but be touched by this loving personality. She began her business life as a Bryant and May match girl, but her craving for knowledge led her to study and bit by bit she acquired the qualifications which made her later career possible. The wonderful thing about this progress is that she won against great odds, but never at other people's expense. So every time a certificate was gained, all the other Bryant and May girls would cheer — "Our Elizabeth has done it again" they would say.

Then she went to the Personnel Department of Carreras, the cigarette manufacturers famous for their "Black Cat" cigarettes. Here she greatly influenced the policy of the company at a time when "people" management was not a grave consideration. She encouraged the company to develop advanced liberal staff policies.

After this she moved on to The Industrial Society and set up innumerable courses for women, some of which I was delighted to assist with. A special pleasure of hers were the courses for Supervisors. In those early days — women who had potential at the starting level, were rarely given any chance to train, so it was very difficult for them to acquire managment and supervisory skills. Many excellent women did it by pulling themselves up by their boot straps so to speak.

Elizabeth with her persuasive and logical approach, convinced companies that there was advantage in sending such women on courses and so they were allowed to attend. The gratitude and the enthusiasm which was displayed on those brief one or two-day workshops, sometimes held at weekends because companies wouldn't release the women during the week, was most rewarding. It was generated to a large extent by Elizabeth's personality, which was a most effective mix of gentleness and tenacity. She was indeed inspirational.

Sadly, at the height of her powers, she died after a long and courageous struggle with cancer. It is a splendid memorial to this great lady that there is now a Pepperell Unit at The Industrial Society which offers training to women.

Girl's Education

Another important trend in women's development has been evolving over recent years and will, in my view gather, momentum. I refer to the steadily increasing quality of the education which some, but not enough, girls are gaining at school. Unfortunately there is still too much mediocre education and too much temptation for girls, and boys too, to leave school as soon as possible, with inadequate or no qualifications and no love of learning.

Fortunately, there are many girl's schools, and I would like here to put in a strong word in favour of girls only schools, which are giving their pupils a first class grounding not only in normal school subjects, but in music, drama and sport. This rounded education is imperative if girls are to take up managerial and leadership roles in later life. Project work and field work are important and exciting, but the sound framework of well understood basic subjects is essential. It is an excellent development also that maths and science subjects are now being much more emphasised and imaginatively taught in well-equipped labs and computer rooms.

In the last year I have become tremendously interested in school work, becaused I see the young women at school as the real hope of the future. If they can get their qualifications and a feeling of what the world of work is about early on, they will, I believe, develop the sense of purpose and self-responsibility, which can make a big difference to their own success and also to the contribution they can make to the country in the years ahead. I have given away prizes and conducted one-day workshops in a number of schools and am greatly encouraged by what I see.

Here, as in all areas of development, the key word is confidence — confidence held by the teachers who recognise themselves and are recognised by society as doing probably the most important jobs in the country — confidence by the girls who need to become aware as soon as possible of the great opportunities which now await them if they are determined enough — confidence by the parents to believe in their children, really help and stand by them without aggravating parental interference — so that the whole concept of the pursuit of excellence is a shared experience.

A splendid evidence of this growing willingness to participate, came to me recently at Bolton School when the Head Girl gave a most polished and fluent vote of thanks.

I was also greatly encouraged by a function held recently in Manchester, "The North West Woman of the Year" contest, sponsored by The Prudential Assurance Comapany. The prize was won by a most talented and able woman, Sandra Eckersley, who had just been made Manager of a new important branch of her bank in Manchester. Her gracious acceptance of the trophy and her mention of her Assistant by name, showed her to be an excellent Manager and a worthy "first" for this award. As I looked round the room where some 200 business women were gathered, I had to say to myself, this event could not and would not have happened, dare I say particularly in the north of England, even five years before.

Results

And so what have all these different experiences and developments, both personal and in work, taught me? First and foremost, I think I have to say I have learned and am still learning to look — to observe — to compare more accurately, so that I believe my awareness and sensitivity, so vital to a meaningful life, is growing.

It has also taught me to seek for whatever good elements there may be in people and situations, even if they are hidden. In addition, I have come to recognise that the length of time of an incident or a contact is not the important thing, rather it is the enriching quality which may reside in a mere minute. Innumerable times it has been the briefest of happenings which have provided me with what I call my moments of ecstasy, such as the first time I heard a nightingale singing on a very dark night — or the delicious gurgling, chortle of a happy child, or after a rain storm, seeing the front of St Paul's Cathedral sparkling and bright with a rainbow arching above it.

In people terms a spontaneous smile and the sympathetic meeting of eyes when one is in need of support — or an unexspected sincere thank you, can make the world come alive again.

These brief moments have subsequently illumined so many of my thoughts. Their short duration has been extended into hours of pleasure of feelings of well being.

From a different angle, if I am fully to understand and identify with the people I am trying to help on my seminars, I need the same patient study enthusiasm and involvement that I use to take in the beauty of a large black leopard, lolling relaxed and replete on the branch of a tree in Kenya.

I know that I need constantly to attune my senses as sympatheticallly as possible, to sharpen my mind and direct myself purposefully to my current objective, because this is the only way that I can harmonise my abilities and give more of myself to others and receive more from them.

There also has to be a vision of what could be, so that my spirits are continually raised to the attainment of that vision. This seems to me to support the thought that, "We may only make these times better, if we better ourselves".

Life is indeed unfinished business, but with confidence and determination and gratitude also for the many who have helped me, I still go forward, spurred on by the maxim "Nothing by Chance". I trust that others can also take inspiration from these thoughts.

Hard at work in 1987. In organising events a great deal of time is spent on telephone

typical group on one of my "Building Personal Effectiveness" Courses at indridge Park Management Centre. The use of the centre began 12 years ago when Len Sneddon, then its Director, gave so much support to my activities

Thrushes in a forsythia bush — a painting by Mary Elliot Lacey, which she kindly did for me

Osprey nesting in a dead tree above the St. Jacques river in Western United States

Dogs and cats that have given me so much pleasure over the years
(A) Snooky

(B) Sammy

(C) Nicky

(D) and now Alex

garden. I am very fond of roses, but, like many amateurs, I try to crowd in too many types of flowers. Selection is very difficult for me

S.L. Moore — my gardener mentor

Walking on Dartmoor with April, Mrs. Staples, Nicky and other friends

With my godchild, Philippa Vaughan, in India

The 28 Nigerian delegates who attended the Women Managers Course in Nigeria in January 1987